ELVIS,

MY BROTHER

ELVIS,

MY BROTHER

—

Billy Stanley

with George Erikson

ST. MARTIN'S PRESS NEW YORK

The names of certain individuals described in this book have been changed. In many cases, conversations have been reconstructed from the author's memory and are not intended to be precise transcriptions of what was said.

Design by D. Abbate

Library of Congress Cataloging-in-Publication Data

Stanley, Billy.
    Elvis, my brother / Billy Stanley with George Erikson.
        p.   cm.
    ISBN 0-312-03329-X
    1. Presley, Elvis, 1935–1977. 2. Rock musicians—United States—
Biography. 3. Stanley, Billy. I. Erikson, George. II. Title.
ML420.P96S6   1989
782.42166'092—dc20
    [B]   89-34851
                                                                          CIP
                                                                          MN

First Edition

10 9 8 7 6 5 4 3 2 1

Dedicated to Connie, my wife, and Brooke, my daughter, for all your love, patience and understanding.

CONTENTS

Author's Note

I'm sharing my story with you because I had a distinct advantage over most people. Elvis was my brother. In telling this tale I must be truthful about the positive and the negative times without being judgmental. I loved him unconditionally.

Elvis showed me a world that few can truly comprehend. In doing so he left a part of his undying spirit in me.

I hope this book will help you to understand Elvis, the man, a little better.

—Billy Stanley
July 1989

ACKNOWLEDGMENTS

To my mother, Dee Presley, for without her none of this would have come about.

To Vernon, for sharing his home and his son.

To my brothers Rick and Dave for saving my life and helping me get on the right path.

To Paul and Sissy for your love.

To George Erikson for all the hard work and long hours you put in.

To Sandy, Brett, and Courtney for being my adopted family.

To Mike Sagalyn, for all the time and effort and for pushing me farther than I really wanted to go.

To Eric and Dena for being good friends.

To EB and PE for being there and helping me remember.

To Lewis Tucker for always being there.

And most of all to Elvis, for your loving and giving spirit that still lives in me.

INTRODUCTION

It all began the day my mother picked us up at Breezy Point Farms and introduced us to our "new daddy," Vernon. Mom and Vernon then packed our bags, put us in a black Lincoln limousine, and we started on the long drive from Virginia to Memphis, Tennessee. Mom made a big fuss over us and, along the way, she and Vernon told us about the mansion that was going to be our home. Vernon talked even more about his son, Elvis, who was a famous singer and entertainer and who soon was going to make a movie called *G.I. Blues.* He told us that Elvis was going to make a lot of movies and that we would be able to go to some of them and see them being made. That sounded exciting and I guess Vernon was nice enough, but he seemed kind of distant and we didn't quite know what to make of his being called our new daddy. I was seven, Ricky was six, and David was four, and we were wondering what had happened to our old daddy. It all seemed strange to us.

But we were impressed with the limousine and very happy that our mother had finally rescued us after several months at the boarding school. And, though it was late at night when we arrived, we were even more impressed when we drove through the iron gates of Graceland. It was all lit up. We gazed at tall white columns, stairs flanked by two huge stone lions that seemed to glow in the night, a green lawn and trees that went on forever.

Vernon said, "This is your new home, boys," and took us in to show us around. The house was not only more beautiful and grander than anything we'd lived in, it was grander than anything we'd ever seen! We kept looking to my mom to see if it was all true.

"This is our home, now," she said.

"Do you like it?" Vernon asked.

We just nodded, wide-eyed and amazed. After they showed us

through several rooms, we went downstairs and found Elvis shooting pool. There had seemed to be people in every room of the house when we arrived, but they had all gathered in the poolroom when Vernon and Dee took us down to meet our new stepbrother. When we walked in Elvis had his back to us, and for an instant we were scared. Every castle, I'd learned, had an ogre or a giant, someone who'd make our lives a misery, and I was sure Elvis would be the one. But when he turned to meet us he laughed. He immediately lifted the three of us up in one embrace and said to Vernon, "Daddy, I've always wanted a little brother. And now I have three."

Elvis sat down with us and introduced us to Red West and other guys that we would get to know well, and also to some we would never see again—like this heavyset guy named Fabian, who I thought was funny. Then Elvis asked us what we liked to eat, what games we played, what toys we wanted, whether we rode bikes, what kind of dogs we liked, and a dozen other questions. He even tried to teach us how to shoot pool, lifting us over the edge of the table and directing our shots. We got to bed very late (that night we slept on blankets on the floor next to Vernon and Mom's bed) and even though we were tired it was hard to get to sleep.

Mom woke us up early in the morning. "Elvis wants you to come out in the backyard," she said. We rubbed our eyes and wondered what was in store for us. Would the loving, generous Elvis of the night before be a red-eyed, mean, and demanding brute in the morning air? We didn't know, but one thing my dad had taught us was that when the morning call sounded you responded. And something in Mom's smile told us we weren't exactly in trouble. We hurried out, and next to the pool we found a smiling Elvis standing in the middle of bikes, sleds, games, footballs, bats, toy cars, tractors, rifles, and even puppies and kittens, all in numbers we'd never seen before, not even at Christmas. "Boys," he said, "all of this is for you. To welcome my new brothers to Graceland. I know we're going to have good times together." We were delighted and confused. We didn't know whether to run to Elvis or the toys, so we ran toward him and then veered off at the first toys. We started playing with them immediately, tossing the balls with Elvis, testing the cars, and sighting through the toy guns. "I'll teach you how to shoot real ones when you get older," Elvis said. Then David set out for a swing set, Rick got in a pedal tractor, and I jumped on a bike. I rode it around the pool several times and announced, "I don't need these training wheels!"

"Billy, if you can ride it without, we'll take them off," Elvis said.

"I can, sir," I said, still not sure what to call Elvis.

"Charlie," Elvis commanded, "get those training wheels off 'Sir's' bike. He doesn't need them." Charlie Hodge took them off and I set out again. Elvis ran after me with his arms wide apart, ready to grab me if I fell. He was laughing and whooping and when I wasn't concentrating on staying upright I laughed a little too. Vernon, Charlie, Red West, and the rest laughed with us but my mom, when I caught sight of her, had hidden her eyes and was sort of collapsed against the wall of the house. But I didn't fall.

At some point Elvis picked up a football and motioned us toward him. "Boys, do you like football?" We said we did but we weren't sure. In Germany everyone played soccer, but our dad, Bill, had told us football was a man's real sport and Elvis seemed to be of the same opinion. "We don't know how to play," I said.

"You'll learn," Elvis answered. He organized a game. Looking back I realize that the game we played wasn't really football. Not by the rules we soon learned. But it was a game designed to permit us to excel and triumph—whatever we did led to a score, a victory. Catching the ball didn't really matter as long as we pursued it, scooped it up, and continued toward the goal line. Maybe it was closer to rugby. But that doesn't matter. We played the game for hours. We were more than happy. We were ecstatic.

Later I found out he had spent hours the previous night calling department store managers and pet store owners, persuading them to open their stores so that he could shop for the things he thought we'd want. He bought three of everything so we wouldn't fight over the bounty. Then he'd spent the rest of the night and early morning pacing the backyard waiting for us to wake up. We really didn't know who Elvis was, but we knew we liked him, and that we wanted to be with him from then on. That was in the spring of 1960 and for the next seventeen years I was with him. He was my big brother, my role model, my god.

It ended, for me, twenty-seven years later in a psychologist's office in a drug abuse center in Florida. After a battery of tests measuring depression, anxiety, anger, interpersonal relationships, alcohol use, and drug abuse, they presented me with a typed "Psychological

Evaluation." Each paragraph began "Mr. Stanley," and what followed jumped out at me and hit hard. "He is compulsively driven toward people. . . . His high level of socialization reflects both a need to belong and a fear of rejection. . . . His relationships are extremely superficial and shallow in nature. . . . He is easily bored. . . . He may start many projects but finish few. . . . He is moderately depressed. . . . He is extremely anxious and angry. . . . He is quite impulsive and it is difficult for him to delay gratification of his impulses. . . . He has a poorly developed conscience, easy morals, and fluctuating ethical values. . . . He is rebellious, resentful, and nonconforming. . . . He may be described as being narcissistic, selfish, and a self-indulgent person."

I looked up at the psychologist.

"That's Elvis," I said.

"That's you," he answered.

I nodded and smiled. But deep inside I had the same feeling of desolation and abandonment I'd known at Breezy Point Farms. So I'd become Elvis. It had always been my goal and I'd achieved it. But not as an entertainer, not with his money, not with his fame, not even (perhaps) with his humor. I'd become his psychological problems, his evasion, his predilection to self-destruct. And I was there alone with it, thirty-four years old, undereducated, and broke. I had loved Elvis. I adored him. I suffered at his death and for years after that. And now, ten years later, I felt I was present at my own death. I had "bottomed out" on alcohol and drugs. I had no income, no prospects, and no interest or even concern at my lack of prospects. And my wife, Connie, the only woman who had loved me for myself, had filed for a divorce. What had gone wrong, first with Elvis, now with me? People have always befriended me because of my close relationship with him, asking me, "What was Elvis really like?" The answer was in front of me, staring me in the face from those sheets of paper, and it was shattering. What had happened to Elvis? What happened to the three stepbrothers who loved him? Everything had been great, and then everything became so chaotic, so full of hurt. The psychologist's assessment did leave one hope, I realized, and that was to try to put the pieces back together. I started remembering. . . .

ELVIS,

MY BROTHER

1

"WELCOME TO MY WORLD"

(December 1958 ▬ Summer 1961)

It all began in the early winter of 1958 in Germany, where my natural father, Bill, was stationed. More than a decade before, he'd been General Patton's personal bodyguard, but now he was just a sergeant in a peacetime army. At the same time, Elvis was in Germany to serve his own celebrated hitch in the U.S. Army. And it was there, in Frankfurt, where Vernon Presley had gone to live near his son, that our mother and Vernon first met. Years later I learned what most people now know: Dee, my mom, had called Elvis to offer him some southern home cooking and Elvis arranged a meeting between Dee and Vernon at a restaurant. Shortly after that Vernon started showing up at our apartment in Bad Neuheim. That Christmas I got a new sled and Mom told me it was from Vernon, but I still didn't know who he was. I knew that he had been coming around, but we were kids and we paid little attention to him. I had thought that he was a friend of my dad's. The odd thing, as I later learned, is that I was right. While Vernon pursued my mother, he befriended my father. For a time they were a threesome, but my dad was a drinker and liked to spend his time off with his army friends. Whether it was that or something else that provoked my mom, I don't know. But in the spring of 1959 she started seeing Vernon on her own and I guess they spent a lot of time together when Bill was out on maneuvers.

That summer their relationship must have come to some crisis because Ricky, David, and I were taken to the airport to fly back to the States with our mom. We were told simply that we were going to visit our Aunt Peggy in Virginia for a few weeks. But from the way they packed all of our things up, and from the general tension, we knew something was wrong. Both Vernon and Bill were at the airport to see us off. And, except for one occasion, I didn't see my real father again for another fourteen years. It was only then that I learned some of the details of their breakup. Apparently Dee had told my dad what was going on and Bill had been shocked. He saw Vernon as a buddy to both of them, and had actually been flattered that Vernon was willing to escort Dee places that Bill didn't want to go. When he found out the truth, he tried to fight. But Dee was determined, and though Bill was a tough guy—he'd been a much decorated war hero before Patton made him his bodyguard—he had finally given in. Bill realized his drinking and neglect of my mom had been a big part of the problem and that he hadn't earned much sympathy from anyone. Even his commanding officer had told him, "If you raise any hell about this you can forget your pension." I do remember that my dad looked on proudly as we boarded that plane.

A year later, the one time I did see him, he was calmly sitting and having a drink with Vernon and Dee at Graceland. He got up to leave and then, before he got to the door, he picked me up and hugged me. "I want you to listen to me, Billy," he said, softly. "Mr. Presley is going to be your new father. I won't be here anymore. I want you to say, 'Yes, sir' and 'No, sir' to him." I was confused and I was starting to cry but I bit my lip and said, "Yes, sir." "And remember to always take care of your mother," he said. Then he put me down and went out the door.

A few weeks later I walked up to Vernon and asked, "Sir, may we call you Daddy?" Vernon said, "You sure can, son."

When we arrived in the states from Germany we did go to my Aunt Peggy's house in Virginia. But after a short time my mother told us that she was going back to Germany and we were sent to Breezy Point Farms. At first it was impressive . . . a large estate on the banks of a wide river. While my mom was there they were really nice to us but as soon as her car left the driveway things changed fast. The other kids were mostly older than we were, and didn't seem to like us much. They told us we were "army brats" and that their parents were much more important. The teachers were worse. They all looked grim-faced and sickly, and they put Tabasco sauce on your tongue when you were bad. The main entrance had big soft furniture but after the first day we never got to go there. The classrooms all had hard wooden benches and the dorm where we slept at night was always cold and dark. David was three at that time and they made him sleep across the dorm from Rick and me in this section they had for infants. We had slept together all our lives and the sudden separation was difficult for David. After the lights were out we could hear him crying, so either Rick or I would sneak across the room and sit on the edge of his cot until he quieted down and went to sleep. Some nights he wouldn't sleep until one of us got in bed with him. Occasionally we'd get caught and that meant more Tabasco sauce on our tongues.

The only fun I remember having was when some older boys put me up to opening the girl's bathroom door one night. There were three girls, probably eight or nine years old, all in this one tub together. They screamed and one stood up to throw a bar of soap at me. Then she realized her mistake, screamed again, and fell back into the tub. Other than that we were just counting the days until someone came and got us out.

Dee took us there in late summer of 1959 and by Christmas we were still there. Alone. It seemed all the other kids went home for Christmas. But all we got was a call from my mother. No one even came to see us. By then we'd started calling Breezy Point Farms "the orphanage," and we'd begun to think of ourselves as orphans. One of the older guys, the last to leave for the holidays, told us that he was getting out for good, but that it looked like we'd been left there and that we'd probably be there forever. Then his parents came to get him, and by the size of his parents' car and the way they dressed we at least figured that we weren't in an orphanage for the poor.

When we did get that call from Mom on Christmas day we immediately asked her where she was. She told us she was with Vernon at Elvis's house in Bad Neuheim. In the background we could hear a lot of people and laughter. "I sure wish you boys were here with me," Mom said. We wished it too. We didn't know what had happened when we had all been in Germany, but we knew that everyone else was there now and that we only had each other. My brothers and I banded together, determined that nothing would ever separate us.

On January 19, 1960, my seventh birthday, there was another call from Mom. By now we were sure we'd never get out of the "orphanage." Mom kept telling us we'd all be together soon, but she'd been telling us that for months. And I guess my mother was telling us about Elvis and Vernon even then. She remembers calling and asking us if we ate our cereal for breakfast. She recalls that we'd ask, "Does Elvis eat cereal?" and she'd say, "Every morning." I don't remember that. But either Rick or I must have mentioned Elvis at the school because I remember these girls who were much older, teasing us. They had this plastic guitar with Elvis's picture on it. They would say, "This is your new brother. When's he going to come and get you out of here?" Then they'd start singing his songs—"Love Me Tender" and "Heartbreak Hotel"—and they'd laugh. When Dee and Vernon finally came and got us, we had the last laugh.

Graceland is a colonial mansion situated south of Memphis on Highway 51 (now Elvis Presley Boulevard) in a suburb called Whitehaven, just a few miles north of the Mississippi border. It sits on a hill overlooking a rolling fourteen acres of fields and trees, mostly oak and magnolia. A stone wall seven feet high separates it from the road in front and from the church grounds to the right. The stone wall also separates Graceland from the backyards of the houses to the right (they face on Dolan Street), while an equally high wooden fence surrounds the larger back grounds to the property. (David and I helped build that fence.) From the road a circular drive winds up the hill to the columned entrance and then back down to the wrought-iron front gates. These are called the Music Gates, with metal figures of Elvis, his guitar, and floating music notes welded on the perpendicular bars.

At the top of the drive a low stone wall surrounds the house. When we first arrived, Graceland was all natural-colored limestone. On the exterior of the mansion only the shutters around the windows are painted green. Shortly after we arrived Elvis had everything else painted white, and he had soft blue spotlights installed. They circled the house, and at night they made the limestone facing glow like a ghostly apparition from the antebellum south. (I helped with the painting and the maintenance of the lights.)

As you enter the mansion the formal dining room is to the left and the living room, with its deep red carpet and white baby grand piano, is to the right. All of the walls on the main level are a deep purple with gold trim and all the draperies are of white corduroy. At the end of the large main foyer is a winding gold and white stairway leading up to Elvis's room and the other bedrooms. At the left of the main foyer a staircase leads down to the TV-projection room, with a full bar and the poolroom. These two rooms had been a dirt-floored basement when Elvis bought the house, but he put in wood floors, carpets, and paneling. Years later he had the walls and ceiling of the TV room completely enclosed with mirrors to make it look larger. He also had a colorful fabric lining put in the ceiling of the poolroom. But when we first got there, they were wood-paneled.

Just past the foyer stairs, on the left, is the door leading to the large kitchen. Straight ahead and up a few stairs is the garden room, also called the den, which was a screened back porch when we first saw it. Shortly after our arrival Elvis had it enclosed with glass and had a waterfall built at one end. This was generally the most popular room in the house.

We lived at Graceland for the next two years in what had originally been a garage for Elvis's many cars and motorcycles. In anticipation of our arrival it had been completely redone into one huge room that housed Dee and Vernon and the three of us. The room was just a few steps outside the den (then a porch), with a connecting walkway covered by an awning. Another huge awning covered a newly paved carport area where all the vehicles had been moved.

Vernon still had his bedroom on the second floor down the hall from Elvis's. We'd all slept there those first few nights and Mom could have stayed there with Vernon. But she didn't want us to be separated. So all of us slept together in the converted garage. I guess our mom just felt cautious about her new environment and wanted us under her wing.

I think there was another reason Dee rejected the upstairs room. It had been Vernon and Gladys's room and the closets were still filled with Gladys's clothes. Her side of the family, the Smiths, would meet often to say prayers in remembrance of her. At that time we really didn't know much about Gladys except that she was Elvis's mother, Vernon's first wife. Later Elvis told us that he had been very close to her and that he had always honored her wishes and followed her advice. "Boys," he told us, "I want you to take care to be the same way with your mom because she's the only one that you'll ever have and if you ever lost her you'd be losing part of your soul."

I was later to read of a supposed resentment Elvis had felt when Vernon started dating and later married Dee so soon after his mother's death. Elvis reportedly couldn't understand how Gladys was replaced so quickly in Vernon's heart. But if he harbored a resentment we never saw it.

Our room was filled with bikes, sleds, toys, and television sets, and if they spilled out into the yard and were temporarily forgotten there were maids to pick everything up. The fourteen acres of the estate were our playground. The pool, the rolling hills, and the oak trees (we climbed every one) became our territory. The huge house was an indoor playground with only Elvis's room off limits. We got into everything, testing our "new daddy" and our mom in every way we could think of. We must have tested Elvis, too, but he never said a word about it. I remember when I discovered that the phone system with its five lines and blinking lights could be a source of great amusement. I'd try to catch the incoming calls before anyone else could get to them just so I could answer "Graceland." Or I'd listen in on calls in progress and push the hold button just to see what would happen. Once when Elvis was on a call to the West Coast I managed to cut him off several times before finally jamming up the phones altogether. I heard him upstairs, slamming the phone down and exclaiming, "Damn those boys!" All afternoon I expected him to come down on me. But Elvis was silent. Later, when Vernon got home, I heard plenty about it.

In the mornings we were driven to school in the limo or the pink Cadillac that had been Elvis's gift to Gladys. Usually Vernon took us, but sometimes it was Alberta, the maid, who drove. And sometimes Lamar Fike, who'd been with Elvis since the day Elvis entered the army, drove us in the BMW sports car Elvis had bought in Germany. It was a two-seater with a jump seat in back. We'd take turns to determine who got to ride up front with Lamar and who got to ride in back. We loved it either way because of that jump seat and because Lamar drove fast. And we loved to joke with him. Our day really began when we got back from school and asked, "Is Elvis home?" Our favorite way of greeting him was to catch him unawares and throw a cross-body block at his knees. Sometimes we were actually able to knock him down. Then there'd be a four-way wrestling match. But more often, we'd just hang on his legs, wrapping ourselves around him to try and trip him as he walked around the house. We could hang on a long time.

Elvis wasn't much for discipline, but Vernon was. We'd listen respectfully to Vernon's warnings and then go out and do the opposite of what he said. There was a house at the back of the property that Elvis eventually bulldozed. One day we went out and threw rocks through all the windows. We even broke all the light fixtures inside. We just wanted to see the glass breaking. Vernon found out and came after us to give us a whipping. Elvis heard him cussing us.

"What's the problem, Daddy?" Elvis asked Vernon.

"It's these damn kids. They broke every window in the back house and I'm going to whip their asses!"

"Now, Daddy. Kids will be kids. They probably didn't have anything else to do."

"All the same," Vernon vowed. "I'm going to whip them!"

"Now, Daddy," Elvis went on, "you don't want to hurt these boys. They know they've done wrong. And they're sorry for it."

Vernon, of course, had to relent. He preached the rules, but Elvis was the law and when he was around we were saved.

Another time Elvis left his motorcycle in the front drive and I climbed on. I was having a good time pretending I was Elvis racing down the road when all of a sudden it fell over, throwing me clear. Vernon was right on me, yelling and cussing, and Elvis heard the commotion from upstairs.

"What's going on?" Elvis called down. "Is he all right?"

"Now he is," Vernon said. "But he soon won't be. This time I'm going to whip him."

Elvis said, "Daddy, don't you worry about it. The bike just fell. It was my fault for leaving it there." I was saved again.

Of course there were a few times when Elvis wasn't on the spot to stand up for us and we would go running to find him with Vernon in hot pursuit. But we couldn't always get to him in time. Once David came in the house wiping away his tears with one hand and rubbing his sore behind with the other.

"Damn that Daddy!" David said. Elvis just roared with laughter.

There were always a lot of adults around the house. The "Memphis Mafia" of Red and Sonny West, Joe Esposito, Lamar Fike, Charlie Hodge, Gene Smith, a guy called Chief, lots of others. Other people would call them the Memphis Mafia, a term coined by some journalist, but we never used that expression except in jest. All these adults and just us three kids. I liked Sonny West the best. He played games with us, taught us how to fight, how to work the slot cars, and later, how to ride motorcycles. All the good stuff. We also liked Vernon's brother, Vester. He worked the grounds and we'd follow him around, sometimes riding on the tractor with him. Our favorite was Uncle Earl Pritchard. He had married Nash, one of Vernon's sisters, and he took over as the head groundskeeper when Vester took over security. Earl had a great sense of humor and was always telling us jokes. He once told us, "Vernon wouldn't go to hell for a nickel but he might just get so close trying to pick one up that he'd fall in." Other favorites were Gladys's brother, Travis Smith, and his sons, Billy and Gene Smith. Vester Presley had married Gladys's sister, Cletus, so brother and brother had married sister and sister, and all lived and worked at Graceland. You could say it was a family affair.

In those days in the early sixties there were peacocks all over the grounds, and guinea hens and some mules out in the pasture. There was even a chicken coop that Vernon had put in so that we'd all have fresh eggs. Usually we'd chase the peacocks, circle the chickens, and steer clear of the mules, but if we got bored or mean we'd throw rocks at all of them just to stir them up. It was a fantasy world for us, but in a sense it was also a fantasy world for Vernon and Elvis, because they could have all the things that they could never have afforded for themselves on a sharecropper's farm. My brothers and I even made up new words for an old song and sang, "Old Elvis had a farm, ee-i-ee-i-oh." Elvis folded his arms in front of him and said, "Uh, now just who are you calling old?"

We had fun with most everyone, except maybe Vernon. I guess it was Vernon's job to look after the mansion and its finances and make sure that expenses were kept under control. He really got upset one time I was shooting pool and the cue ball hopped off the pool table and landed on a glass-topped table, cracking the glass. Vernon started moaning and cussing me. But Elvis said, "Whoa now, Daddy." Vernon said, "Damn that Billy. That glass is expensive." Elvis said, "It's only money." Vernon looked aghast. Only money! He'd lived most of his life in harder times. But he never questioned Elvis and never gave us a whipping when Elvis was around. When Elvis was out of town, he got a few licks in.

But even Vernon could be funny at times. He loved those mules, and one night in the kitchen he was telling us boys about his mule down in East Tupelo, Mississippi. "That mule would get to farting," Vernon laughed, "and if he farted once you knew there were bigger things to come. On a cold winter's day if you got behind him and lit a match at the first rumble you could get a blast of blue flame ten feet long!" Elvis had been passing the kitchen while Vernon told that story and he must have heard some of it because he swung the door open with an expectant grin.

"What did you say, Daddy?" Elvis asked. But Vernon was laughing too hard to repeat himself. So it was up to eight-year-old Billy to retell the story word for word just as Vernon had. "Why Billy!" Elvis roared.

My mom had been watching all this with a faraway smile. Although she probably didn't think the story was funny, she wasn't going to spoil everyone else's fun. But then she narrowed her eyes at me as if to say, "I hope you're good and proud of yourself, acting up and talking that way." I just kept laughing with Vernon and Elvis.

At school we were somewhat aloof from the other kids. My brothers and I had become very close when we felt we were orphans, and we hung pretty much together at Graceland Elementary. There was some taunting, because of Elvis, and we all got into a few fights just to let the others know we weren't sissies. Elvis told us never to back down, particularly when some kid was being a bully. He told us he had been harassed, too, and that he had always looked for a peaceable way out. But sometimes you just had to stand up for yourself and be prepared to fight. So we were ready when some kid would say, "Hey, there goes Elvis's little brother. Let's see how tough the little big shot is."

One day there was a knock on the front door at Graceland and I opened it, expecting to look up at some adult. Instead there was a six-year-old blond kid about my size. He looked puny. And arrogant. I didn't know how he'd gotten past the gate but I disliked him immediately.

"What do you want?" I asked in my toughest tone.

"Have you got a brother named Ricky?" he asked.

"Sure do."

"Well, I've come here to fight him."

I closed the door behind me and walked out on the porch, almost bumping chests with him. "Why wait for Rick?" I asked. "Why don't you fight me?"

"No. I think I'll wait for Ricky," he said. He walked away a few steps and sat on one of the stones that lined the driveway. I picked out a larger stone and sat down on it with my arms folded.

"I'll wait with you," I said.

I kept my eye on this kid, thinking that Ricky was going to whip him but that if he said or did something wrong, I might just do it first. Finally Ricky came up on his bicycle and I soon realized that the kid and been leading me on. The two of them were friends!

"This is my new buddy, Jackie," Ricky explained. It seems the two of them had almost gotten into a fight outside the school and Jackie had had a bad attack of asthma. Ricky put him over his bike and rode him to Jackie's house for medication. "Seems like he saved my life," Jackie said.

I was a little disappointed that there was no fight but I was glad Rick had made a friend at school, so I went with them into the house. Elvis was there and he asked, "Who's this?"

"This here's my friend, Jackie Stovall," Rick said.

Elvis said, "Well there's a Stovall who sold me my radio control airplane and there's another Stovall who handles all my money. You related to them?"

"That's my daddy and my granddaddy," Jackie said.

"Well, son, you're welcome to come up here anytime you want," Elvis said.

The granddaddy Jackie spoke of, I soon learned, was a vice-president of the National Bank of Commerce, one of the largest in Memphis. He happened to have been closing the vault of the downtown bank years before when Elvis was there asking for a loan. Elvis, then nineteen, had a chance to work as an apprentice for the Crown Electric Company but he needed a pickup truck to do it. He went to every bank in Memphis looking for a loan so that he could buy a used truck. Elvis spotted the elder Stovall, asked a teller who he was, and strode right up to him. "Sir," Elvis said, "I've come to ask you for a loan to buy a truck."

"Have you spoken to one of our loan officers?" Jackie's granddaddy asked.

"Yes, sir. He turned me down."

Stovall asked him what kind of credit he had and what kind of collateral he had. Elvis replied that that's just what all the other bankers had asked him before they turned him down.

"Mr. Stovall," Elvis asked, "how do you get started if all you have is the desire to work and to honor your commitments?"

The banker responded by arranging to give him the loan on the spot. Six months later Elvis cut that record, "That's All Right (Mama)" and "Blue Moon of Kentucky" over at Sun Studios and was on his way to becoming a millionaire. Later Elvis went back to the senior Stovall and said, "Sir, you believed in me when I had nothing. Now I'm going to believe in you." And Jackie's granddaddy and his bank handled all of Elvis's money from then on.

So Ricky liked Jackie, Elvis liked Jackie, and I decided I liked Jackie. When Elvis talked to him, man-to-man, he stood there and responded in kind. He spent so much time with us that he became, in effect, the fourth "little Presley" at Graceland.

Dinners were usually our quiet time. Alberta (Elvis called her Alberta V.O. 5 or just O-Five—he would burst into the kitchen and say, "O-Five. What's cooking?") would set up ours in the kitchen. Vernon and Dee liked it that way. Our family kept its separate identity with the three hellions under their watchful eye. This way they could have us quiet and ready for bed by the time Elvis and the others were sitting down to their typically late dinner in the main dining room. We got to go in and say goodnight to Elvis just as they were sitting down. Elvis would say, "Come on, Dee. Let them stay up and eat with us." Dee would say, "Elvis, they've already eaten and they need their sleep." But occasionally, if there was no school the next day, we'd all get to eat with Elvis.

Usually Elvis's pleas on our behalf would work. "Come on, Dee," Elvis would say. "I've been on the road and I haven't had any time to spend with them. Let me take them to the movies tonight. I've already got the theater rented." Dee would see us jumping up and down in anticipation and would finally relent. The next day she'd have to call the school to give an excuse for our absence.

In those early years when we all ate together, Scatter, Elvis's chimp, usually had a place at the table. Elvis would dress Scatter up in some weird outfit. He even put glasses on him and tried to get him to serve us food. That was always a disaster. Sometimes he'd stick a cigar in Scatter's mouth and we'd all address the chimp as Colonel. Scatter would just eat the cigar. Scatter had other tricks. The

Memphis Mafia brought a lot of pretty girls around. Some were their regular girlfriends who knew to watch out for Scatter, but others were there for the first time, all agog at the chance to meet Elvis Presley. They were the easy targets for Scatter, who made their visits miserable. All of this delighted Elvis.

We'd already learned to be wary of Scatter. Shortly after we arrived at Graceland the three of us were sitting quietly in the TV room one afternoon when the door opened and Scatter came screaming into the room. We chased him over the furniture, up the drapes, and back over the furniture. Then he turned and chased us! The damage we could cause was nothing compared to what this monkey did. He practically destroyed the place. Then we heard Elvis laughing in the hallway. We hadn't even known he was home.

We had trouble with one of the dogs at Graceland, too. Elvis had a mean dog, a basset hound, that would chase us whenever he saw us. But Elvis had another dog named Rebel, a collie that defended us. Once Rebel grabbed that hound by the neck just before he got to me. He was the greatest dog Elvis ever had, with the possible exception of Git Low.

We had a myna bird that could talk quite well. Actually it was Elvis's bird but we kind of considered anything at Graceland to be ours as well. This myna bird must have picked up his vocabulary from Vernon, because most of what he said was in the nature of orders: "Turn that light off!" . . . "Shut the door!"—that kind of thing. He sat on his perch in the kitchen at night, a black bird in a dark room. One night Elvis came into the kitchen late looking for something in the refrigerator. He had just got it open when the myna bird cried, "Close that damn door!" Elvis jumped a foot in the air. "I'm going to shoot that damn bird!" he said. Other times he'd say, "We're gonna have that bird for dinner one night."

Also at that time we had a Siamese cat named Wendell. But cats didn't fare too well at Graceland. Scatter terrified them.

Elvis had fully embarked on his film career by now, making *G.I. Blues*, *Blue Hawaii*, *Flaming Star*, and *Wild in the Country*. Elvis always brought one copy of the movie home with him and a couple of nights later, if we could wait that long, we'd all gather in the TV room and Vernon would play it for us on the sixteen-millimeter projector. Elvis wasn't much for watching his own movies, but he did watch *Flaming Star* with us. He told us that what impressed him most was his costar

Dolores del Rio. "Look at her!" he exclaimed when she appeared on the screen, "That woman is fifty-five years old and she's beautiful! Even her skin is beautiful." Elvis also said that his role as a half-breed son of a Kiowa Indian in west Texas was a natural for him because he was one-quarter Cherokee himself. We were impressed with that but Vernon let us know later that it was an exaggeration. The next day we challenged Elvis on it but he stuck to his version. "Daddy just doesn't want to admit it," he said. "Everyone from East Tupelo has got some Cherokee or Chickasaw blood. Tupelo comes from a Chickasaw word meaning lodging place. One of these days I'm going to take you boys back there and show you some caves where Indians lived. There might be some arrowheads. Maybe even a live Indian." So we were impressed all over again.

I particularly liked *Flaming Star* because of the difficulties Elvis's character faced and the nobility and independence (or rebelliousness) with which he faced them. Looking back, I feel we sometimes fail to appreciate the effect that a favorite movie seen at an impressionable age (I was eight the first time I saw it) will have on our basic views of the world. Particularly when it is our main hero who is forced to deal with the problems. For me that movie was *Flaming Star*. And it was Elvis. He was handsome. He was strong. He was noble and just. And he was my brother.

When we watched *Wild in the Country*, Elvis wanted to be sure Dee watched it with us. "I want you to watch Hope Lange," Elvis told her. "Dee, that woman reminds me so much of you. Not just her looks but the way she carries and expresses herself."

"Fiddlesticks, Elvis. You're just trying to flatter me. I don't look like any elegant movie star like Hope Lange."

"Yes you do, Dee!" Elvis answered. "Doesn't she, Daddy?"

"She sure does, Sonny."

"Dee, you don't know how hard it was for me to do those love scenes with Hope. I kept looking at her and seeing you."

Dee wasn't buying it, although everyone described her as pretty and vivacious and she surely was (and still is today). But I wasn't much of a judge of Elvis's comparison. I barely noticed Hope Lange. That was because of Tuesday Weld. I was beginning to notice girls, though I'd never at that time admit it, and Tuesday Weld was a lot of girl to notice. Elvis couldn't have been too happy with the movie, though, because halfway through he got up and went out riding on his motorcycle. But I kept my eyes glued to the screen for every glimpse of Tuesday Weld.

We first saw Elvis on television on "Frank Sinatra's Welcome Home Party for Elvis Presley" in May of 1960, a few days after we arrived at Graceland. The first time we saw him perform live was at a benefit show in February, 1961. That show at the Ellis Auditorium in Memphis and another benefit in Hawaii a few months later (we didn't get to go) turned out to be his last live performances for over eight years. I can't say we were disappointed—we were so young and we were excited—but we were in a balcony with Vernon and Dee that seemed far removed from the action, and the performance didn't have the rocking, leg-thumping wildness that we'd seen in film clips of earlier performances. Apparently Colonel Parker had wanted to present a new, subdued Elvis with shaved sideburns and a lot less leg movement. The songs were mostly ballads: "Are You Lonesome Tonight," "Surrender," and "It's Now or Never." But by the time Elvis got to his closing song, "Hound Dog," it was rocking and the jammed house of more than 5,000 were on their feet.

Still, the thing I remember most about that night was the drive back to Graceland. Vernon and Dee got into a terrible fight and Dee had opened the door and tried to jump out while the car was moving at full speed. We had no idea what it was all about at that time but later we found out that Dee had learned she was pregnant. Elvis's reaction was one of delight. "You mean I'm going to have a baby sister, too!" he had exclaimed to Dee. But Vernon's reaction was darkly clouded by an almost insane and unfounded jealousy of which we, at that time, had no understanding. "Well, that's fine, Dee," he reportedly said. "But just whose child is it?" I don't know if that was the cause of the fight. Mom later lost the child and I've never asked her about it. But I do know there were some strong emotions on display that night.

The first filming Elvis took us to was *Follow That Dream*. It was shot in 1961 near Clearwater, Florida, during our summer vacation, and the whole family took over a motel close to the action. It had a pool and everything, but we had the most fun at the set. We got into everything. After awhile Vernon and the security guards tried to keep us in a car, but we kept getting out and going up to the film crew. "How come you do this?" we'd ask them. "What's this for? Why do you do that?" They knew who we were so they had to put up with us.

Sometimes word of our mischief would get back to Elvis. They thought Elvis would put a stop to it. But usually he'd just laugh. Once a particularly disturbed assistant director scolded us within earshot of Elvis. He came over, pointing a finger at the offender. "Don't be telling them what to do," he said. The guy backed off fast. Elvis was our buddy.

Once the security officers at the set put us in the back of a police car. They were real nice about it, making our "arrests" into a game, and we thought it was great fun until we tried to get out. Then we realized that there were no handles on the doors in the back seat. We wailed and pounded on the window for an hour before they let us out. But afterward we thought it was a great experience.

There was a lot of water-balloon throwing, squirt-gun fighting, and pie throwing on the set. Mostly it was Elvis who started it, but if we had a chance to join in we did. Elvis always said if you couldn't have fun then it wasn't worth it.

It was at *Follow That Dream* that I first became aware of Colonel Parker. He strutted around with his hat and his big cigar. I noticed that everyone jumped when he appeared on the scene, everyone except Elvis and us boys. (Elvis called us "the boys" even if there was only one of us present.) Later I found out why. The colonel thought Elvis had too many camp followers and if one fell into his disfavor, he'd say to Elvis, "What do you need that guy for?" Elvis would answer, "He's here because I want him to be here." It was odd. To us, the colonel was a joke. But to others he was a real menace. If the colonel didn't like them, they could be gone. Not always, but sometimes the colonel would have his way. Nobody else could do that with Elvis.

Back in Memphis, though, Elvis had a more formidable opponent: my mother. Sometimes Elvis rented out the fairgrounds for his entire entourage. He'd rent it from closing until the next morning with instructions that all the rides, games, cotton candy, and hot dog stands were to be open all night. Everything was free for us, and there were no waiting in lines. One night Elvis told us, "Boys, we're going to have some fun tonight. Go tell Dee you're coming with me." We were excited but we were sure we wouldn't be allowed to go. School had started and Dee had issued her decree. No late nights.

We told him, "Elvis, it would sure help if you spoke to Dee." It had always been automatic if it was Elvis doing the asking. But this night it was different. Elvis had to practically beg on our behalf. We heard

16

him say, "Aw, come on, Dee. What's school for, anyway? And you know we'll take care of them." He had to stand and listen to her protests for several minutes. But he wouldn't leave without us and finally she gave in. We were on our way to the fairgrounds.

We arrived there in a string of limousines with Elvis driving the lead car. Rick, David, and I always rode with Elvis, and as soon as we got there we'd head straight for the bumper cars. We'd ride them for hours, smashing into Red, Sonny, Elvis, each other, and anyone who dared move. Then we'd head for the carnival games. There was one with about twenty wooden hoboes moving in a line behind walls, doors, windows, fences, and the like. They all wore hats and the idea was that as soon as they appeared in a window, or a door swung open, you threw a softball and tried to knock the hat off. Red West got the idea to go in back and climb up on the moving conveyor belt between two hoboes. He put one of their hats on and wore this big grin. Naturally, we all let fly at him. Someone caught him right above the eye and he had a big bump there for weeks.

The main attraction was the big roller coaster. The first couple of years we wouldn't go on it. We'd ride the smaller coaster, eat hot dogs, candy, everything there was, and then we'd go to sleep somewhere. Elvis or Sonny would carry us back to the limo and then Elvis would post someone to sit outside the car and watch us until everyone was ready to go back to Graceland. But one time Elvis and Sonny shamed us into going on the big roller coaster. Elvis rode in the car with us, looking perfectly relaxed and happy as we made the ascent up the first incline. We were ready to jump out of our skins. It seemed we would never get to the top, but when we did, the terror began. Going down the first hill Elvis spread his arms wide while we hung on to the bars and screamed. The rest of the ride was a nightmare. I was never so happy as when I saw that the ride was over and we were back at the beginning. But it wasn't over. Elvis just waved us through and we started climbing that steep first hill again. We were terrified but Elvis just said, "This is funsies, boys." As we neared the top he said, "I'm going to show you how easy it is. I'm going to let you go down on your own." Just then he leapt from the car, landed on the narrow walkway, and grabbed the wood railing with one hand. We rode the coaster not really sure what had happened to Elvis. But when we came through for our third ride we could see him at the top, waving and waiting for us. He hopped back into the car just as we reached the peak and started another fast descent. I thought, if Elvis can do that and not be scared, then I'm pretty stupid to be scared just sitting inside the car. From that point on it was all fun.

I guess Elvis was just a big kid in those days. But to a real kid he seemed like something else. He was older brother and substitute father all rolled into one magnetic person.

2

"PROMISED LAND"

(Summer 1961 ▬ Fall 1962)

None of this set too well with my mother. She knew about the roller coaster ride because, of course, we'd bragged to her about it. Dee disapproved of that and thought that Elvis was spoiling us. The worst part was the hours we kept when he was home. Elvis was a very late riser and stayed up well into the early morning. Naturally, we wanted to stay up with him and, despite Dee's protests, we sometimes did. She had other concerns on her mind as well. The lifestyle at Grace-land was not to her liking. Anita Wood, a former Miss Tennessee, was Elvis's girlfriend. She lived at the house, and all the other guys had girls coming in and out too. There were parties going almost every night. Usually we were asleep in our separate quarters by the time they began, but Mom still thought that they were disruptive to a normal life.

Of course, when Elvis was out of town, things quieted down considerably. We'd have to toe the line, go to Sunday school and church, wear ties, all that. We were raised by two opposing influences. Dee was determined to raise us by southern middle-class values as set out by the conservative Church of Christ, while Elvis's rebellious, fun-loving nature drew us toward the other extreme. At Elvis's parties you could meet anyone, and (if you were old enough), do most anything. There was always a party atmosphere at Graceland. Anyone present was drawn into it, and made part of it. Elvis never said, and to our knowledge never felt, "Well, you guys are kids. This is adult time." He never made distinctions for age. He did nothing he was ashamed of or would ever want to hide from either his parents or his children. (Officially we were his brothers, but in our youth we fit the latter description). We were welcome and wanted at any event Elvis sponsored, and encouraged to participate fully, just as Vernon was. I may have seemed a nuisance to some of Elvis's guests but I basked in the light of his acceptance. At those parties Elvis always chose us as his opponents in his karate demonstrations. He broke a lot of our toy guns, but he also made us feel important. And when there was music, and if anyone encouraged me, I'd dance in front of everyone for as long as I could stand up.

If one of us Stanley boys had his own party, usually only on birthdays, Dee and Vernon would screen the guest list. Our friends were welcome only (but only!) if Dee knew their parents through the church. Everyone who came had to be announced at the front gate and escorted up to the house. The few parties we had seemed to occur when Elvis was out of town, but even when he was in town he was careful not to interfere with Dee's well-organized plans. And no one from his so-called entourage dared appear at Graceland at those times.

Sometimes Elvis created chaos even my mom couldn't control. Usually he'd be coming back from Los Angeles after filming at MGM studios. We'd come home from school, excited, waiting for the big tour bus to roll in. Before it did, the street in front of the mansion would fill with fans waiting for a glimpse of "the king." Finally Elvis would pull in, having driven nonstop from L.A.—at the wheel all the way. There'd be quite a commotion until late that night, with Elvis relating stories about the film, his costars, what happened. On the first night Elvis was home we wouldn't have a curfew. Then we'd steer clear of his room for a couple of days while he rested and slept off the ordeal of the movie and his long drive back. But when we knew he was up and about, we'd greet him with our usual body blocks and mischief.

It was at one of those times that I finally did something to get the king's goat. He had Anne Helm, his love interest in *Follow That Dream*, visit the mansion. She was sitting with him in the den and

Elvis had lapsed into the low monotone he used when he wanted to romance women for the first time. I could hear phrases like, "I need someone," and "That would make me so happy." Anne was so pretty and I had a crush on her myself. Only weeks before she had played Frisbee with us on the set of the movie and I still hadn't recovered. But I guess I recognized something different in his voice and I piped up with, "Anita Wood says hello." Elvis turned and stared at me with a mean look. I'd seen it before, but it had never been directed toward me. He said, "You git now, boy." I got. The next day I went up to Elvis to apologize. Elvis didn't seem to know what I was talking about.

That fall Elvis left with the gang for the West Coast to begin production on *Kid Galahad*. Anita was agitated. She came around to our room shortly after he left, grabbed my two brothers and me, and said we were going after Elvis. We piled into the car and tried to catch up with the bus, but after hours of fast driving it was still nowhere in sight. We loved it! We were already deep into Arkansas and we were hoping she'd chase Elvis all the way to California. But finally she turned around and took us home. We could tell she was very upset. We didn't know what it was all about, but we did know that Anita had been hearing a lot about a girl in Germany and she once confronted Elvis about her in front of us.

"Aw, Anita. She's just a kid," Elvis had told her. But there was a lot of tension around Graceland and I know my mom was concerned about it. Anita packed her bags and moved out. With Elvis on the West Coast we had the entire mansion to ourselves. By that time Dee had decided that the whole place was a bad influence. And I guess it was when my teachers called her and said that I was failing the second grade that she became determined to move out of Graceland.

Elvis had a different idea. He was making three pictures a year on the West Coast and he said he was tired of the ordeal of driving the touring bus back and forth each time. He had leased a house formerly owned by the Ali Khan and his wife, Rita Hayworth, on Perugia Way in Bel Air, and he called several times urging Dee and Vernon to move out to California with him. He told Dee how big the house was, how the boys would love it, and how the family could be together all the time. I remember because Dee and Vernon quarreled over the subject of a move. At that time Vernon never traveled without Dee and us at his side. But it pained him to be separated from Elvis. So Vernon argued for the move. But his heart wasn't totally in it. When

Vernon asked Elvis, "Well, Sonny, how will we all fit in out there?" Elvis could only reply, "Daddy, it doesn't matter. The family will be together." But Vernon must have had visions of us living like the "Beverly Hillbillies." He left the decision up to Dee. We heard her tell Vernon, "Elvis has some ideas for those boys. But I'm their mother and I have different plans." She flatly refused to consider any move. Elvis was unhappy, at least at that time. Years later, in Los Angeles, he told us, "Daddy was right. And so was your mom. I was wrong. This is pretty country. And you can make a fast buck. But the way they've got it set up you never know if your feet are on the ground. It just isn't the right place to try to hold family together."

In December of 1961, while Vernon was having our new home on Dolan Street built, we made a sudden move to a house on Hermitage Street. Looking back, I now know that the reason for the rushed move was that Elvis was out of town at the time. If he had been there he could have charmed Dee out of it. He had that power. So with a dreary, snowless winter, a newer and much smaller house, and Elvis still off making his picture, things got a little somber. Dee took control and Vernon watched us like a hawk. It was early to bed, early to rise with our older brother gone. And then a strange thing happened. That Christmas, for the first time anyone could remember, Elvis didn't come home to Graceland. We were crushed. We asked Vernon about it and he said, "Well, boys, it seems that with us moved out and Elvis and Anita broken up, Elvis just doesn't feel he has a home to come back to. He's been talking about all of us moving out to the West Coast so we can be together. You know he's got to make these movies and they take up so much of his time. But your mother won't hear of us going out there."

"Will he ever come back? To live here, not just to visit?"

Vernon laughed. "Of course he will, boys. Sonny's not likely to leave kin behind. Ever. He's not built that way."

When we thought we'd figured out what it was all about my brothers and I came to a decision. We felt that we had to make a choice between our mother's program for us and Elvis's. We decided that if the conflict arose again, we were going with Elvis.

Work on the house on Dolan Street house moved quickly, and we could see that it was going to be a big home. All the rooms were large; in fact, the living room and dining room were actually larger than those at Graceland. They opened onto a patio and a swimming pool that was also bigger than Graceland's. Upstairs there were five bedrooms opening onto two large balconies. The best part was that the back gate opened onto Graceland's seven-acre back meadow. We had our direct connection with Elvis restored! Now we couldn't wait to move out of the house on Hermitage. After school we'd check out the progress on the house and then head onto the Graceland property. Vernon was usually at one place or the other and we'd play there until he gathered us up and took us home.

At last we moved into the house at 1266 Dolan Street. The odd thing was that when it was finally completed, Mom immediately started remodeling. It seemed she had every wall in the back of the house knocked out, and had sliding glass doors put in where the walls had been. I guess she didn't like that "closed in" feeling. Vernon had overseen the construction, with crews working overtime and, I guess, an unlimited budget from Elvis. But you'd have thought they would have planned for some of those things while the house was being built. When we asked Mom about it she just said, "Hush, boys. Vernon built it his way and now I'm rebuilding it mine."

She also had her bedroom expanded and a sauna installed in her bathroom. She even had a white marble pool put in her bedroom. The walls were lined with mirrors everywhere except our bedrooms. We wouldn't have stood for that.

With Graceland as our backyard we hung out anywhere we wanted to on the grounds, usually in oak trees. From the trees outside the office annex, we could look over the wall to the neighboring church parking lot and see fans in trees looking at us. It was like a zoo, but who was inside and who was out? We'd go up to the wall and start talking to them, acting like we ran the mansion. Then we found out what they wanted: autographs! We'd make a deal and then run to the house and have one of the secretaries sign Elvis's name to whatever sheet of paper or book they gave us. They didn't seem to know or care that he was out of town. We started out charging fifty cents for the service but soon we had it up to five dollars.

One of the secretaries was very nice to us, often signing Elvis's name for our scams on the fans. But one day she went to lunch having promised David that she would come back with a Twinkie for him. She forgot, and David repaid her by stealing Vernon's keys and locking her in the office. She banged on the door and yelled for some time before Vernon heard her and found a key to let her out.

We tried to avoid bugging Vernon, but we followed his brother, Uncle Vester (then in charge of the grounds), and Uncle Harold (from Gladys's side of the family) all over the property. We played in the barn, jumping from the loft onto bales of hay. This eventually led to a competition in which we'd see if any of us could do a swan dive without getting the wind knocked out of him. I lost. Rick and I rode Elvis's tandem bike and ended up smashing it into a wall. It had hand brakes and all we knew about was back-pedal brakes. We even took Elvis's go-carts out and ran them down the front drive, engine off. If we'd started the engines Vernon would have been on us in a flash. Even Elvis jumped the few times we actually started the motors to those things. We ended up with a lot of cuts, bumps, and bruises but just like Elvis movie characters, we didn't cry about them; we just went on to the next game.

At that time we liked to play a game in which Rick was Ricky Nelson, David was David Nelson, and I was Elvis. You could call it a movie game because we'd usually decide we'd make a movie. That's what Elvis was doing. Being Elvis, I'd say, "Well we're at my home, Graceland. If we're going to make a movie we're going to have to go out to Hollywood." So we'd ride our bikes across the grounds pretending we were going cross-country just the way Elvis did with his bus. The bikes played a pretty big part in our movie-making. They were our cars, tanks, or motorbikes, depending on the scripts we created; and most of the action featured races, chases, and battles, with the Nelson brothers and Elvis working as a team against imaginary opponents. We were invariably victorious, with David, Ricky, and Elvis emerging in turn as heroes. (Later in 1964 we were all thrilled to meet Ricky Nelson in person when he came to Memphis to perform in a concert. But we weren't brave enough to tell him how great his deeds were in our games.)

I was nine by this time and beginning to feel pretty grown up. But sometimes we still did stupid things. Uncle Harold was the guard at the front gate in those days (he's still there today!) and one late fall day it rained hard and turned the soil into sticky mud. We started throwing mudballs around and soon discovered that if we put a rock in the middle, they flew much farther and truer. We needed a target and Harold was it. We just wanted to get his attention and have him chase us. But one of the "mudrocks" hit him on the shoulder and splattered mud all over his face, and we suddenly had more attention than we wanted. Vernon was in the office working on the books as usual, and for some reason we ran to him for help with Uncle Harold right behind us cussing and yelling. We soon realized our folly in seeking Vernon's assistance and we raced through his office to the front driveway. But by then it was too late. Vernon shouted for us to stop and we froze. The two men grabbed us by our shoulders and then Vernon took us into the annex one by one for a whipping. We came out crying, and Vernon gathered us together before Uncle Harold. He said, "Harold, if they act up again you don't have to come to me. You just whup 'em yourself." After that, in front of Harold we were on our toes.

We made other mistakes that cost us. Like the time we decided to smoke the cigars the colonel had given us. We lit them up in our room and started strutting around pretending we were Elvis and the colonel discussing a recording date. When Dee caught us, Rick put his cigar (still lit) in his back pocket. He jumped around pretty good before they got the fire out. Then Vernon made us smoke whole cigars in front of his whole staff, Uncle Earl, Harold, and the whole landscaping crew—there were a lot of them whooping and laughing as we lit up. We turned green and other colors before going out back to get sick.

In the spring Elvis returned. Vernon told us he was back, and we raced to Graceland. Elvis was talking to some people in the front hall when we came bursting through the door. He just turned and smiled and said, "Hi, boys." I remember that particular grin because Elvis really didn't smile that often. He laughed a lot, but smiles were rarer. At that time I thought it was because he had to smile so much in those movies. But later I remember seeing pictures of Elvis with Vernon and Gladys back in East Tupelo, Mississippi, when he was young. There wasn't a smile in any of them.

Things were back to normal at the mansion. Every day we looked forward to coming home from school. Dee tried to keep us away from Graceland but it was "See you later, Mom," and we were gone. "Where's Elvis?" we'd call as we went through the door. We'd never have to ask him if he wanted to do something. As soon as he saw us he'd come up with the idea. Often it was football. If it was raining outside, no matter, we'd move the living room furniture, set up boundaries, and start a game.

Anita Wood was back and we were glad of that because she'd always been our friend. She took us to parks, took us swimming in the summer, talked to us, played with us—to us she was family.

And the house was full of other people too. While Elvis was away, there was only Grandma Presley (Elvis called her Dodger) watching TV up in her room, or Aunt Delta and Billy Smith, or Vernon and the secretaries out in the office. With Elvis back, every room had people in it, all the TVs were on, and there was music everywhere. We'd stay until either Vernon or Dee came to get us and then sometimes we'd hide. When they found us we'd be curled up together asleep. Dee would wake us and take us home.

There was music in our house on Dolan Street, too, because Vernon had put in a stereo system that went to every room in the house. And sometimes Elvis would come over through the back gates and play the piano and sing and we would all join in. It would always start out as gospel music, but Elvis would and could play anything, any instrument, any kind of music. But as we got older and started buying records and trying to play the ones Elvis and his friends gave us it became apparent that our tastes (and our fondness for volume) were not to our parents' liking. Eventually, Vernon had to have a "playhouse" built for us at the far end of the pool near the mansion wall. There we could play our music loud and carry on without disturbing their peace.

Jackie Stovall was the one friend we could have over at any time. Otherwise Dolan Street was just like the mansion, with potential friends screened through the Whitehaven Church of Christ and delivered to our door by fretful parents at appointed hours. I guess everyone, including Elvis, was afraid of our falling in with the wrong people or of innocently saying the wrong thing to some member of the press. The golden rule was never to reveal anything about Elvis to the public or the press. I think the other rule must have been that we couldn't have friends unless our parents had known their parents for five years. And Dee hadn't been there that long. Except for when we were with Elvis, we felt stifled.

Vernon still drove us to school every day in that pink Caddy and there was a mean old dog who followed us down the road at the end of Dolan Street barking and snarling until we drove out of sight on Highway 51. We'd see him coming and we'd call to Vernon from the back seat, "Hey, Daddy. There's your friend."

"My friend?" he asked once.

"Yeah, he's too mean for any one else to like him."

Vernon laughed at that. Sometimes he'd look around while driving and say, "Where's that dog that's as mean as me?"

Dee was just as strict as Vernon. Elvis had gone off to make his second picture of that year (*It Happened at the World's Fair* followed *Girls, Girls, Girls*) and when he got back he planned a big party at the fairgrounds. We thought Elvis had cleared everything with Dee and we were all excited. Finally the black limo pulled up outside and honked and Elvis waved from the window. Dee looked at us and said, "You're not going." Ricky came running down the stairs yelling, "Mom, Elvis is outside. He's waiting for us." Dee said, "Yes, he's outside and you can just go tell him to leave." Ricky went back upstairs and slammed every door in the house. Elvis continued to wait outside. Finally I said, "Mom?" But she said no. We couldn't believe it.

Around that time both Vernon and Dee talked to us about our having our last name changed to Presley. We were all for it at first, particularly when we learned from Elvis that it was his idea. "You boys are my brothers," he told us. "I lost another at birth [his twin, Jesse, was stillborn] but now I have you. I want you to carry on my name. But it's up to you. No one else." Then Vernon told us that with the Presley name we would have to be even more careful outside the Graceland grounds because we could easily be kidnaped and held for ransom. That soured us a little on the idea, because we felt the restrictions we had already were heavy enough. Just the same, Vernon was for it and so were we because we knew it was what Elvis wanted. Our mom finally said no to the idea. She reminded us that maybe someone should carry on the Stanley name. That we hadn't thought of this shows that we were young, and, more important, shows how much life around Graceland had wiped memories of our real daddy from our minds. My father, who's still alive in Florida, was totally out of picture by that time. I think my mother felt that Elvis already had too much control over us and if we took his name, her influence might weaken further.

If Dee was overprotective, she had her reasons, and if Vernon was strict, he had his. Apart from Elvis and Dee (and Gladys before her death), Vernon was close to no one. In Memphis, in the early fifties before Elvis had gained his fame, Vernon had worked for years packing cans of paint into boxes at a factory. He was always torn between the desire to make more money for his family and the fear that if he made too much he'd be evicted by the Memphis Housing Authority from the only decent place they'd found to live. They occupied a two-bedroom apartment with a kitchen, private bathroom, and running water at the red brick Lauderdale Courts—all for $35.00 a month so long as Vernon's income was less than $3,000 a year. But though he could still have been considered poor at that time, it was quite a step up from what the Presleys had been used to in Mississippi. Back there Vernon had even gone to jail for a year and been put on a chain gang for writing a bad check at a grocery store, a fact Dee didn't learn until years after they were married. Vernon had paid a high price for trying to get food for his family. So he had developed a hard-boiled and self-protective view of life. Elvis had become his entire life, and he didn't want anything to upset what he viewed as a precarious hold on riches.

That fall Elvis took us out to hunt snakes at Ensley Bottoms on the Mississippi River near McKellar Lake. We were probably too young for this but Elvis gave us twenty-gauge shotguns. Elvis, Gene and Billy Smith, Red West, and a few other adults who were with us carried twelve-gauge shotguns. We got some instruction on how to use them. It was a thickly wooded area but there was a trail that ran along the river bank. We must have walked five miles that day, and a couple of miles before we saw the first snake. Rick, then eight years old, saw it first and he fired immediately. But he was at the back of the pack and his shot went between Billy Smith's legs. Billy jumped in the air crying, "What the hell?" and Elvis screamed, "Rick, you got to tell people you're fixing to shoot!" But pretty soon we saw a lot of snakes, some on the bank and some swimming with their heads up like periscopes in the water. "Splash that SOB!" Elvis yelled, and we killed several of them, always with Elvis giving us instructions like, "Don't close both eyes!" and "Hold that thing close to your shoulder!"

After we'd killed several snakes, Elvis decided it was time for a new game and he devised a contest shooting at trees. I know it will sound odd—northern Mississippi boys like Elvis are supposed to hunt bears when they're three—but Elvis never did hunt while growing up. And he didn't really like killing animals, not even snakes.

After taking us out snake-hunting one day that fall, Elvis sat us down and said, "Daddy never did take me hunting. Matter of fact Daddy never took me fishing. He was a sharecropper and he just never had the time." And sometimes Elvis would just put his arms around us, and I felt that his daddy had never done that either, not when Elvis was a boy. But it just must have been that Vernon couldn't help it, that his world was different and harder—we'd learned that Vernon's father regularly beat him—and that he was aloof with us because he'd been that way with Elvis when Elvis was a child. It could have ended there between Elvis and Vernon. But it didn't because Elvis's wealth and fame gave them a second chance. And unlike many others who experienced a sudden rise to stardom, Elvis never turned his back on his family. Elvis and Vernon became more like brothers, at times arguing over how the family wealth and business should be governed, and at other times laughing and delighting in each other's presence. And they hugged a lot. I believe that's something Elvis taught Vernon.

All that fall Graceland was alive with music, guests, parties, and football games on the weekends. And shortly before Christmas it snowed. It wasn't much, just a few inches, but it possibly equaled the previous winter's total snowfall. We were all out on the hills riding sleds until late at night. Elvis was still out there when Dee made us come home. When she got us inside, she said, "Boys, Priscilla's coming from Germany to spend Christmas with us. She's going to be staying here with us." She asked what we thought of that.

We looked at each other and said, "That's great." Then we all scratched our heads and tried to remember who Priscilla was.

3

"BABY LET'S PLAY HOUSE"

(Christmas 1962 ■ Summer 1965)

I first became aware of Priscilla about a year after we'd moved into Graceland. Elvis was sitting in the kitchen holding a photograph of her and talking to Mom.

"This is the one, Dee," he said.

I looked at the photo. She seemed pretty enough. She also looked pretty young. Beyond that I didn't pay much attention. She first came for Christmas in 1962, and Christmases at Graceland were filled with people, presents, expectations, and just plain good times. There were trips to the fairgrounds, all-night movies (Elvis rented out the Memphian theater), and parties at Graceland. Then we had a second winter storm that resulted in a big snow. In Memphis anything more than an inch was a big snow, and this Christmas we had four or five inches. That meant the sleds were out all day and on until three or four in the morning. Since it was Christmas vacation we got to participate in everything as long as we could stay awake.

We built a snowman at least seven feet tall and we spent all day packing the snow against the curbs of the driveway so that we had a track for sledding that we could either bank down for increased speed or bank off to fly several feet in the air before crashing into the yard. Elvis always led the way with the sleds, inventing new ways to increase the speed and flirting with the dangers of a crash. We just followed his lead. Happily.

Christmas itself was celebrated on Christmas Eve. The front lawn was adorned with a nativity scene and there were lights everywhere. Inside, Elvis would sit beside the tree in the living room surrounded by gifts from all over the world. Of course there were plenty of presents for everyone, but Elvis liked to open them one by one, with his whole entourage and their families at hand. Sometimes the proceedings got too drawn out for us and we'd end up in the basement with the other kids.

Now what we called the basement—because it was downstairs—consisted of the TV room with several monitors, a thickly carpeted floor, a complete bar, several lounges, a large walk-in coat closet, and the poolroom. This was all different from the concrete floors, exposed light bulbs, and rafters that had meant "basement" before we moved to Graceland. In our basement we were kings, and though we were usually nice and protective of the other kids, sometimes we could get bossy or mean. One of Elvis's aides, Marty Lacker, brought his kids every Christmas. They were a couple of years younger than we were and this time we decided to scare them by showing how we could turn off a TV screen by remote control. Then we pointed the remote at them and said we were going to erase them. Very few people had remote control back then and we succeeded in terrifying them so much they went yelling and crying upstairs. Marty came down to give us hell but was followed by Elvis who gave him hell. "The kids are just having fun," Elvis threatened. "If yours are crybabies about it then it's their fault." When he was upset about something Elvis could rage and threaten but somewhere in the middle of his worst outburst he'd wink at us and we'd know that it was just playacting. On that occasion, when the storm had quickly passed we all went back upstairs and the long pageant of present opening continued.

Every year it was the same procedure. First Elvis opened all his presents. The gifts came from all over—network executives, movie producers, recording companies, fans. Then he would open the smaller things those closest to him could afford. And then my brothers and I opened our packages. The bounty was always magnificent. After that everyone else would get their checks and presents, with the final gifts being given to Vernon, Dee, and to the woman at Elvis's side.

Before it had been Anita, but this year it was Priscilla. By the oohs and ahhs of everyone there I could tell Elvis gave something beautiful to Priscilla: it was a cute little puppy. But I hardly noticed. My brothers and I were too busy with our loot to know what anyone else had.

A week later Priscilla went back to Germany, and in late January Elvis and his crew drove off to begin filming *Fun In Acapulco*. When he returned to Graceland, Priscilla was with him and shortly there-after her stepfather, a Captain Beaulieu, whom we quickly decided to avoid, was strutting about the grounds. In addition to our personal distaste for this captain, we had Elvis's appraisal to go by. "That guy just likes to push his weight around," Elvis told us. Of course Mom and Vernon said that he was a nice guy and all that. Unconvincingly. But it was Elvis's opinion that mattered.

After a few days of hard questioning of Elvis and my parents, some of it in our living room—we watched and listened from the stairs—the captain went back to Germany and Priscilla moved into the house on Hermitage Street with us. She seemed all right, a little stiff and preoccupied at first, but soon she warmed up to us. When she settled into a routine she'd go to school, come home, change (she was enrolled at Immaculate Conception High and had to wear a uniform), and go over to the mansion to see Elvis. The only difference I could see in having her around was that we saw less of Elvis. And even when Elvis left for a recording session in Nashville she still spent most of her time at Graceland, either with Elvis's grandma, "Dodger," or with Elvis's cousin, Patsy Presley, who worked for Vernon. We could understand why. Vernon had the same rules for Priscilla that he had for us: No friends allowed to visit the house without previously arranged permission, no use of the car except for specific church functions, no spending money if it came out of his pocket, and so on. Within a few weeks she had moved all her stuff into the mansion. I guess that was in violation of the agreement that, I learned later, had been made between Priscilla's stepfather and the Presleys. She was supposed to be living with my parents. But nobody cared except Captain Beaulieu, and he was in Germany.

We really started to get to know Priscilla in the summer of 1963 when Elvis left to make another movie, *Viva Las Vegas*. We started spending more time with her at Graceland and we discovered that she was fun to have around, even if, at seventeen, she was seven years older than I. We were learning football, Elvis's passion, and Priscilla got into most of the games with us. She was a pretty good athlete. Because we were more aggressive we had an edge at blocking and tackling, but we were no match for her at running. She'd burn us with her speed. That speed also gave her the edge in games of tag or hide-and-go-seek, usually played in the mansion at night.

We didn't always plan the games, sometimes they'd just happen. One night we were teasing her about all the makeup she was wearing. Elvis was encouraging her to wear heavy black mascara and false eyelashes and to dye her hair black (Elvis had begun to dye his hair black for the movies). We told her she looked like Lady Dracula. She started chasing us around the house pretending she was going to bite our necks and suck our blood. The game of hide-and-seek with the "vampire lady" went on for hours, and was revived from time to time thereafter whenever we teased her about how she made herself up. Often on Friday nights she'd take us to the midnight horror movie. If the movie featured Dracula or some other vampire we'd tell her that she should be on the screen instead of sitting with us.

Over all she was pretty tough and able to hold her own. But she wasn't fearless. When she graduated from high school Elvis bought her a little red Corvair. I remember one of the first times we all rode with her she was going over to the house of one of the maids, Ernestine, to pick up a cat she wanted. It was a rainy afternoon; in fact it had been raining for a couple of days. We ended up lost in one of the tough areas of town. We had been passing groups of hard-looking young men standing at corners and in front of stores. After awhile we realized that we'd passed some places twice because Cilla wasn't sure where Ernestine's house was. We ended up in a wooded area with nothing but dirt roads and big mud holes completely covered with pools of water. Sure enough, Cilla got the car stuck. Priscilla had attracted considerable attention in the neighborhood. She was a pretty girl with lots of makeup driving by in a shiny new Corvair. We had a difficult time convincing her to leave the car for by this time it was getting dark. We told Cilla she couldn't stay there and that we had to go find Ernestine's house or get help from somewhere. When we all finally got out of the car we realized that the house was on the other side of the cemetery. Now it was starting to rain again and we had no choice but to cut across the graveyard. Priscilla didn't really want to go but it was either that or be left behind. I took the lead through the water, muck, and tombstones. Eventually Cilla followed, yelling, "Would you guys stop walking over the graves!" I remember how scared Priscilla was that time. But later, for Elvis, she had a different version. "I wasn't scared," she said. "I was just hoping your brothers weren't." In any event we got the cat, and it was some of those young men we had feared who, laughing and joking, pushed Priscilla's car out of that mudhole.

Cilla was something of a tomboy and, aside from Jackie Stovall, she became our best friend around the mansion. Of course it was years before we could beat her in a foot race or most any other athletic event. David, being the youngest, should have known that he would come out last in most of our contests, but he never seemed to learn and would get mad every time he lost. Priscilla would tease him and that only made it worse. She teased Rick, too, because he had developed a crush on her. Finally the day arrived, about three years after Priscilla came to Graceland, when Ricky beat her in a foot race. Then I challenged Rick and beat him—for the first time. Then I challenged Priscilla and she refused to race me. She knew she would lose. She had by this time lost her edge over us.

Of course she would have preferred to be with Elvis rather than with his little brothers. When she first came to Graceland Priscilla wanted to go with Elvis to the sets of his movies but she had to stay in school. (After high school Priscilla enrolled in the Patricia Stevens Finishing School in Memphis.) Even when she did get to go, she and Elvis would argue and he'd send her home after the first few days. She got very jealous after being sent home from the set of *Viva Las Vegas.* Even while the film was being shot, tabloid and gossip column rumors about a smoldering romance between Elvis and Ann-Margret, whose sexual charisma was publicized almost as much as Elvis's, had Priscilla beside herself. Apparently she drove Elvis crazy for several days until he put her on a plane back to Memphis.

But we'd seen Priscilla's jealousy before. When she first arrived at Graceland, she was fresh from a week of hanging around the set of *Fun in Acapulco,* which Elvis had made with Ursula Andress under the ever watchful eye of John Derek, Ursula's husband at the time. When they were back at Graceland, Priscilla demanded that he tell her about Ursula.

"Cilla, are you worried about her?" Elvis responded. "She has no hips and she's got shoulders a yard wide. Built like a man. I don't like any woman who I think might be able to outwrassle me. God, you should have seen the way she moved me around in our love scenes just so she could get the best camera angles. And she had a bone structure so sharp it could cut you in half if you moved too fast. You don't ever have to worry about her."

Priscilla seemed to buy it. She also wasn't aware that for a time after that, Ursula was calling Graceland several times a week. Vernon, as usual, screened most of the calls, and he came out of the office one time shaking his head and laughing. "Man that Ursula sure wants to talk to Sonny."

A few years later, after I'd seen the movie on TV, I asked Elvis about women who could outwrestle him, "You know, Elvis, like Ursula Andress."

Elvis just looked at me and laughed. "That John Derek had eyes like a hawk."

I don't think Elvis ever saw Ursula again, but I'm sure he dallied with Ann-Margret both during and after their film. And, years later, I was present at subsequent intrigues between the two of them.

After *Viva Las Vegas* Priscilla had a fit every time Elvis got the tour bus ready and rode off to shoot another film. There was always a party atmosphere as the closest members of the Memphis Mafia, Joe Esposito, Red and Sonny West, and Charlie Hodge, prepared that bus for the cross-country trip. Cilla wanted to go (we did too!) but this was the territory of "the guys," and Elvis didn't feel it was appropriate for Priscilla to ride along.

I want to say something about Elvis's supposed fear of flying. He did mention to us the number of recording stars who'd been killed in plane crashes: Buddy Holly, Ritchie Valens, Jim Croce, Patsy Cline, the Big Bopper, and others. But fear for his own safety was unlikely in a man of his natural daring. In fact he had told us about how he took over the controls of a helicopter while on location for *Blue Hawaii*, and how much fun they were to fly. But in the early and mid-sixties Elvis wasn't comfortable with air travel. His main fear sprang from the way it had affected his mother. Gladys couldn't understand flying, leaving the earth on a metal machine, and was almost berserk every time Elvis did it. The flight Elvis made to Europe after he enlisted in the army was apparently the worst. He and Gladys were so close that every time Elvis went anywhere he talked to her before he left and then called again immediately upon his arrival. But the flight to Europe took so much time, and he was delayed by military procedures for so long, that it was nearly twenty-four hours before Gladys heard from her son. She apparently went almost crazy with worry during that time. Elvis told us that one of the last things his mother said to him was that he had to promise to never fly again. When she died not long after that, Elvis couldn't help but believe that the long and desperate anxiety she felt when she was on the ground and he was in the air had contributed to her demise. Once he said to us, "It was like I tore a piece out of her heart every time I went up."

After a couple of occasions that Elvis regretted, if Priscilla went to a filming she went with us. In 1964 we drove to Florida for location shooting of *Girl Happy* in Fort Lauderdale. But most summers we'd fly out west as a family—Vernon, Dee, my brothers, Priscilla and me— to visit Elvis on the sets or at one of the houses he leased in Bel Air or Palm Springs. On one occasion in Palm Springs we were watching some show business news about the "best-dressed" list and Elvis objected that he hadn't made it. He pretended to be angry. Later that afternoon Ricky, David, and I decided to style our hair like Elvis's. Charlie Hodge helped us. We even wanted to dye our hair black as he did (he was a natural dark brown like me) but Charlie thought that might be going too far. Then we unbuttoned the fronts of our shirts and turned the collars up, and went to dinner. We weren't mocking him, we just loved the guy and thought it would be great to look like him. When he saw us he dropped his head and wouldn't look up at us. We just sat there watching Elvis, wondering whether he would blow up and what he would do. Finally he looked up at us and we could see he was biting back the laughter. His whole body was convulsing but he was trying his best to keep a straight face. Then he pointed his fork at my slicked back hair.

"Billy. Ever see 'The Munsters' on TV?" Elvis asked. He knew I had because we'd often watched it together. "Well, you look like Eddy Munster. Yes sir, Billy. That's who you look like. Little Eddy Munster." Then he couldn't contain it any longer and he started laughing. We were a little hurt but we weren't about to say anything. But Priscilla leaned forward very calmly and said, "Why don't you take a look at yourself, Elvis?"

Elvis stopped laughing and reddened, and I got ready to jump from the table for fear things would start flying. "What did you say?" he asked. Elvis bit down into his burned chopped steak and looked up at her with a sneer.

"Just take a good look at yourself, Elvis," she repeated. "That's all."

The three of us laughed a little, nervously, and then shut up when

Elvis glared at us. But Elvis didn't say another word. He just hurriedly finished his dinner and left. My opinion of Priscilla rose a notch that day. She was certainly one of the boys at that time. But, of course, things have a way of changing.

4

"LIVE A LITTLE, LOVE A LITTLE"

(Secrets of the King)

(1963 — 1966)

Elvis was very interested in our athletic development. In the summer he would sit for hours by the pool watching us swim. But in the fall it was football. Elvis called it "the gift from the gods," and on weekends if we weren't out on the grounds playing we were in the TV room with three sets going. Today there's a big L-shaped couch in that room (put in after he married Priscilla) but back then there were just two recliners. Elvis would sit back in one of those recliners as if he was on his throne and the rest of us were his subjects. He would explain the strategy of each play and each game as it unfolded. Elvis liked the Green Bay Packers back then, and Vince Lombardi, the Packer coach, in particular. Elvis ranked Lombardi with some of the great generals (Elvis also was fascinated by generals and was very proud that we were the sons of General Patton's personal bodyguard).

Elvis liked to play quarterback himself, and he was taken with Johnny Unitas (because he was a winner) and later with Joe Namath (because he brought personality to the game). But he also liked the physical aspects of the game as personified by Dick Butkus and Ray Nitschke. He called them "mean mothers." After the games were over he would take us out in the backyard so that we could practice key plays and techniques of throwing, running pass routes, blocking, and all the rest. Sunday football, both in the den and out on the lawn, was more like a party for some of the guys and their guests (I remember after one game a girl jumped in the pool with all her clothes on), but Elvis concentrated on the football.

I was the oldest and grew up to be the smallest of the three brothers. Rick was born in the same year, eleven months later, and grew to be lankier and taller. David was two years younger than Rick, but by the time I was twelve, and David was nine, he was as big as I was. We continued to be the same size until our mid-teens when Rick grew taller and David filled out into his 6'3", 200-pound frame. Somewhere in there Elvis took to calling me "Nub." Of course I had the edge because I was the oldest and, I thought, the scrappiest. But you couldn't tell that to David. Even when he was little we'd go out in the backyard, put on our football pads and just ram into each other for hours before we'd give up.

My brothers and I played football for our school teams from the fourth through the tenth grades and Elvis had every game in which we played taped. He ran all the games back in their entirety at Graceland, pointing out the things that we were doing wrong and praising us for the things we did right. From the fourth through sixth grades we weren't doing much wrong because we won every game. I was the fullback and main ball carrier for the team in the fourth grade, switched to halfback in the seventh, and was a wide receiver by the time I got to high school. (As I said, I didn't grow all that much larger so as I grew older I had to compensate with speed.) David with his bulk and natural athletic ability was always a linebacker or a tight end. Rick was the quarterback in elementary school but played second team when we got to Hillcrest High. Rick didn't have my scrappiness nor David's size. His long-muscled, lean frame was better suited for other sports; with his blond hair and blue eyes he looked more like a California surfer. But looks can be deceiving. In truth he had more natural ability than any of us, and at one time he was considered one of the top quarterback prospects in the city. But his involvement in football was inspired more by Elvis's enthusiasm for the game than the natural zest that David and I had for it.

Elvis was always sorry that he couldn't go to our games himself. We'd tell him, "Come on, Elvis. You can come. Just show up late. Sit at the back." But he'd say, "No. I'd only be a distraction. It's your game. Besides, I can watch them all from here." We called him our second coach. We even took to calling him Coach all the time for a while. You might be surprised at how much that pleased him. When he was a teenager back in East Tupelo his dream was to be a professional football player. His mother tried to discourage his interest in the violent sport and, instead, encouraged his secondary interest in music. And he could hardly complain at the outcome.

Out on the West Coast he'd have his famous touch football games on the lawns of the houses he leased on Perugia Way and Bellagio Drive in Bel Air. Roman Gabriel, Rosey Grier, and other members of the LA Rams as well as actors like Robert Conrad and Max Baer, Jr. joined Elvis and his friends. (Max is best known as Jethroe from the "Beverly Hillbillies" . . . a role that had originally been offered to Elvis). It was rough tag football, seven-to-a-side games that were played for fun but with intensity. Although the pros were just out there to take it easy and have some fun, they'd occasionally lay a block into someone, like the boisterous Red West, that let him know what their profession was all about. They weren't afraid to level Elvis, too, once in a while, and he wasn't afraid to take it and dare them to try it again. But it seemed that we were always too young to do anything more than be waterboys or spectators. Of course, every year we thought we were finally ready to join in the fray but Elvis would tell us, "Naw, not yet boys. Another year or two. Another thirty pounds." Then when I was sixteen he finally let me play. "We'll take it easy on you, Nub," Elvis said.

They told me I could play center, which in some ways was the least skilled position on a seven-man team (there were two Ram wide receivers at my natural position and the guards had to be big men) but in our game the center was also eligible to catch passes. My duties were to hike the ball and try to hold out whoever it was that was rushing the quarterback, and then to try to sneak off under the deep coverage for a possible reception. To my surprise Elvis lined up opposite me. I'd never seen him play anything but quarterback and defensive back! At the signal I hiked the ball and immediately got hit by a forearm that knocked me back several yards. There was Elvis standing above me with a leer. On the next play the same thing happened, but this time I stayed on my feet and was able to put a partial block on Elvis before he got to our quarterback. On the third play I was prepared and I caught Elvis just under the chin with my forearm as soon as I'd snapped the ball. Now I was smiling and Elvis was scowling something fierce. From that point on it was a "give as you get" situation, with me doing most of the getting but doing some of the giving as well. Elvis loved to put you to the test, but also I think there was a little of the feeling, "Did this guy ever learn anything from all that I tried to teach him? If so, let's see it." From then on we all got to play, David and I lining up opposite Elvis (counting, more or less, as one player) and Rick lined up opposite Red. They didn't give us any slack but they didn't break our bones either.

But Elvis was concerned with more than our progress in athletics. Unlike Vernon, who kept aloof, Elvis would take us for drives in the evening to "go get a 'burger." He'd ask us how we were getting along in school and with other kids. Once, when I was only in the second grade but doing poorly at school, he said, "What's this about you failing in school?" "I can't seem to pay attention," I said. "I don't like the people there and they don't seem to like me. Sometimes there are older kids picking on me. I don't think about it for myself but I worry about Ricky and David. I don't know, Elvis. Maybe I'm just dumb."

Elvis grabbed me by my shoulders and threw his head back so that I did the same. He said, "Hey, there's nothing wrong with you. Don't get that in your head. Your grades might be a little down but that's my fault for keeping you up so late. But don't get down on yourself. Just try a little harder. And don't worry about being picked on. It's the anticipation that wears you down. So don't anticipate. You'll be able to handle it when it comes your way."

"Shoot, Elvis," I said. "David's the one who knows how to handle it. There were some seventh-graders getting on us saying, 'Elvis Presley's brothers. What can we do to get his autograph?' David said, 'Do you want mine?' One of them said, 'Sure.' So David gets out his crayon and starts signing sheets of paper." Elvis just laughed.

Elvis didn't have much respect for schooling as such, although, unlike Vernon, he never said that. He thought that individual expression and achievement depended on courage and the ability to act in ways that the schools, with their emphasis on conformity and toeing the line, thwarted. He didn't like the bad grades I usually got simply because he didn't like underachievement of any kind. He'd made his mark with long sideburns, and a lot of natural talent, and he felt that if you couldn't dare to be an individual, a rebel if necessary, you couldn't really achieve anything. I think he wanted most for us to know that no matter how much others might get down on us, if we didn't get down on ourselves we'd be all right.

If we had problems at school or with other kids it was always Elvis we'd go to with our problems. Vernon couldn't handle problems, and Dee, if anything, was worse. She saw even the slightest problem as a symptom of a "personality disorder" and was ready to rush us off to a child psychiatrist. She must have felt some guilt at taking us away from our father because if we ever said so much as, "I hate you," to each other she would exclaim, "Oh, my God, my son's going to grow up with a warped personality!" So, just as we ran to Elvis to escape a licking from Vernon, we went to him with any problem we had, just to keep it away from our mother.

Elvis always told us, "There's nothing in this world that you can't do. Believe in yourself." And I believed him. Elvis established this rule by his actions. Other times Elvis told us, "When I'm gone you'll be the only ones who can tell the real story." I was only thirteen when he said that to us for the first time, but since his death I've thought about it often. Elvis was totally relaxed with us, to a greater extent than he was with anyone else with the possible exception of Vernon. Elvis always had a role to play with Priscilla and all the other women he knew. And to a lesser extent he played roles with all the guys who worked for him. I've seen him ride Lamar Fike for hours, never letting up and not letting Lamar leave the room either. With us, even if he was angry, he'd say it once and then forget it.

We did many things together but a lot of our time was spent simply watching TV. We learned a lot about Elvis just by observing his reactions and listening to his comments. I remember how much he loved the "Johnny Carson Show" and how thrilled we were when we were allowed to stay up and watch it with him. We all laughed at Carson's monologues, but Elvis was particularly interested in Johnny's guests and how Carson could draw out their personalities even when they were reluctant to reveal anything about themselves. He loved Johnny's quick wit and would often comment, "You can't get into a battle with him. He'll lay waste to you!" To my knowledge Elvis never appeared on Johnny's show but I know he was always getting himself mentally prepared in case the situation arose. Under Colonel Parker's management it never did, but I'm sure Elvis would have loved it.

Elvis disliked performers who, he considered, had "all technique and no heart." Robert Goulet was one he put in this category. Mel

Torme was another. And, of course, when I was older I was present at a few of those infamous occasions when Elvis pulled out a gun and shot the TV while Robert Goulet was singing. Elvis was also irritated by performers who used their talents to make a political statement. He was particularly upset with Jane Fonda when she was carrying on about Vietnam. "I hate uppity broads," Elvis said once. The Smothers Brothers got his goat as well. While we laughed, Elvis fumed and exploded at their political satires. But if a national leader said the same thing, Elvis had no quarrel with him. I remember the day that Martin Luther King got shot. I was sitting in the front drive in a '57 Cadillac Vernon had bought that I was allowed to drive (sort of) in the front of the house—driving forward several yards, backing up, driving forward, backing up. I was listening to music on the radio and then the news bulletin came on saying the civil rights leader had been assassinated in Memphis. I didn't really know what to make of it but around Graceland there were a few irresponsible comments made (I won't say by whom) to the effect that maybe King had brought it upon himself, and worse. When Elvis came home later that day a few other comments were made that Elvis obviously didn't like. He called us all into the house. Just from his demeanor everyone knew that they'd better shut up until he had his say. Elvis sat down and said, "Today we lost a great man. A man who has done a lot for his own people. It's bad for Memphis. But more than that this whole country has suffered a tragic loss. I don't want to hear anything different than that said around here." And, of course, the room fell silent and no one dared contradict Elvis's viewpoint. Later I heard some comments that Elvis was grandstanding, that he couldn't really hold a black civil rights leader in such high esteem. But at the time I remembered how, less than a year before, a temporary assistant groundskeeper had come to our house on Dolan Street after Vernon had let him go. He was white, while the regular man, who'd been sick for a time, was black, and he couldn't understand why he was being replaced by a black man. Vernon told him that he'd made it clear that the job was temporary, and that now the regular man was back. The groundskeeper said he couldn't believe that Vernon would give his job to a "nigrah." He said he was going to get both Vernon and Elvis. Later he appeared at the Graceland gate and Elvis, having been forewarned by Vernon, went down to meet him. They exchanged some words and he took a swing at Elvis, missed (Elvis was by then a black belt in karate and not an easy target), and Elvis laid him out with one punch.

Elvis never forgot where he had come from. We could be watching "Gunsmoke," "Star Trek," or "The Twilight Zone" and something would click. He'd say, "You boys should see the place I grew up in." Then he'd be silent. We'd wait for him to go on but Elvis never said more than a sentence unless you asked him to elaborate. After a while we'd ask, "Elvis, what was it like where you grew up?" "We had two rooms, both smaller than any in this house, bare floors, no heat 'cept when we were cooking, and no running water. And those were the good times! When we came to Memphis it got worse."

We'd heard the story before, but when Elvis told us it made a deep impression. The Presleys were considered "white trash" in East Tupelo, and when Vernon moved the family to Memphis to seek better work opportunities they ended up living in a one-room apartment that didn't even have a kitchen. They hauled water in and prepared food on a hot plate in the bathroom. But Elvis had his first opportunity to play organized football and made the squad as an end for the Humes High Tigers. Because he wore his hair long and grew sideburns in emulation of truck drivers (and, probably, because he was the son of a poor Mississippi sharecropper), Elvis was often picked on by other players on the team and bullies in the high school. He had found one friend at Humes High, Red West, a year older, one of the toughest guys on the football team if not in the entire school. Red stuck up for Elvis when half the team was determined to give him an impromptu haircut, and Elvis never forgot that support. But Elvis let us know that even if you had to go it entirely alone (as he was prepared to), you had to just hang in there and show them that you could play just as tough as they could. Tougher if need be. And you should never give up your style.

Elvis didn't have much in the way of mementos from those years, just a few photographs and a '53 Ford panel truck. But Elvis had some stories about that truck and the girls he'd been with. And one thing Elvis obviously had was girlfriends. The attraction didn't start when he was rich and famous. He had a talent for attracting the fair sex long before that. He told us that first we had to show some interest in the girl. "Just get her attention. Then, if the girl shows any interest in you for whatever reason—she thinks you're smart, she thinks you're dumb but beautiful, she thinks you're funny or a rebel, whatever—explore it! Don't shy away. And don't worry what you'll say to them. Just say, 'How do you feel about it?' When they state their position, just hold their hand and say, 'That's just about what I was feeling.' It works every time! And boys, there's a bonus. Sometimes they'll tell you things you never even thought of."

"Wow!" we said. And our reverence extended to the Ford truck itself. When Vester was in charge of maintenance he used that panel truck to haul garbage to the dump, with my brothers and I usually riding along. Later, after Priscilla had settled into a house in Bel Air, Elvis had it restored and he'd use it, again, to take girls out for late night drives. It was the one vehicle he owned that the fans didn't recognize; he could park it and neck with his date just like old times. He just didn't want to lose that good-time feeling.

Elvis, despite his promise, never took us to the house in East Tupelo, but Vernon and Dee did once. If anything, it was smaller than Elvis had described it. Just a wood-framed building fifteen feet wide and thirty feet deep with a wall dividing it into two rooms. Vernon called it a "shotgun" house, because the way the three doors were lined up you could shoot a shotgun in the front and it'd come out the back. He told us about how he'd worked as a sharecropper and a milk delivery man and as a laborer in various factories. He told us how tough it was to make a living. He'd told us all that many times before and it all seemed a little remote to us. But standing there with him before his old house, we appreciated it a little more. And when Vernon told us he had bought Elvis a push lawn mower and that Elvis had gone out and mowed neighbors' lawns and repaid Vernon the cost, it really got our attention. Back in Memphis we all got mowers and worked out different routes in the neighborhood for lawn-mowing jobs. Of course we had power mowers and we never had to repay their cost—they were part of the equipment at Graceland—but we did earn our spending money that way. (Vernon was never quick to pass out allowances.) And when Elvis told us how many years he had to wait for the bike he always wanted and how the one thing his parents had been able to buy him, a $12.50 guitar, went months with only two or three strings, we soon appreciated all the bikes and musical instruments we had.

One afternoon we were all watching TV together and the program was interrupted by a tornado watch. We looked outside; the sky had become black and still. So we just went down to the basement and turned a TV on there. "Don't worry, boys," Elvis said. "Nothing can touch us here." Then he went on to tell us how none of the houses in East Tupelo had basements and how, when the sky grew angry, Gladys would take him some distance to a cave shelter cut into a hillside—

one of the very caves the Chickasaws had lived in. He and Gladys would huddle together and sing and try not to worry about Vernon, who was out working in a field somewhere. When he told us stories like that Elvis would cry. He didn't try to hide it and he wasn't ashamed of it. He'd say, "It's all right to cry."

Really, in a way, we had two daddies. Vernon would tell us what we couldn't do and Elvis would tell us what we could do.

While Elvis was truly obsessed with football, he'd have temporary "obsessions" that would occupy his time for a period and then be dropped forever. One was radio-controlled airplanes and another was slot cars. He got into the airplanes through Jackie Stovall's dad, spending thousands on the equipment and then searching for fields big enough to fly them. He tried it at Graceland a few times but there were just too many trees. Later he would drive us out to a big open field and parking lot near a church. Once he lost control of the plane trying some fancy hell-bent maneuver and it crashed directly into the church.

He got so involved with slot cars that he had a large building constructed at Graceland between the house and the swimming pool. There he had his track built. My brothers and I got the job of putting the cars back on the tracks when they fell off. It could get pretty exciting because they didn't necessarily stop racing the cars just because one went off. We had to get in there and get it back on track and we had to be pretty quick to keep those cars still racing from slamming into our feet. Elvis played with the slot cars every day for about six weeks. He had everyone else involved; each person had his own race car, teams were formed, tournaments held. One day he stopped playing and he never played with them again. Some months later the tracks were torn out.

Elvis bought bikes for everyone. By bikes I mean motorcycles, in this case Triumphs. Except us—we were still too young. He'd gather everyone together just like a scene from *The Wild One*, everyone gunning their bikes behind Graceland and then pulling down the driveway several abreast and roaring out through the gate en masse to cruise Highway 51. I got to ride a lot with Sonny West. Sonny was a big man, about 6′3″ and 215 pounds. He'd had parts in several biker movies, usually playing a heavy. He liked to ride fast and I just hung on. Elvis, of course, didn't have a Triumph. He had a Harley Davidson just like Marlon Brando. And he rode at the front of the pack. No one passed Elvis. You could pull up beside him to say something but after you had your say you pulled back behind him. He was the leader of the pack. Even old Vernon was out there riding a Triumph. He really enjoyed it.

At first Priscilla couldn't go. Elvis would give her rides sometimes, but cruising on the bikes was for the men. Then he bought her a pink Honda 300. To make it democratic he bought himself a black Honda 300. They rode those bikes together maybe twice. Then Elvis went back to his Harley. Priscilla tried to keep up, but that made it worse. There they were, a group of tough-looking hombres on Harleys and Triumphs with black leather jackets and black caps, with a seventeen-year-old girl in heavy mascara and a bouffant hairdo tagging along on a pink Honda. Elvis would send her home crying. If she refused to leave, they'd just turn up the throttle and lose her.

In a way we had our own Harley. In his quieter moments Elvis liked to drive around the Graceland grounds in a Harley-Davidson golf cart. But he hated the slow pace, so he had the governor, which regulated and limited the speed, taken out. Before his daughter Lisa Marie was born Elvis didn't use golf carts all that much, but we did. We rode them all over the grounds. One day there were a lot of fans at the gate (the end of the downhill first turn in our track), and I guess Rick wanted to see how close he could come to them. Instead of backing off the accelerator for the curve, he gunned it and went flying down the hill straight toward them. At the last moment he hit the brakes, but they locked and he crashed into the gate. He'd gotten a little past the point of no return. The fans just jumped away from the gate at the last moment and no one was hurt.

Elvis was all for using the front drive as a race track, but he thought golf carts were too slow and unresponsive. He and the guys raced go-carts. Vernon had made it clear that we weren't to touch them unless Elvis was present and said that we could. One day Elvis had them all brought out and announced. "OK, boys. Let's see what you can do." That's when the real racing began. We used the circular front drive at Graceland as our private race track, timing each other in heats. Then Elvis climbed into his and showed what an experienced driver could do. He was king of the road at Graceland, and not above blasting you off the track if you were going too slow or taking what he considered to be his lane. But it wasn't too long before we could give him a good race. Elvis also owned an Indy-type racer that we kept in the back garage, but except for a few wild rides he never really used it much. The go-carts were a wonderful substitute.

One night I saw Elvis drunk. Generally he hated alcohol. It had killed his mother, Elvis told us. (Apparently there have been a variety of reports on what lead up to the acute hepatitis and liver failure that killed Gladys, but Elvis laid the blame squarely on alcohol.) And he saw how it had ruined the lives of a lot of good musicians. He always warned us to stay away from it, and although he kept a bar at the mansion he didn't like to see anyone even walking around with a beer can in his hand. If you drank a beer you drank it from a glass and you didn't carry it around. But that night someone had given him a margarita, and he liked it. When Elvis liked something he went full bore. He drank them down like soda pop. Soon he was very happy. Someone put on some music in the garden room. Elvis started jitterbugging with this girl, throwing her out and catching her hand before she went flying into the furniture just like in one of his movies. Everyone was laughing and applauding when Elvis missed her hand and sent her smack into a glass wall. It shuddered but didn't break and the girl slumped down to the floor, momentarily stunned. But when she got up laughing and Elvis saw that she was all right he broke out laughing so hard that he fell, first on the couch and then on the floor, where he promptly passed out. Several of the guys had to help him to his room. He was still giggling and saying that he wanted to dance and that maybe another margarita would help, but his legs were rubbery and he couldn't stand on them. They put him to bed.

That was the only time I ever saw Elvis get drunk for he almost never consumed alcohol. A few years later he would have an occasional glass of wine with Priscilla because she liked it and she told Elvis that it would relax him. But he always regarded alcohol as the enemy.

By this time some of the movies Elvis had made were starting to be shown on TV. My brothers and I thought this was a great event, particularly when they showed *Follow That Dream*. We could reminisce about our escapades on the set, playing Frisbee with Mary Ann Mobley and Anne Helm, and all the fun we had. And we loved the film. It was good. It was funny! But we couldn't watch any of Elvis's movies if he was around. He couldn't stand it.

I remember one night Elvis was driving us around Memphis talking about football and school and how we had to prove ourselves, and all of a sudden he slammed on the brakes. He had spotted a wino who looked down and out, as if he hadn't slept under a roof in months and hadn't had a good meal in as long. Elvis told me to get out his wallet. (Elvis never carried his own money. Even though I was only twelve at the time he gave me his wallet before we went out.) He called the wino over to the car. Elvis started peeling off twenties until they got to be a couple hundred dollars and he held them out in front of the guy. "This is for you," Elvis said. "It's to buy you a place to stay, some clothes, and some food. But first you've got to tell me you're not going to blow it on cheap whiskey."

The guy stared at Elvis for a long time, making no move to take the money in front of him. "Are you Mr. Presley?" he asked. Elvis said he was. "I used to see you in the movies," the guy said.

Elvis said, "Well here, take this. It will help you forget some of them."

"Why, I can't take money from you, Mr. Presley. I just can't. I feel I know you."

Elvis laughed. "I give money to people who know me all the time."

The guy still didn't grab the money. Elvis got out of the car and pressed it into his hand. "Take this," he said. "But get yourself something good to eat."

Finally the man accepted the money. "God bless you, Mr. Presley," he said.

"Don't worry," Elvis replied. "He already has."

Now when I read and hear of those years in the sixties when Elvis was making movies and driving his bus nonstop between Graceland and Hollywood I keep learning that Elvis was "a living ghost." According to all reports his music got lost, his movies got progressively worse, and Elvis himself was reduced to a brooding recluse within the bleak confines of Graceland Mansion—brooding and ashamed even to come out of his room for days and even weeks at a time. I lived with him then and I know all of that to be untrue. He *was* disappointed in the movie contract, he *was* discouraged by the quality of the scripts, and he *did* yearn for dramatic roles that would enable him to express himself as a serious actor. Also, his music output was low and few of his songs made the charts. (They were mainly "situational" songs for silly movies, and one gospel album.) He was sensitive to criticism from critics and fans alike. But if he withdrew from anything, it was only from the demands of those critics and fans who wanted to interview him to find out when his next big album was going to come out or when his next big appearance would be, or why he was in seclusion, or when he would next do something for them. Elvis wasn't mooning away. He was doing something for himself. He was enjoying life to the fullest. You had to live with him to really know. His "toys"—the Indy racer, the Harleys, all the cars and exploring what they could do and how he could perform with them—these made him happy. Graceland, the grounds, the horses—these made him happy. Priscilla made him happy. Giving made him happy. Gospel made him happy. Reading, religion, philosophy, and exploring the limits of his mind made him happy. His entourage of friends, us boys, Vernon, his animals—all made him happy. His body was in top physical condition, honed by the sports he loved, football and karate. He was rarely more than a pound or two away from 170 pounds; he had no need of dieting or working out to lose weight or regain lost physical conditioning. He hadn't lost a thing. I may have been young but I can tell you what life with Elvis felt like in those years—the energy we felt when he walked into a room, the mischievous humor and daring that always seemed ready to explode into some happy act, the radiance he carried with him. He was like the sun to us; we just wanted to be in his glow.

It has always struck me as odd that later, when he was back on tour and reestablished as the "king," and lacing himself with a variety of drugs to manage the rigors of the schedule and please the fan hysteria, no one in his inner circle criticized his moodiness or seclusion. And no one in his "public" seemed to care that he was killing himself to do it. The charisma was still there, but maybe he used up too much of it on stage. Even offstage there were times when the radiance would shine again and you'd get that warm feeling inside, but never for long.

5

"RAISED ON ROCK"

(1 9 6 5 ━ 1 9 6 6)

The summer of 1965 was one that didn't end in a family trip to the shooting location of one of Elvis's movies. Probably that was because *Paradise Hawaiian Style*, Elvis's only movie that summer, was shot in late August, and a trip to the set might have interfered with school.

Other than that it was a full summer. I was mowing lawns for some of the neighbors, and then I was given a job working for Uncle Earl. It was a hot summer, and the maintenance shed didn't have air-conditioning then. Earl, fun and humorous as he was, worked us hard. And he made sure we were up early. The fourteen acres of Graceland had to be mowed every two weeks, but this summer it was not only hot, it was wet. Thunderstorms rolled in every third or fourth day, and we were mowing that lawn once a week. It was a big lawn. The mansion was repainted (I was spared from most of this) and we re-painted the fence and curb that lined the driveway. (Once these had been painted white there was no end to it. They had to be repainted over and over again. I did most of that.) When the painting was done we put in shrubs behind the rocks to line the driveway. Probably to test me, Uncle Earl put me on a gas-powered posthole digger. Heavy equipment. I was so light (about 115 pounds) that I'd hit a big root or a rock and it'd just spin me around. Threw me all over the place.

We had tractors too, all shapes and sizes. Most of the time they'd be used for work, but when Elvis was home anything could happen. He and the guys got to racing them, rain or shine, and when it rained they'd dig deep ruts across the grounds. It had Uncle Earl shaking his head, but he couldn't say anything because Elvis was having fun. Then someone built a big, flat trailer that could hold fifteen to twenty people and hooked it up to one of the big diesel tractors. They'd fill the trailer up with eager, laughing volunteers and then Elvis would start the tractor and drive it across the fields. The ride in the trailer was rough: no cushions, no springs, and Elvis at the wheel, crisscrossing the hardened ruts that were left when the rains ended. Bodies bounced crazily against each other, against the sides, and even against the hard wood floor of the trailer. Everyone would eventually get thrown off (or, if they were smart, jump off when they spotted a soft place to land), and soon the ground in back of Graceland would be strewn with bodies, some of them bruised. After a while it became difficult to fill that trailer up. People would make excuses: "Uh, Elvis. I've got to take my kids to a ballgame this afternoon." Or they wouldn't show up at all for a few days after they'd been knocked around. But this is what Elvis wanted. He wanted to see who could take it and come back for more. And Elvis was very disappointed if too many people backed down. Really he was a kid at heart, and he wanted to know who else was. It was important to him. If you weren't a kid in that sense and you weren't family, he really didn't want you around. My brothers and I were always game. And in the trailer we bounced the highest. Sometimes one of us would get thrown off the back and after he finally heard us shouting Elvis would stop the tractor and come back to see how the fallen brother was. "You OK?" he'd ask. We'd nod. "Had enough?" We'd shake our heads. "Then get back on the trailer."

Billy Smith came up with the idea of putting a saddle on the tractor, and Elvis would drive it as if it was a bucking bronco, hitting the biggest bumps and deepest ruts as hard as he could. When Elvis left for Los Angeles to record songs for *Paradise Hawaiian Style* in late July, it was back to work as usual. Often our work was to repair the damage to the grounds inflicted during his last stay, and Earl, his good humor now tested, kept us at it, mainly with hoes and shovels. By noon I'd already have put in five hours and I'd go into Graceland and ask Mary Jenkins—Alberta, Elvis's "O-Five," had died—to make me a sandwich. Then I'd get a Pepsi, find a cool spot, and start watching TV. They'd have to call for me. "Where is that boy?" Uncle Earl would ask. "We're just getting started." I'd make them hunt me down, but Uncle Earl was always good-natured about it. He'd laugh and say, "That boy'll hide if I don't keep an eye on him."

About this time my voice was changing. One time I'd open my mouth and there'd be this deep voice, and the next time I'd sound like a girl. Once when I was hiding out from Uncle Earl the phone rang and I picked it up and said, "Graceland."

"Daddy?" Elvis asked. He was still on the West Coast.

"No, this isn't Daddy. It's Billy." My voice cracked.

"Billy!" Elvis roared. "Is your voice changing already?"

"I guess," I said, trying to keep it low.

"Damn!" Elvis said. "Where's Vernon?"

When the tour bus got back to Graceland, Elvis, Joe, Red, Sonny, and the rest would go around deepening their voices every time they talked to me. "Uh, Billy. Can we consult your opinion on this matter?" Of course Elvis did it the most and the longest, and I didn't have to guess who put the others up to it.

As soon as my voice made a decision as to which direction it was going, my brothers and I had started our own group, calling ourselves "The Brothers." We'd practice at the clubhouse Vernon had built at the end of the pool. Sometimes Elvis would hear us and come over through the back gate to listen to us play. Most often we'd get records of the top songs and play along, making our own tapes. We'd take them over to Elvis. He'd laugh and say things like, "Well, Billy, you need to work a little on your vocals." Then he'd come over to our clubhouse and show me different chords that I could play on my bass guitar. He was very patient. Very tender. I had small hands, so my fingers just weren't big enough to do all the chords. But Elvis would stand over my shoulder making sure I repeated my attempts without getting discouraged. "Hang in there," he'd say. "There are great piano players with small hands. They just had to learn how to move them."

It's hard to express the joy of Elvis's physical presence or the feelings we had when he was with us. But I do remember them vividly. Mostly he encouraged us and told us we were doing a pretty good job. He'd ask us, "Who are your favorites?" We'd laugh and say, "The Beatles."

Elvis would say, "Well, they've got some pretty good songs. But did you ever hear this one?" Then he'd do his fifties stuff. He'd sing and have us play the background—"I Got a Woman," "Ready Teddy," "All Shook Up,"—and he'd play the drums, base, acoustic guitar, electric guitar. He was good on all of them. Priscilla would come with Elvis in those days. Usually she'd just sit by the side of the pool with Dee and they'd talk. But there were a few times when she joined in with us and sang.

Elvis loved to sit down at the piano either at our house or at Graceland with a group of people he liked. We'd just jam. Besides his recording he'd sing Beatles songs and the music of Marty Robbins, Ray Charles, and Jerry Lee. About the only thing Elvis couldn't do was duplicate the three-octave range of Roy Orbison singing "Cryin' " or "Oh, Pretty Woman." But he tried. Sometimes he'd come close. And a few times he actually did it. Then he'd beam. Elvis thought Roy Orbison was the greatest singer ever.

Sometimes we'd just make the music up. I wrote a song that began

> Let me tell you about my brother
> A brother like no other
> His father married my mother
> But he's more than a brother to me
>
> Wherever I go
> The people keep asking me
> What's it like to be the brother
> Of a celebrity . . .

I know Elvis came up with better lyrics than that but, try as I might, I can't remember the words. But at the time he remembered mine. "Billy," he'd say, strumming a guitar, "Now just how does your song go?"

One song Rick and I loved was "Don't Hand Me No Boogie-woogie, Because I'm the King of Rock 'n Roll." We rehearsed it for days and then played it for Elvis. He just shrugged, but then he came back with a song we'd never heard. He always had a musical challenge. He loved it. At the time we were disappointed in his reaction to the song we'd practiced. But some months later I was sitting in the dining room at Graceland, where Elvis could not have seen me, and I heard him coming down the steps from his room singing, "Don't Hand Me No Boogie-woogie, Because I'm the King of Rock 'n Roll."

We never thought to tape any of the jam sessions. We were having fun and thought it would go on forever. But maybe we should have known better. The year before, a local radio station has polled its listeners as part of a nationwide poll on who was the biggest force in popular music. In Memphis Elvis won. Nationwide the Beatles were first and Elvis was second. My brothers and I couldn't believe it. Elvis was second only to the Beatles! We knew Elvis made movies and had been a big recording star in the fifties, but to be mentioned so close to the Beatles blew our minds.

Only weeks later the Beatles had come to Graceland. We'd just missed meeting them. This was in the fall of 1964 and "I Feel Fine" was their fifth consecutive number one song. They were on their U.S. tour and we had heard on the radio that they were in Memphis. Then a limousine pulled up in front of our house on Dolan Street. Brian Epstein, the Beatles' road manager, got out and came to our door. Apparently they had tried to visit Graceland, hoping Elvis would be there. Finding he wasn't (he was in L.A. filming *Tickle Me*), they still wanted to visit the shrine but were told that they'd need permission from Vernon. Vernon was in his office but someone misdirected them to our house. We were so excited we could barely contain ourselves. Dee invited Epstein in and the three of us shook hands with him. He talked with us for awhile, trying to be friendly, but we kept running back to the window where we could see the Beatles in the back of the limo. Brian Epstein was praising Elvis to my mom and asking if the Beatles could visit Graceland. Dee told him that she'd call and arrange it. Meanwhile we were jumping up and down in excitement. We asked her (begging, pleading) if we could go out and meet them. Dee just said, "Hush. You're staying in here. Now settle down." Then she went to the phone to call Vernon. We asked again, but we could see it would do no good. Here were the Beatles twenty yards away and Mom wouldn't let us meet them! She wasn't even interested in meeting them herself. That, at least, we could understand. If it had been Hank Williams or Bill Monroe, someone she respected, she not only would have let us out there, she would have led the way. Because Mom loved music. But only her kind of music. The Beatles didn't play her kind of music. They didn't sing her kind of lyrics. I know because we'd made her listen to Beatles songs (that we sang), and her response had been, "Now, will you listen to those words! That song doesn't tell any kind of a story." And later she would exclaim, "How can they sing songs that teach things like that?"

"What do you mean, Mom?" we'd ask. "It's just a song."

"Don't think your mother is so stupid," she said. "I don't like you listening to their songs. And I don't want you playing them either." We did anyway. And Dee's motives in preventing us from meeting the Beatles were obvious to us. In her mind one rock star was already keeping us from the true way of the Church of Christ. She didn't want to encourage our experience with other rock stars.

A few weeks later, in Los Angeles, the Beatles and Elvis met for the first time. Elvis told us all about it when he got home for Christmas. Elvis liked them. He told us he gave them all full-dress cowboy outfits and told them, "When you're the top gunslinger in town everyone takes you on." He said John Lennon told him, "Before you there was no one."

"What were they like, Elvis?" we asked.

"They seemed clean-cut. Straightforward. Paul McCartney was very quiet. Maybe even shy. And George Harrison was quiet too. Lennon and Ringo Starr did most of the talking. Ringo's got an ear for country music. He knows a lot about it."

"How long were you with them? What did you talk about?" we persisted.

"I told them about you boys. I told them my three brothers really love you guys."

Needless to say we were in ecstasy. Elvis meeting them, and liking them, and mentioning us made up for our earlier disappointment. But one night that next summer when we were practicing our music, Elvis came over and I started talking about their latest songs and lyrics. Elvis said, "Yeah. Well don't listen to all of them."

"What do you mean, Elvis?" I asked.

"Billy. There's stuff about drugs and political stuff. It's John Lennon, not the others."

But I kept talking about the Beatles and about how I heard that their sudden rise to stardom was likened to his in the fifties. I must have gone on about it a little too long. Some of the guys who'd come over with Elvis and picked up on the comparison must have become a little obnoxious about it because Elvis suddenly got up and said, "Yeah. Remember Elvis?" and walked off.

We were crestfallen that night. And for several days thereafter. I felt I was mostly to blame. Elvis was getting testy. Looking back, it wasn't my fault any more than it was the Beatles'. The problem was his music. While the Beatles were doing their record-breaking songs Elvis was recording "Song of the Shrimp," "No Room to Rumba in a Sports Car," "Kissin' Cousins," "Fort Lauderdale Chamber of Commerce," and "Do the Clam." Not exactly the quality of song you'd expect from the king of rock 'n roll. My brothers and I, like millions of others, collected Elvis's records from the fifties. They were always our favorites. We knew the names of the guys Elvis played with and the stories of his rise from one-night stands to national stardom. We knew that in 1956 alone he recorded the Drifters' "Money Honey," Ray Charles's "I Got A Woman," Carl Perkins's "Blue Suede Shoes," Little Richard's "Tutti Frutti," as well as "Love Me Tender" and "Don't Be Cruel." We weren't questioning Elvis in a critical way, but after the "remember Elvis" incident we once got bold enough to ask him about it. We knew that our favorite musicians, the Beatles, the Rolling Stones, Led Zeppelin, and the other big names of the times, like Bob Dylan, were all writing their own music. But Elvis didn't write music and depended on material brought to him. So we decided to ask Elvis why he wasn't getting any of the top songs. "Because the colonel doesn't get any of them for me," he growled. And I could tell by his glare that Elvis didn't consider it our place to question him about his music. But others were questioning it too.

We never brought the subject up to Elvis again but we did ask Vernon. He told us that Colonel Parker had signed Elvis to a long-term contract with RCA and apparently had worked out deals whereby all songs were published by companies that gave a piece of the action to Elvis and to the colonel. By the early summer of 1966, there were growing signs that Elvis was becoming disillusioned with the colonel. Once when we were watching *West Side Story* on TV Elvis complained about the lead, played by Richard Beymer. "That should have been my part. This guy they've got looks like a choir boy."

"He sings pretty well, Elvis," I said.

Elvis sneered, "Billy, he's no more singing those songs than Scatter there. He's just mouthing it. But I could've sung 'em. Natalie wanted me for the part. They all did. After *King Creole* they were calling me the new James Dean and comparing me to Marlon Brando. That picture won an Academy Award but Colonel thought we were too good for it. He doesn't care anything about quality. Just how fast we can make them."

"Elvis, you knew Natalie Wood?" I asked. Elvis laughed. "Nub," he said, rubbing my hair. "I guess you could say I knew her." Later I learned they had conducted a well-publicized "motorcycle romance" in the late fifties with Elvis's buddy, Nick Adams, as a constant compatriot. But I never heard any more about why the colonel had prevented Elvis from doing *West Side Story.*

So the problem also was with his movies. After *Flaming Star* and *Kid Galahad,* two movies that allowed Elvis to work on his dramatic skills, he was given a string of "beach 'n bikini" musicals set in Hawaii and other exotic locations. Elvis had fun with *Follow That Dream* and *Viva Las Vegas* (Ann-Margret's presence helped!) but soon got bored with the worsening string of formula musicals that followed. He'd look at a script and say, "This is nothing but a setup for a bunch of lousy songs." It had begun with *Kissin' Cousins* (Elvis hated that film) and after that it didn't matter how bad the scripts were or how cheaply the movies were made, as long as they had exotic locations, lots of pretty girls, and Elvis crooning, the public ate them up. It was a double triumph for the colonel, an ex-carnival barker who believed in giving the public as little as possible for their money, in that the songs from each movie could be made into an album for RCA. Colonel even openly bragged that he never read the scripts and that all he wanted from the movies were enough songs to fill another album. The plan was working as far as the colonel was concerned. But it was getting Elvis down. Elvis was at his peak but he was not performing the kind of music he wanted to do and he was making silly movies. My brothers and I decided the problem was the colonel. We couldn't figure out why Elvis didn't get rid of him.

We thought things might change after *Easy Come, Easy Go* when Elvis came back to Graceland in a foul mood and festivities were kept to a minimum. Elvis went straight to his room, stopping only long enough to give the order that he was not to be disturbed and to tell everyone that if the colonel called he was not available. In the weeks that followed Colonel Parker repeatedly called the mansion and spent long hours on the phone with Joe Esposito, Marty Lacker, Vernon, and anyone else he thought might be able to intercede on his behalf. But Elvis let it be known that he wasn't speaking to the colonel and that he wasn't doing any more movies. Apparently the colonel begged, threatened, cajoled, screamed, and pleaded—he could do all that within a few minutes—but all to no avail. Christmas came and still Elvis wouldn't talk to him. If ever there was a time that Elvis "hid out" at Graceland, this was it—but only from the colonel and the press. Was Elvis just being moody? No. We saw him. Elvis was determined. My brothers and I were happily convinced that Elvis was soon to be rid of the colonel forever.

That Christmas season a lot of our time was spent with horses. In the summer he'd bought Priscilla a black quarterhorse she called Domino. At first he'd just watch her ride but then Elvis tried it, liked it, and bought himself both a golden palomino named Rising Sun and a Tennessee walker named Bear. In a few days Elvis was buying horses for everyone. He already had a stable out in the back grounds near the back entrance to our house on Dolan Street (which Vernon had been using as a storeroom for old furniture) and soon every stall was filled and the tack room was a center of activity.

Then Elvis bought me my own horse, Flaming Star. It was a great-looking animal but the first time I got on it, Star walked slowly away from the barn and no amount of urging on my part could get it to move any faster. After a while I got impatient with the pace. I was afraid Elvis had bought me a "dog." When I'd given up on it, I turned it back in the direction of the barn. Suddenly the horse had more speed than I had ever dreamed of. It thundered along at a full gallop. I was just barely hanging on, screaming for it to stop, when we came flying back to the barn where Elvis and Priscilla were standing alongside their horses. I jumped off and came tumbling to rest at Elvis's feet. The horse continued into the barn, back to his stall and feed. Elvis laughed. "Enough horse for you, Billy?" he asked.

Soon I had Flaming Star under control and I became one of the better horsemen around the place. By this time everyone was getting into the act and there were sixteen or seventeen horses at Graceland. The afternoon rides were becoming so routine that hundreds of fans would line the walls to watch. Elvis had bought the best western saddles and riding gear for everyone and he struck quite a figure strutting before the fans in full attire.

One day Elvis wanted to know which of his horses was the fastest. He got everyone out in the front grounds and staked out a course. Ricky was to ride Bear and I rode Elvis's horse, Rising Sun. Sun won, but I was riding so hard that I forgot we had to stop. I rode Sun right up to the Graceland fence at a full gallop. The horse stopped but I was thrown head over heels right over the fence. Apparently I landed with a thud and didn't move. Elvis was the first to reach me. I was still in a daze when my stepbrother picked me up in his arms and asked, "Are you okay, Billy?" I said, "Yeah, I'm fine. I won the race didn't I?" Everyone laughed this time.

Elvis liked to ride in the late afternoons and early evenings after most of the fans had left for home. Sometimes he'd be riding along the wall that separated Graceland from the row of houses on Dolan Street and he'd catch the aroma of a neighbor's barbecue in his backyard. Elvis would peek over the fence and ask, "What are we having for dinner?" Sometimes he'd stand up on the horse and jump over the fence to check it out. To my knowledge he never actually joined them for a meal but the neighbors got a big kick out of the visits.

And during the Christmas holidays Elvis would ride Sun down to the Music Gates every day just to chat with the fans, sign a few autographs, and wish them all a Merry Christmas.

I got to see a different side of Elvis myself that winter. One night about a week before Christmas he took me shopping with him. I had always watched Graceland fill up with gifts before Christmas but I'd never before seen Elvis doing the actual shopping. We went to Sears and Goldsmiths and Elvis delighted in picking out individual gifts for everyone. My delight was in watching him examine a stereo and say, "I'm getting this for Red," or in picking up a sports coat and saying, "I think Rick would like this one."

Among my presents that Christmas was my first "bike," a Honda 50. Originally it had been meant for my birthday (that was to come three weeks later), but Elvis held fast to the equal treatment policy that began the day we met him. So this present was "moved up." Ricky got one too, and David, though only eleven, got a minibike. The only problem was that we couldn't go anywhere outside of the estate with them. But within the grounds of Graceland we were terrors!

After New Years our spirits were only dampened slightly when we learned that Elvis had signed a new deal with Colonel Parker. At that age, and for a long time to come, we simply followed Elvis's lead. If he was unhappy with Colonel, we hated Colonel. If Elvis signed a new deal with Colonel, then it must be okay. We didn't question Elvis. Years later we did feel a little betrayed when we learned that it was Vernon who beseeched Elvis to make peace with Colonel Parker and give in to his plans.

6

"SPEEDWAY"

(February 1967 — Spring 1969)

During the fall of 1966 we often heard Priscilla urging Elvis to buy a horse farm somewhere, a retreat where they could go by themselves and just ride for miles and miles without being disturbed. But Elvis was still thinking of moving the whole family out to the West Coast and, in the meantime, he thought the grounds of Graceland were big enough. However, something in those confrontations, and signing again with the colonel in early January, had changed Elvis's position on several matters. He stopped objecting to air travel and soon sold the tour bus. He never again mentioned a move to the West Coast, and he granted Priscilla her fondest wish.

In February of 1967 Elvis bought the Circle G, a 160-acre ranch about thirty miles south of Graceland in Mississippi. But if Priscilla thought it was going to be a place where they could get away from everyone, she just didn't understand Elvis. No sooner had they fixed up the main house than Elvis was making plans to have houses built all over the property for "his boys." (Not only did Elvis call Rick, David, and me "the boys," he often referred to the inner circle of Joe Esposito, Alan Fortas, Charlie Hodge, Red and Sonny West, Richard

Davis, Marty Lacker, Lamar Fike, and Richard Geller, and his cousins, Gene and Billy Smith, in the same way.)

Priscilla had a fit, and Vernon backed her. In matters of finance and privacy they were of one mind. Even so, when Elvis took a project to heart he'd develop a sheer lust for it. And Elvis was determined that there would be a place at the Circle G for everyone. When plans for a community of houses fell through, he ended up buying mobile homes so that he could have his wish.

By this time I had a car, a 1960 Valiant that Vernon had given me, but I was only fourteen and had no license to drive. I had been driving around the grounds at Graceland, but the ranch was over ten times as big. So we took that and the '57 Caddy down to the Circle G. Whenever I didn't have to go to school, or if I got a ride down after school, I went to the ranch. Ricky and David were right with me. We could ride horses, drive cars, fish in the lake, and pretty much do as we pleased until it got dark and we had to find a ride home. I rarely stayed overnight because I usually had school or some work or church activities the next morning. But getting a ride was easy enough because there was by this time a constant stream of people going back and forth between the Circle G and Graceland.

The rolling hills were great for horseback riding and I drove that Valiant all the time. The center of attention was usually the fourteen-acre lake. We used it for swimming and fishing, and it was Elvis's favorite spot for skeet shooting. Skeet shooting was something we could all do for as long as eight hours at a time without getting tired. Elvis loved it so much he would quit only when it finally got dark. We kids were slowed down when Elvis decided to let us try out his twelve-gauge shotgun. Man, that thing packed a wallop! Elvis let each of us try it in turn, and all three of us got knocked over backward. I decided I knew how to handle it, and backed up to a tree to brace my shoulder. When I fired, the big gun drove me back into the tree and practically broke my shoulder. Normally, Elvis would be the first to me when I was hurt, to find out if I was OK, but this time he was laughing so hard he simply fell to the ground and lay there as long as I did. Except I was gritting my teeth to hold back the pain and Elvis was gritting his to try and hold back his laughter.

By now the Circle G had become a second Graceland. Same people, same games, just a bigger playground, with, often, bigger crowds. None of this exactly pleased Priscilla. In fact she was very upset, and while she had always been cool to the guys who worked for

Elvis, she no longer tried to hide her resentment of them and their families. "Bossy," "bitchy," and words much worse were now commonly used to describe her. And it wasn't just at the Circle G Ranch. Back at Graceland there was the feeling that she had taken over; when Elvis wasn't around everyone steered clear of her. She reorganized the kitchen so that there was a set menu and certain hours when it would be available. This was probably a good thing, because the guys were ordering sirloins and T-bones at any odd hour while Elvis himself was eating hamburgers and fried peanut butter and banana sandwiches, but the way she did it antagonized everyone. Even with Elvis there, she would get on the guys pretty hard. Elvis would kid them and sometimes ride them, but Priscilla could be downright cruel. She'd call them "hangers-on" and ask them what they thought they were really contributing. She still treated the three of us OK but our friend Jackie told me more than once, "Man, I just try to keep out of Priscilla's way."

Then on May 1, 1967 something unexpected happened. Elvis and Priscilla got married. I first heard about it at an assembly at my school when a friend told me she'd heard it on the radio. Then the girl asked, "Didn't you know they were getting married?" I didn't. Mom and Vernon had known since shortly after Christmas but they hadn't wanted to tell Rick or David or me because it was to be a secret. They thought we might spill the beans to someone at school, rumors would start, and somehow the press would get wind of it, which eventually happened anyway. But not telling us fit right in with Vernon's idea of security and caution. After all, except for Jackie, Vernon still didn't let us bring our friends over to our pool on Dolan Street for fear one of them would fall in and drown or sue us. At the wedding Elvis and Priscilla were whisked from one hotel to another in Las Vegas until they were finally married at the Aladdin Hotel. A small group (Vernon, Dee, Joe Esposito, Marty Lacker, Charlie Hodge, and Billy Smith) tagged along. The colonel had orchestrated the wedding throughout, and his arrangements managed to irritate and confuse everyone. Elvis and Priscilla, after an embarrassing press conference, went to Palm Springs for a few days of what was supposed to be their honeymoon, which was cut short so that Elvis could finish some voice-overs on his film *Clambake*.

It did surprise a lot of people that Elvis would have let the colonel control and manipulate his wedding like that. Looking back, there are probably two good reasons why that happened. First, Elvis was definitely not one to want to look after such arrangements himself. He had to give the job to someone and that person would have to be in complete control. And second, though they'd had a little feud, Elvis was no longer upset with the colonel. We didn't know any of this then, but my brothers and I later reconstructed the important points that brought the two men back together. They were: Colonel was to desist from making further movie deals—Elvis would decide what pictures he would act in; Colonel was to pursue Elvis's wish to reestablish himself as a performer, through the media and on tour; Colonel was to provide Elvis with the best songwriters and musicians so that Elvis would record and perform only quality music, not movie songs. In return Elvis would fulfill the existing movie contract; would agree either to marry or drop Priscilla; and would pay the colonel fifty percent of all proceeds after Elvis's expenses. As a kicker, either they decided or Elvis determined that to accomplish all that he wanted to do, he'd need to make extensive use of airplanes. All of this is conjecture. But it's based on many things that Elvis and Vernon said to my brothers and me about what was expected. Whatever had been agreed between Elvis and the Colonel sealed the eventual outcome—and it followed those lines. And it would explain a lot, including Colonel's orchestration of Elvis's wedding. But what could never be explained to my brothers or me was why, at this point, Elvis needed the colonel at all.

Roughly a month after the wedding, on May 28, 1967, Elvis and Priscilla threw a big reception at Graceland, inviting all their friends. Elvis was particularly cordial to those that he knew should have been at the wedding but were excluded by the colonel. Red West refused to come, but those who did seemed to have a pretty good time. At the dinner Elvis sat at the head of the table with Priscilla, and then Ricky, to one side. On the other side were Daddy and Mom, and then David and me. Elvis wore the tux and Priscilla wore the gown that they'd worn at the wedding. Then Elvis stood up and made a short speech about how he was glad everyone had come. There was a lot of applause and I know few of those gathered heard him comment, softly, "I wish the wedding had been here, at Graceland." When he was seated Elvis turned to David and said, "I'm sorry you boys weren't there. You should have been. It's just that damn colonel and his secrecy."

"That's all right, Elvis," I said. "I'm sure this is better anyway."

"Maybe it's for the best Ricky wasn't there," Elvis replied. "With the crush he has on Priscilla he might have tried to stop it. I'm just sorry to have taken her away from him." We all laughed at that but Rick and Cilla had their heads together in their own conversation and didn't hear it. Realizing that, we laughed all the harder. I remember someone asking Elvis if he'd had such a good time at the actual wedding. "It was a shambles," Elvis answered. But this night the champagne and good times flowed and it was one of the few times I'd seen Vernon so inebriated or so happy. He danced with some young blond and even Dee, this time, laughed and clapped her hands to Vernon's version of the jitterbug. Elvis said, "I love seeing Daddy have such a good time. I just love it!" Later Elvis had Jerry Schilling drive us home. Even though it was only a quarter of a mile by car, Elvis wasn't taking any chances. Vernon was still singing when we got back to our own house.

Elvis and Priscilla left for what was supposed to be a two-week honeymoon in the Bahamas, but for some reason they were back at Graceland within a week. They did manage to slip off for a few days to the Circle G and spent their second honeymoon in Lamar's house trailer. (They could have stayed in the house but Elvis loved those trailers.) Lamar slept in the front room and Elvis and Priscilla stayed in the back.

When they were back at Graceland, Elvis and Priscilla didn't get along too well. Even while people were still congratulating them on their marriage they seemed to argue and bicker over everything that came up. No one else seemed to notice it. Vernon in particular was going around beaming and shaking everyone's hand. But the couple didn't seem like newlyweds to me.

A few weeks later, in the grandest send-off ever, Elvis and the gang left for L.A. to film *Speedway*. It was to be the last time the tour bus was used on a cross-country junket and spirits were high. The last week in June 1967, when my brothers and I were on our summer vacations (another cause for celebration), Vernon, Dee, and the three of us flew out to join them. We were met by a guy named Stan, who always seemed on the spot to meet us whenever we flew out to one of Elvis's movies. Stan was always friendly and anxious to please but we couldn't exactly figure out what he was doing there. He'd tell us about the movie, the story, Elvis's character, who was in the movie with him, the roles they played, and then we'd hardly see him again until Dee or Vernon had some special request, or it was time to leave. At

Speedway I asked him what he did and he told us that he was a publicity man. Ricky immediately came up with, "Stan, Stan, the publicity man," and we began chanting that phrase whenever we saw him. We didn't know his last name or whether he worked for the studios or the colonel. We did know that he didn't work for Elvis, but at that time we really didn't pay attention to who worked for whom. That knowledge would come later when we all worked for Elvis and understood that there were cliques and loyalties. Many years later I repeatedly heard a story to the effect that Stan, either as the studio's or Colonel's man, would approach Elvis with someone who wanted to meet him. Stan was fine dealing with the press or other celebrities but very nervous when talking to Elvis. He'd try to get Elvis's attention, but when he succeeded he'd hesitate, trying to make sure he was phrasing his request properly. Of course Elvis, who was always moving, had no patience with that and Stan would be left talking to himself. As the story goes, Stan finally cornered Elvis on one occasion and told him that some starlet was waiting to meet him, and that she was not only beautiful but smart and had the right connections. Elvis said, "Uh, Stan. That's OK but—"

Stan pressed on. "She's beautiful. She's from a wealthy family. And, Elvis, she's a big fan of yours. She loves your pictures and she has every record you've ever cut."

Stan went on celebrating every quality she had including being a nonsmoker and nondrinker until Elvis finally cut him short with an impatient glare.

"Stan," Elvis finally asked him. "Does she fuck?"

I don't know if this story is true or not. There are so many Elvis stories that could be. I probably don't know them all. There are new ones created daily. But when someone repeats one and asks, "You were his brother, is that a true story?" I often only have my feeling for it to go on. If it doesn't sound like Elvis, or something he'd do, I say, "No, that's bull." But if it's a story that I don't know but sounds likely, I'll say, "Sure sounds like him." This one sounds like Elvis, not as I knew him then so much, but as I finally got to know him.

They were shooting *Speedway* at the MGM studios and high jinks, practical jokes, and general fun dominated the set. Of course not everyone liked it, especially when the water pistol fights escalated (as they always did) into water balloon fights. Some of them dropped like bombs from the rafters above the set. Then there were cherry bombs. I think Red brought them, and they were setting them off everywhere,

once even catching Bill Bixby in his dressing room. He was a good
sport about it, but there were others who got pissed. To those who
didn't like it, Elvis had one answer. "If you can't take the heat, get
off the set." But what did you do when the door to your small dressing
room opened and in came a handful of lit cherry bombs?

The sets at *Speedway* were elaborate. One was a restaurant with
mock convertibles as tables, cars protruding from the walls, and dozens
of beautifully built and scantily attired women. Rick and I must have
felt our young hormones churning because we took one of Elvis's
tandem bikes and rode it right across the set while the cameras were
rolling. No one yelled at us right then, but later it was carefully
explained to us what the red light on the camera meant.

Stan "the publicity man" tried to find other activities to occupy our
time. We had been told that we could visit the set of "Rat Patrol,"
one of our favorite TV series, but the cast and crew were all out in the
desert shooting location shots while we were there. Stan had something better to offer. He took us over to meet Robert Vaughn and the
rest of the crew from "The Man from U.N.C.L.E." This was one of
our favorite shows (and Elvis's) and we were very impressed. We met
David McCallum, too, but he was kind of cool to us. Robert Vaughn
was just like the guy he played—in control! He and Stan took us
around and showed us their dressing rooms, their sets, and told us we
were welcome to stay and watch the taping they'd be doing over the
next several days. Then Vaughn remembered that they were about to
blow up a set, a lobby of some international hotel, that afternoon. He
asked us if we wanted to see it and, of course, we were all for it. But
by the time he figured out where it was going to happen and got us all
there it had already been blown up (they'd used a double for Vaughn
in that scene) so we missed it. Then he gave us cards that said we
were part of "The Man from U.N.C.L.E." team and that we agreed,
if called upon, to participate in any future mission or adventure. I
carried mine for years. Sad to say, I no longer have it or any other
memento of those years.

Elvis was spending a lot of time with his costar, Nancy Sinatra.
And she was spending a lot of time with us, taking us around the sets,
out for walks, out for ice cream. She was treating us the way Anne
Helm, Shelley Fabares, and Mary Ann Mobley had done in the earlier
pictures. Or Joanna Moore, who'd taken us out fishing off a bridge on
the set. Winning the hearts of the "little brothers" was part of a
possible path to Elvis's heart and we loved the attention. Nancy

Sinatra was fun to be with. The first day we met her she was wearing shorts and sandals. We told her how much we liked her song, "These Boots Are Made for Walking," and the next day she was wearing white boots and a white miniskirt. She had the prettiest eyes, so bright, and she drove us around the sets in a golf cart. She asked us if we wanted to be entertainers like our big brother. "I wish," I said.

She introduced us to other stars at the studio. We met and had our pictures taken with Nelson Rockefeller, and with Ernest Borgnine and Jim Brown who were making *Ice Station Zebra* on the next set. We liked them and they seemed to like us. We spent almost as much time on their set as we did on Elvis's. Really, it was our best movie experience ever. And Nancy Sinatra was the best part. I just loved the sound of her voice, so smooth, so in control, so like Elvis when he wasn't mad about something. She even invited my brothers and me over for dinner at her house. We told Dee, but she said, "Boys, Nancy's been nice to you. But you're pushing it." "No," we said. "She wants us to come." But Mom wouldn't let us. Even Elvis finally approached her one day and said, "I may be missing something. But are you trying to kidnap my brothers?"

Elvis didn't miss a thing. He and Nancy had their times together off the set. And on the set they resembled high school kids on a first date, gently touching, laughing, then touching each other again.

I don't know where Priscilla was at this time—she had been on the set earlier—but I think she'd gone back to Germany to visit her parents. I do know that when we got back to Memphis Priscilla was as testy and domineering as I'd ever seen her. Of course there were tabloids and gossip columns trumpeting Elvis's friendship with Nancy Sinatra, but at the time I didn't know anything about that. And Priscilla had to be thinking about her pregnancy, which Dee had carefully explained to us.

Soon we were back at Graceland for our summer schedule, working again for Uncle Earl on the grounds. We worked hard and willingly at whatever task he gave us. Dee used to complain that we would do anything to improve the grounds at Graceland but we wouldn't even clean our own pool. She was right. Our own pool was boring. Elvis and his land of adventure was at the other side of the gate. Anything could happen there. So that's where we wanted to pay our dues.

That August, Dee took us off to her brother Richard's house in Huntsville, Alabama, where we'd spent the last few weeks of several summers. We had total freedom as to dress, friends, schedules, anything. We built a raft on the river, had plum fights, and made friends with other kids in the area. Our best buddies were the Mullins brothers, Mike, Delbert, and Dude (I never knew him by any other name except that Dee called him "Kitten" because he once had a kitten who looked just like him). They were the ones who taught us how to build a raft and to explore the back country. Up till then our back country had been at Graceland or the Circle G. They had a cousin we all called "Measles." He got that nickname because he once told us he could drink gasoline. Naturally we got a glass jar and filled it with gasoline and dared him to drink it. To our great surprise he did. He immediately went into convulsions, started vomiting, wheezing, and generally acting as if he was about to die. By the time we got help and they got him to a hospital, his entire throat and upper chest looked as if he'd contracted the measles. To this day (I saw him three years ago) he speaks with a deep rasp. But of all the opportunities, falling out of trees, near drownings, encounters with water moccasins, and the like, that was the only serious injury any of us sustained. And our few visits to Richard's house were probably the most normal, maybe the only normal times we spent as kids. They contrasted sharply with the hectic, distracted life we led in Memphis, to which we soon returned.

Months before, we'd become aware that Priscilla was pregnant, had watched her grow big in the stomach, and had wondered what was going on. But she'd continued to ride horses, dance, and do what she'd always done, so we came to think little of it. Then one night about three weeks before Lisa Marie was born (February 1, 1968), it snowed. That night we were all out building a snowman, riding sleds, and throwing logs on a huge bonfire in the yard. Then Elvis got to fooling around, roughhousing as always, and Priscilla took a hard fall. Later when we were back in our house Dee asked us if we'd had fun. I believe it was David who piped up, "Yeah we had a great time. Except when Cilla fell." "What?" my mother gasped, "Is she all right?" "Sure, Mom," we quickly replied. "It was OK. We just all picked her up." But I could tell by the look on her face that we probably hadn't convinced her. Fortunately Priscilla truly hadn't been harmed.

7

"GIRLS! GIRLS! GIRLS!"

(1966 ▬ 1969)

It was the spring of 1969. I had turned sixteen, drove fast bikes, and had my driver's license. I was the uncle of a one-year-old girl, and my brothers and I were making new and different friends. And I was noticing girls in a different light. More than noticing, I had begun dating. I felt I was ready to become a man. The times were changing.

Elvis had taught me quite a few things about women. First and foremost among these was self-confidence. Even when we were at Graceland Elementary and pretending that we weren't interested in girls he would tell us, "That's too bad. They're interested in you. And you know why? Because you're somebody. And they can see it." Later, when Ricky and I did confess to some interest and asked Elvis how to handle it he told us, "You don't have to worry about it. You're the king's brothers and it's just going to come naturally to you. Just have confidence in yourselves." So we were self-confident. But by the sixth grade I figured it was time to start trying that confidence out.

Connie Gregory was one of our neighbors and she was one of the few that we could invite over to our house and to the pool. Dee knew her parents, they met the proper criteria, churchgoing and all that. So she became one of the "guys." One day at school she introduced

Ricky and me to Dena Scott. We couldn't have helped but notice
Dena because she was one of the prettiest girls in our school, and one
of the most popular. And she seemed quite interested in us. Within a
few days she was inviting us over to her house for a party that Friday
night. She told us there would be music, dancing, refreshments, and
a lot of fun. Then she read us off a list of the kids who would be
there. It included just about every pretty girl in the sixth grade at
Graceland.

We beamed. "Of course we'll be there." We'd heard a little about
Dena's parties and they sounded like the place to be. Almost as an
afterthought Dena said, "Oh, I think that some of us are going to play
Spin the Bottle."

Wow! Now Ricky and I were really excited. But there was one
major problem. Dee would never let us go. She didn't let us go to any
social gathering that wasn't sanctioned by the Church of Christ. And
this was not only outside the church, it was people she didn't know,
it was dancing, and it was possibly Spin the Bottle and who knows
what else. (The Church of Christ not only frowned on dancing and
mixed gatherings, but was also adamant in the belief that young boys
and girls shouldn't swim in the same swimming pool—a rule we
broke.) So there was no sense asking. The answer would be no and
we would be watched.

How were we to do it? The obvious answer was to go to Elvis, tell
him the situation, and have him arrange to get us out of the house
and over to Dena's. But Elvis was in L.A. making *Harum Scarum* and
of no use to us. The irony was excruciating. Here we were, younger
brothers to the star of *Girls! Girls! Girls!*, *Fun in Acapulco*, and *Kissin'
Cousins*. We were cocksure replicas of the king as we strutted the halls
of Graceland Elementary, and when push came to shove, we were still
at the age when kissin' was about the last thing we'd ever do. But
somehow I swallowed a little pride and went to Dena the day before
her party. I told her my parents were pretty strict and that it might be
tough getting out. She seemed really disappointed, thinking that
meant we weren't coming. "We'll be there," I said. "We'll find a way
out of the house." The problem was that we weren't sure how we
could get to her house once we'd escaped our own. (It was at about
that time that we decided that it was no longer cool to ride our bikes.)
"That's no problem," she said. "Just get to a phone and call me. My
mother and I will pick you up."

"It might not be until after nine or ten," I warned.

"Anytime is OK," Dena said.

So that Friday night we dressed up in our best pants and shoes. I finally had grown into the size six, felt "Beatle boots" that Elvis wore and that I had coveted for some time. We wore casual shirts as we watched TV with Mom and Vernon. At nine-thirty, as always, Dee yawned and announced she was going to bed. We watched TV with Vernon for a few minutes and then said we were going upstairs too. Immediately we changed shirts and went out on the metal awning off our bedroom on the second floor. From there it was only a short, calculated leap to the roof of the garage (with our shoes off it seemed like a long leap, with nothing but hard concrete below us, but I'd seen Elvis do stuff like that a hundred times in the movies and at Graceland). We made the leap and then we climbed over the wrought-iron grillwork to the street. In a few minutes we were at a pay phone calling Dena, and twenty minutes later we were at the party.

Now this was excitement, first being there, and then the expectation of what might come. Of course, we were "cool," and when the first announcement of Spin the Bottle came, the boys huddled in a far corner of Dena's den. But after some coaxing and taunting, I was the first to cross over to "enemy" territory. The bottle spun with me and five girls. As I recall they were Dawn Perry, Carol Couvier (on whom I had a tremendous crush), Ruth Ann Cockrel, Judy Clark, and Michelle Ferguson who'd later be a "steady" with me. I think it was Michelle Ferguson who was the target of the bottle, and she had to choose me to kiss, or kiss a girl! I had never kissed a girl but as we approached I could feel Elvis over my shoulder and see him in his many movies. I didn't put my hands around Michelle's waist or anything as dramatic as that, but I did place them surely on her upper arms—thinking of how Elvis would do it—and opened my mouth, before our lips touched. All the girls let out a squeal. Some had played the game before, but they had never encountered open-mouthed kissing before. I was an immediate success. My emulation of Elvis made me Elvis—at least for that moment—and I felt the power and ecstasy, at least as clearly as a sixth-grader can feel it, and maybe it was as clear and powerful as it would ever be. And it wasn't just power for me but for Elvis as well, because I felt how proud he would be of me.

I may have kissed all the girls before the other boys joined in. I know I was a huge success and that Dena called it her "greatest party ever." And I swaggered as I walked for some time to come. Of course we told Elvis about it at the first opportunity, and he laughed and cherished the story just as we did. From that time on the episodes were repeated. We went to Dena's house often, always the same escape route, always with Dena and her mother willing to pick us up and drive us home, and never a suspicion by Dee and Vernon.

From that time on the world had an added quality: girls. It was the one adventure in those days, unlike racing or shooting or fighting, that Elvis could not share with us. Fortunately it was knowledge that I was quite happy to discover for myself.

Elvis had a second rule for us. After confidence came awareness. "You're my brothers," he said. "There are women who will want to take advantage of you only for your name or position. Keep an eye on it. Because you're the ones who can take advantage of them." And we did. My friend Charles Boozer and I even had a contest during the spring of that sixth grade year to see how many girls we could exchange ID bracelets with. I won. A lot of the matchups began at Dena's parties. A short flirtation, some kissing, a lot of time on the telephone. Then an inevitable misunderstanding, and it was on to the next "steady." The funny thing was that Dena was never among my girlfriends, although I've got to admit, she was sometimes part of my fantasies. She was always just a friend. It's as if I was copying Elvis and his pattern of multiple girlfriends. He'd first seen Anita Wood, who I thought was the most beautiful woman in creation (though I was only seven when I met her). Then came Anne Helm, who played with us on the set of *Follow That Dream* and later Nancy Sinatra (*Speedway*) who looked at me (so I imagined!) as if I were Elvis. I was in the seventh grade but I couldn't get her out of my mind. I thought she was just great. At any rate, my social life had certainly picked up.

Dena, almost as much as Elvis, opened a world to me that I might otherwise have missed. Recently I got together with her, and I asked her if she could remember me in those times. Her response was, "Billy, I not only remember you. We were all struck by you. We'd seen Elvis playing football with his bodyguards and we'd seen him in the movies and driving around on his motorcycles, but to us you were the real 'Elvis experience.' More than your brothers, you looked like a Presley, carried yourself that way, wore his clothes, a lot of black with your collar turned up at the neck. And you were older! You and Rick were in the same grade, but something had happened and you were in our grade. So sure of yourself and wearing the best clothes.

You had that long hair that you had to shake to keep out of your eyes. You don't know what a commotion you created."

Whew! It isn't all true. I don't think I ever turned my collar up—that went out in the fifties—and except for that one time in Palm Springs, I did not consciously mimic Elvis. I emulated him, and I asked myself what he would do in a particular situation, and usually that meant being bold. So I was. But I did have a Beatles haircut, almost down to my ears. And I was a sudden hit with the girls.

Elvis's third rule was "Treat them special. Compliment them. Open doors for them. Make a fuss." And I worked on that, too. I always thought of the character Elvis had played in the movie, *Kid Galahad,* protective, sweet, but tough when he needed to be. The girls thought Ricky and I were such gentlemen (their parents sometimes had doubts), and that counted for a lot. Again I would watch how Elvis treated the women in his movies and then I'd try to do everything the same, everything except sing to them.

One thing we couldn't do was bring girls back to Graceland. I don't know if it was because Vernon and Dee didn't want any family goings-on exposed to outsiders—were they afraid Elvis could do something embarrassing that could end up in the papers?—or if it was just Vernon's fear of being sued if some accident happened, which is how he explained the prohibition. Once I did bring a girl over to ride horses, but she had to ride on mine with me. She wasn't allowed to ride a horse by herself even though there were several available.

Things were going beautifully until Dee decided that instead of continuing at Graceland we would all go to the Harding Academy, a private school under the patronage of the Church of Christ. That was when I was in seventh grade, the year Elvis and Priscilla married, and therefore we were basically out of it socially for the entire year. As usual, I didn't do much of note in the classrooms, but I can say, in all honesty, that apart from my mom's fervent desires, I didn't have much help. Elvis was, at best, indifferent to school learning—even though he loved books he disdained the school approach to learning. Elvis was happy when we made good grades (the good grades were mainly Ricky's doing), but when David and I didn't perform well he'd say, "Don't pay any attention to that. Their measure is only as good as the people measuring. I'll be your measure." Furthermore, Vernon was positively antagonistic to book learning.

When we were home trying, at Dee's behest, to do our homework in algebra, English, or history we'd invariably run across some problem and ask Dee for help. She'd puzzle over it for a time (Mom was good in English but algebra was a foreign matter to her) and say, "Well, what does the book say?"

"The book says this is the answer," we'd respond. "But it doesn't make sense and I can't figure out how it came to that answer."

Then Vernon would appear and take the book in his hands. It didn't matter what the subject was; Vernon would immediately announce the answer to the question. Usually he'd be wildly wrong—at least according to the book. We'd say, "Daddy, that can't be right. Look what it says here."

Vernon would take a quick look at the book and say, "No, that ain't right. This book's got it all wrong."

Later we might find the right answer or the right method to find it and we'd show it to Vernon. His response always was, "The hell you say! That book's got it all wrong. It ain't right. That's all."

It was fortunate for me that my parents never expected much from me in school. If I ever had any "smarts" I never showed them. I consistently underachieved. Rick was the one who made A's (but not all the time), was popular with the girls, and was voted class president one year. Early on, Rick had been targeted as the young Stanley capable of doing great things. But all it got him at home was a lot of flak. If David and I got in trouble in school once in a while, that was expected. We were emotional misfits. But if Rick screwed up, he was in it deep with Vernon and Dee. Dee expected Rick to become a doctor and to attain a new and higher level of respect for the family. When his conduct and achievements were in line with those expectations Dee's attitude was, "Well, that's good. Now let's see where you can go from here." And when they didn't measure up she would go haywire. Vernon, following Mom's lead, made Rick the whipping boy, so that he was held accountable and sometimes punished when David or I got into some mischief. Looking back, I can see that it wasn't at all odd that Rick would be the first to drop out of high school to join Elvis on the road. Not odd to my way of thinking, at least. But to Dee Rick's decision would be devastating.

Though they expected the minimum from me in terms of conduct and academics, they got a little less. The contrast between being the "king's little brother" at Graceland and on motion picture sets, and being a newcomer at a grim and bleak Christian school, the easy target of bullies who were waiting to pounce on Elvis's brother, was extreme. Being the oldest of the brothers in an alien and unkind world, and being the smallest (by now everyone called me "Nub"), my main task was to be the toughest. I got into more than my share of fights and run-ins with the authorities. Rick made good grades but his conduct wasn't any better than mine. So in the eighth grade we were allowed to go to Hillcrest and rejoin our classmates from Graceland. But a year away can make a big difference at that age, and when I first was back in Hillcrest I'd become shy with girls again.

Elvis sensed my predicament. Before, we had asked him, "Elvis, what is the secret?"—to getting along with girls, whatever. Now he knew how confused I'd become, being pulled back and forth between the public school and the teachings of the church. He asked me how I was doing with the girls and I answered, "OK, Elvis. They all seem friendly enough. But they all have new boyfriends and I'm not sure how I fit in. From what I hear it's all gotten to be a little faster now. I guess it's a little hard getting back into it."

"Just have confidence in yourself," Elvis said. "And remember who you are." Then he cleared his throat. "Nub, has anyone told you the facts of life? Where babies come from, and all that?"

"Well, Elvis," I said. "Mom told me that I should have a conversation with the preacher about all that. But somehow I wouldn't feel comfortable with that." So Elvis told me a little about biology and passion and possible problems and how to avoid them. He said there are women and men and they fall in love. Really nothing I hadn't heard before from other kids. But he made it all seem natural and fun and that was not what the church told us. Elvis wouldn't say anything against the church but he did say, "There's nothing unclean about sex. Don't let them tell you that." Then he asked me if I had any "protection," just in case anything did happen. I told him no. Elvis said, "Well you ought to."

I was then fifteen but in the eighth grade just the same because I was never a good student and because Dee kept moving us back and forth. Each time I was put in a new environment I temporarily lost confidence. And whenever I was confined to the rules of the Church of Christ and made to wear sports coats and ties and told about the evils of sex, sinning ways, unclean thoughts and all that, I believed it. I believed in my mom and I was probably more obedient to her wishes than either of my brothers ever were. But all of it confused me. Everything that seemed right to me was wrong to the church. The Church of Christ always made me feel inadequate, sinful, dirty, and bad. When Elvis told me that he thought I was doing 'just fine,' it was such a relief I just can't describe it. But life felt good again.

I set out to find a "rubber" but was too ashamed to ask for one at a pharmacy. Then I bought one from a senior at Hillcrest and carried it proudly in my wallet for several months. Dee finally discovered it one day and got rid of it, but never said anything about it. In the meantime with the "protection" in my pocket, never used, I resumed my social life. The parties at Dena Scott's house were better than ever. We still had to sneak out to them by the familiar route and be picked up by Dena's mother. By now we had it organized.

Everyone knew about Dee's and Vernon's strictness and we were even able to get our musical equipment to Dena's. We'd take out the TV in Dena's den and set up Ricky's drums, and with Ricky or Jackie on drums, our buddy Lee on guitar, me on bass, we'd hold Friday night jam sessions there. We all took turns on lead vocals. The music we played was mainly the Rolling Stones, Led Zeppelin, and the Beatles. We tried one rendition of Elvis's "Jail House Rock" but we couldn't get it down right. We never did his movie music.

Donna Downing had a party house too, but it wasn't like Dena's. Her parents were stricter, though nothing like mine, and the parties were more organized. At Dena's it was anything goes, almost. Dena's mother was all for anything we got into and the house was open to parties at any time. I only remember seeing Dena's father a few times. He must have had some soundproof room to retire to at night. But Dena's mother was right there, in with whatever mischief we kids were up to. It was an open house, with Dena's mom as the house-mother. Nothing ever got out of hand. It was just good clean fun.

I had my first Harvey Wallbanger there. If anyone drank too much Dena's mom drove them home. She always said that if anyone wanted to drink she wouldn't stop them, but it should be somewhere where an adult was present and could look after the situation. Man, that was so different from what we expected from Dee and Vernon. Dena and I remained friends for the whole time I was in school.

On Saturday nights it was the movie theater at the Whitehaven Plaza Shopping Center. Dee would let us go there but she or Vernon were always on the spot to pick us up. We could flirt with the girls and sometimes sneak out later, but the only alternative was the bowling alley and that crowd was too rough for us. Our arrangements were always to meet our friends somewhere else. Graceland was out.

Elvis wouldn't have cared but Vernon was always concerned about lawsuits, pressure on Elvis, exposure to Elvis's crowd, and the like, and gatherings at our house were out of the question.

I was concerned at what was going on in our country. But, like all kids, I was obsessed with other matters. I couldn't wait to turn sixteen so that I could get a car. A car, to me, represented freedom—the ability to go anywhere I wanted, hang out with anyone I chose, and do anything I wanted to do. My sixteenth birthday, in January of 1969, provided me with a license to drive on the streets and highways of the world.

When I finally did turn sixteen Vernon and I had a common interest: cars. The same vehicle that represented my freedom proved to be his release as well. On that birthday he gave me a '57 Cadillac, and when he saw that it wasn't my style he gave me a '59 Chevy. That was better, but by now we were talking cars and Vernon was teaching me not only the basics—changing the oil every two thousand miles, watching the tachometer, and so on—but showing me how to take care of an engine, how to increase performance, and how to assess a car's abilities. I learned what one could do and another could not. One day I had a flat on the '59 Chevy and went to school on the bus. When I got home I had a shining '57 Chevy with a 402-cubic-inch engine! Now we were talking business! When *that* engine blew he bought me a '58 Ford, for which he bought several "continental kits." None of them fit so they ended up just sitting against a tree in the backyard. Uncle Earl, always trying to keep the grounds in the best possible shape, would come around and ask what I was going to do with them but Vernon would tell him, "Earl, hold your pants on. My boy and I have plans for all that."

Later I had a '57 Chevy Nomad, followed by a '65 Starfire and a '65 Nova. Jackie Stovall had a '65 Nova before I did, and it was one of the fastest cars in town. When I told Vernon about it he said, "Well, let's just check the paper, son. I think I saw something. . . ." I had one the next week. Of course we got to dragging them, but I always had something go wrong, a blown tire once, a transmission the next. I still think mine was faster than Jackie's. The old cars disappeared as fast as the new ones arrived. Vernon's taste in cars mirrored my own. He knew what I wanted and there was nothing he loved better than to wheel and deal, trade one for another, sell this one to buy that one. Now when I walked into his office, long off-limits to me and my brothers, Priscilla, and most everyone else, he would welcome me with circled listings in the daily want ads for different buys on used cars. He always handled the negotiations but he knew what we both wanted. Any Ford, Thunderbird, Chevy or Pontiac from '55 to '57, if it was in the right condition and had the right engine, was worth our trouble. Chrysler products from '55 on and Fords from '61 on were out, and the only foreign cars that held the least interest, like Elvis's Rolls Royces and Mercedes, were financially out of the question. It was the only interest that Vernon and I passionately shared, outside of his wife and his son. And it was the only one we talked about as equals. Later when I turned twenty-one and Elvis bought me a new TransAm it didn't diminish this bond. We still traded in old cars every time something of interest was available, and by the time I reached the age of twenty-one I had owned twenty-four different cars.

Elvis was having his own problems—finishing the movie contracts he'd come to hate, dealing with the colonel, trying to come to terms with being a married man, and finding a way back to creating real music instead of the movie songs he'd been made to do. But he was always aware of our situation, too. I don't remember when it first occurred but it must have been after I told him about Dena's parties. "Nub," he warned me over the years, "be careful. You fall in love too easy. You might just end up marrying the first girl you sleep with. And that could be a big mistake."

I didn't marry the first but I did fall into the trap Elvis predicted and it turned out to be a bigger disaster than even Elvis could have guessed. And Elvis was a big part of the disaster.

My father, Bill, Sr., and me. (*photo by Dee Presley*)

My father in uniform, with me and a cousin. (*photo by Dee Presley*)

My mother, Dee, married Vernon Presley in June 1960.

From left: Ricky, me, and David in front of our new home: Graceland.

Eventually, we moved to our own house on Dolan Street, just in back of Graceland.

Captain of the Harding Academy Track Team 1968 (I'm second from the left in back row).

1970: following in Elvis's footsteps, I joined ROTC.

Me, David, Lisa Marie's pony and Vernon. (*photo by Jimmy Velvet*)

Elvis riding Sun at Graceland, 1967. (*photo by Jimmy Velvet*)

Lisa Marie in July 1968, she's almost six months old. (*photo by Dee Presley*)

Los Angeles, 1968; you can see the pride in Elvis's face. (*photo by Jimmy Velvet*)

My mother, Dee; Lisa Marie; and Vernon.

8

A LEGENDARY PERFORMER

(January 1968 ▬ August 1969)

Following the rift and subsequent reconciliation between Elvis and the colonel we all waited for the first signs of the changes that Elvis demanded in his career. It began with Colonel's announcement to the press, in January of 1968, that Elvis was going to do a TV special, a Christmas show, later that year. Up to that time the colonel had always been dead set against Elvis doing any TV, on the theory that the exposure would dilute and harm the box office at Elvis's movies. But now the movies were no longer his primary concern. Elvis still had three to make under his contract, which he agreed to honor. Beyond that, the emphasis was on getting Elvis back out before the public, as a singer and an entertainer. That meant the colonel had to go back to work. Yet after his announcement, Colonel seemed primarily concerned with displaying his power. He was making personal demands on Elvis, and they were falling on deaf ears.

During the latter half of 1967 and for much of 1968 Elvis had withdrawn to his own world. The birth of his daughter, Lisa Marie, in February 1968, contributed to Elvis's withdrawal but more than that event was involved. Larry Geller had been Elvis's hair stylist, but his relationship with Elvis had grown much deeper. He had become Elvis's guru, introducing him to metaphysical and new age pursuits like numerology, scientology, and star-gazing, and to a new world of books.

Elvis wanted Priscilla involved too. He was always giving her books and reading her passages from books on Buddhism, Islam, and Sufi ways of knowledge, psychic potentialities, including mental telepathy, mind control, and out of body experiences. Once he took her to a meeting at Yogi Paramahansa Yogananda's Self-Realization Center on the West Coast. (I was invited, but declined. Rick went.) Elvis often held his own Bible meetings both at Graceland and at his house in Bel Air. He'd gather a group, read passages from the Old or New Testament, and then ask everyone their interpretation of what he'd just read. However, Elvis would get so excited he couldn't wait for the interpretations of others. He'd cut them off and tell his own. Priscilla always sat dutifully through these meetings, smiling and assessing the females in attendance to judge if they were any competition for her. Ricky, who would become Elvis's protégé in these pursuits, was fascinated. David, then twelve, didn't care. And, although I would later carry Elvis's personal library, including several copies each of Hermann Hesse's *Siddhartha* and Kahlil Gibran's *The Prophet*—Elvis liked to give these out—these matters held no interest for me. In fact, I avoided those gatherings like the plague. But occasionally I was caught. If you were sitting in the room, daydreaming about something or not paying attention, and one sprang up, you were stuck! Once they got going you couldn't stand up and say. "Uh, excuse me, Elvis. This stuff reminds me of Sunday school." You stayed.

Once Elvis singled me out. Probably he knew my mind was wandering. "Billy," he asked. "There are so many religions. Which one do you think is right?"

I answered, "The only thing that I can say is that I believe in God, Elvis."

"Well you've got your head screwed on right. That's the most important thing. You don't have to go to church or follow one certain religion to prove that you believe in God."

Another time, at his house in L.A., he was reading from the Bible that Jesus commanded his disciples to go forth and spread the word of the gospel. When Elvis got to this point he climbed up on a coffee table and, holding his cane like a staff, exclaimed, "Go ye sons-of-bitches forth and spread the word of the gospel!"

Priscilla, despite Elvis's encouragement, remained aloof from his quest for self-awareness. Then, when Lisa Marie was only a few months old, Priscilla made her move to the West Coast. In December of 1967 Elvis had purchased a home at 144 Monovale in the Holmby Hills section of Los Angeles, also known as Trousdale Estates, and from the spring of 1968 on Priscilla made that house her home.

My brothers and I still did things together with Elvis, and we still had fun. But I could see the change in Elvis's behavior. At first I thought it was Priscilla's presence. She was starting a lot of arguments with him, nagging him, mostly about the guys being around Graceland, and taking care of Lisa Marie, and (an old argument) about standing up to the colonel.

However, we soon realized that Elvis was acting differently even when Priscilla wasn't around. Instead of watching "The Man from U.N.C.L.E." on TV, or starting a water-gun fight, he'd go to a quiet room (usually his elegantly furnished bathroom) and read.

This enjoyment of some solitude was still observable a few years later when I began to work for him. Sometimes a recording executive or one of Colonel's men would appear at the door and ask me if I'd please find Elvis. They'd say it was an important matter, but they just hadn't been allowed to get through to him. I'd go to Elvis's room and tell him about it and he'd say, "Now now, Billy. I'm studying my books. Tell them I'm not here." Now this had been his usual conduct in response to some of the relatives who were just coming for handouts or for Priscilla's dad, Captain (now Colonel) Beaulieu, whom Elvis went out of his way to avoid at all times. But now Elvis was avoiding practically everyone.

Apparently the colonel noticed the changes too, or, since he wasn't exactly welcome at Graceland, found out about it. He started demanding that Elvis stop reading books because, "They clutter up his mind," and he also demanded that Larry Geller be fired. Elvis countered with threats to fire anyone who told Colonel about what he did with his time when he wasn't working. This put Joe Esposito in a difficult position because he'd become the liaison between Elvis and the colonel. He tried to work in the best interests of both of them but he had to be careful. He'd walked that tightrope five years before when he'd infuriated Elvis by giving Colonel daily reports of the progress on the set of Kissin' Cousins. It ended with Elvis's firing his good friend. Six months later Elvis had rehired Joe, but that had been a long time for Elvis to get by without his top man.

Elvis suspected that certain people on his payroll were also on the colonel's payroll for the purpose of spying on him.

While preparations were being made for the June taping of the Christmas special, but before Elvis left Graceland for the West Coast, Joe Esposito remarked to Elvis, "Colonel's got them jumping at NBC. He's got his whole crew working their tails off."

Elvis responded, "Yeah, he better. He gets fifty percent of the take now." That caught everyone's attention. Colonel's deal had always been that he took twenty-five percent, still a very high figure for a manager, even when you consider that the colonel restricted himself to only one client, Elvis. But fifty percent was unheard of, and I think people looked at Elvis as if he must be joking. "That's right," Elvis said. "Colonel gets fifty percent of the net. I get fifty. Then the government gets fifty percent of my fifty. So I guess what you're looking at is twenty-five percent of Elvis Presley. But we're not doing any more movies. Not any more movies that the colonel's going to be involved in."

Was Elvis a "dumb hillbilly," as some people have suggested, to have made such a deal? Not at all. What he wanted to do wasn't something he could handle on his own. He was smart enough to know his own limitations and to know that he couldn't be the "talent" and the manager of that talent and pull off both jobs successfully. And he was smart enough to know that the colonel could do the job Elvis wanted done, even if it cost more than if Elvis had hired someone else. After all, he had done it before. For years Elvis had had to listen to Priscilla and others yammer at him about standing up to the colonel and making his own decisions. On the surface it appeared that all the bitching and complaining did was make Elvis angry at being questioned, but in his own way and at his own time Elvis did stand up and remake the deal.

That summer when all the guys came back to Graceland after the taping of the special, there was a lot of talk about how Elvis had forced the colonel to move his career in a different direction. And there was more talk, and some laughter, about how Colonel was further forced by NBC to accept the talented Steve Binder as the producer of the show. Binder had produced the "T.A.M.I. Show," a rock-only spectacular that had dramatically featured most of the top entertainers in the business, including the Rolling Stones, Diana Ross and the Supremes, James Brown, Marvin Gaye, Chuck Berry—all the recording stars who were now outselling Elvis in the stores. You might think Colonel would be happy with a competent producer, particularly at a critical time in Elvis's career. But he hated it. He wanted the world to believe that he alone decided what Elvis would be allowed to do creatively on the show. Binder and the other producers of the show met with the colonel and were told that the show should have Elvis coming out in a tuxedo saying, "Good evening, ladies and gentleman," and follow that with about twenty Christmas carols, intermingled with a few of Elvis's more sentimental ballads, and a closing of Elvis singing "Silent Night." Then he would wave to the audience, exclaiming, "Merry Christmas, everyone!" They were appalled.

Steve Binder sought a private meeting with Elvis as soon as Elvis arrived at the NBC studios for rehearsals. Elvis told us that they "just talked about music for awhile," and then Binder asked him if he would have first recorded "McArthur Park" if he had had the opportunity. (The song apparently had been turned down by some big names for being too radical.) Elvis's response was, "Yes. I love that song." Then Binder asked Elvis if he wanted to close the special with "Silent Night." Elvis wouldn't repeat his response, but whatever it was Steve Binder knew immediately that he was talking to the man in control and that they were of one creative mind. The work began.

While the critics, and later much of the public, had perceived Elvis as somehow diminished because of the films and the albums cut from them, Elvis knew that he had grown as an entertainer and as a man in control of his life and art. At rehearsals he'd listen to any song or any arrangement that the group came up with. If he liked it he'd try it. Once, twice, twenty times—until either it worked or it was dropped. It was no longer going to be the fast movie philosophy of "shoot it and forget it." Elvis saw the Christmas special as an opportunity for the public to see him trying new styles and expression while still acknowledging his musical roots.

Back at Graceland we all huddled around a television on the night of December third, aware that that night might be one of the most important in Elvis's life. Elvis was in L.A., halfway through production of *The Trouble with Girls,* but anticipation of the special showed in the gleam in Vernon's eyes—as if *he* were going on stage. We were confident, but Elvis was so nervous when he went out before that live audience that, even on TV, you could see his hand shaking when he reached for the microphone. Then, suddenly, there was Elvis looking into the camera with that sly look and saying, "If you're looking for trouble, you've come to the right place!" Everybody laughed at that, and when he whipped into his songs we all knew it was going to happen exactly as Elvis wanted. Dressed in a black leather motorcycle jacket and matching black leather pants instead of the tux Colonel wanted, Elvis appeared both sinister and sensual. And he moved across the stage with a catlike precision that was both powerful and effortless. That night Vernon just smiled and slapped his knee and shouted, "Mah boy!"

The week before the show was to be aired, all our friends at Hillcrest had come up to Rick and me to tell us they were going to watch it and to wish us good luck. That night, after the show, Deana, Carol Cooper, and other friends called to congratulate us, but their parents called as well! "Billy, this is Carol's dad, Jim Cooper. I just want you to know how terrific I thought your brother was." I was amazed. And the next day school was a celebration. Everyone came up to us, laughing, excited, and wanting to congratulate us. Of course, there was some wise-ass, as always, who said, "I think he stunk." But we'd learned not to pay any attention to those comments, and we basked in the glory of our brother's deeds.

Risk and challenge had always been Elvis's primary motivation, and the Christmas special proved to be exactly what he needed. When Elvis got back to Graceland a few weeks later, with Lisa Marie hoisted on his shoulder, he brought a new sense of excitement and impending accomplishment. The year 1968 had been one of changes for Elvis, beginning with Lisa Marie's birth on February 1, and culminating in the Christmas special. But 1969 promised to hold much more. Elvis was renewed, reinvigorated professionally, and Graceland was no longer a recreational retreat from West Coast movie sets. It was swarming with activity and once again was the center of his creativity.

In January, Elvis entered a Memphis recording studio for the first time since he'd left Sun Recordings fourteen years before, to record "From Elvis in Memphis," an album of thirty-six songs including "In the Ghetto," Elvis's first really big single in years. Elvis was determined that the success of the Christmas special would not be a one-shot event. The age of the rock concert was now at full blast, with the Beatles, the Rolling Stones, Jefferson Airplane, and Janis Joplin at the peak of their careers. Comebacks by Fats Domino, Little Richard, Jerry Lee Lewis, Chuck Berry, and Bill Haley and The Comets were well under way. Elvis felt that to rise again to the throne of king he would have to battle the others on the turf they were establishing—the concert tour.

And plans were shaping up. The task of arranging the tour fell, of course, to the colonel. Colonel negotiated a contract with Kirk Kerkorian, owner of the building that was to become the largest hotel in Las Vegas, the International. It opened, with Barbra Streisand as the headliner for the first month, on July 2, 1969. Colonel had arranged for Elvis to come in for the following four weeks.

Financially, of course, it was a great deal. No one ever seriously doubted Colonel's abilities as a negotiator. But choosing Las Vegas as the place to launch Elvis's return to live performance was a colossal gamble. Rock music had never attained any popularity there, the older audiences preferring the sophisticated styles of Frank Sinatra, Sammy Davis, Jr., and Tony Bennett. A concert before long-standing, loyal fans in the South would have made much more sense. Los Angeles, New York, or even London would have been safer—the rock fans would have assembled in droves. But Las Vegas was the gamble and the challenge that Elvis wanted.

Elvis was raring to go but still there were a few movies to take care of. While *Charro* was being released and *The Trouble with Girls* waited its turn, Elvis made his last movie, *Change of Habit,* in March of 1969. With Mary Tyler Moore and Barbara McNair playing nuns and Elvis as a doctor, *Change of Habit*'s story line was a little hard even for a brother to believe. But over the years hundreds of people have told me how great Elvis looked in it, how relaxed and handsome he seemed. That was because Elvis was already preparing for concert in Las Vegas. He'd changed his diet, eliminating almost all fried foods, and had replaced them with cooked and raw vegetables and occasionally some lean meat. And he'd let his sideburns grow back. He looked the way he felt and he felt great. Not just because it was his last movie but because he was working on something new and powerful.

In May Elvis came back to Graceland. I'd never seen him so into his music. He was playing records all the time, and listening to new material. He could get as excited over a particular song as some people get over a touchdown. One afternoon he was sitting in the living room listening to a recording done by Charles Boyer, the actor. On one side was "Softly, As I Leave You," and on the other, "What Now, My Love." Elvis flipped over both of them. "Man, that son-of-a-bitch can sing!" Elvis yelled. "He's tearing my heart out!" Then Elvis leaped up to the stereo and put the needle back a few grooves for an instant replay. He'd listen for a particular phrasing from Boyer, slam his hand down on the coffee table, and pull it back in a fist. "Yeah, I love it," he'd cry. Other times when he heard something he particularly liked he'd say, "Oooo—son!"

Sometimes he'd be at his piano or holding his guitar and someone like Charlie Hodge would say, "Hey, Elvis. What about this song?" and Charlie would start playing it on his guitar. If it appealed to Elvis he'd start playing it, singing it, and fooling around with it. He'd live with a song, feel it in his soul, until he either dropped it or made it his own. It didn't matter if it was Dean Martin, the Beatles, or Credence Clearwater, when Elvis took a song he made it his. The Beatles would still have their "Yesterday," Neil Diamond would still have his "Sweet Caroline," but when you heard Elvis sing his version you almost got to believe that was the way it was meant to be sung. My brothers and I would just sit back and listen for hours. The only regret I have is that we never taped any of it. We just thought it would always be there.

His only diversions at this time were his karate (which, choreographed, would be an important part of his act) and Lisa Marie. He'd take her on long golf cart rides around Graceland (Lisa Marie was almost one and a half by this time), often ending near the Graceland gates where he'd talk to the fans for a while and show off his daughter.

Elvis was animated, alive, vital. We could all sense and see it, just in the way he talked to people and walked around the house. There was a spring in his step. Sometimes that energy could be misdirected. Elvis hated his vegetable and yogurt diet. One time he came raging into the house yelling something about, "The input has to be as great as the energy going out." I was up in the den watching TV at the time, and Elvis couldn't find anyone else around, so he came bounding up and confronted me. "Billy, a man must be replenished. I can't live on just rabbit food!" Then he ran back down to the kitchen and I followed. He was opening and closing cupboards, slamming the refrigerator door, and expounding on his theory of energy input and outgo. Pretty soon some jars and bottles got broken and some appliances got knocked to the floor. Elvis calmed down and said, "Nub, we better clean this up before the cooks get here." So I helped him. Actually, I did all the cleaning up. Once Elvis demonstrated his willingness to clean up some spilt sugar and flour, he must have felt he'd made his point about how helpful he could be, and he left the kitchen. But he didn't eat anything.

Sometimes that new vitality meant trouble for those who surrounded Elvis. He was questioning himself and his ability to do what he wanted to do, and often it took the form of questioning others. He would suddenly fly off the handle. Elvis and Lamar would be joking about something, Gene Smith would join in, and Elvis would tell one of his stories about Lamar. Then Elvis would laugh. We all knew the story was to relieve the tension, but Lamar would sulk. The more he sulked the angrier Elvis would get. He'd swear and get on Lamar all the more. Lamar took it to a point, but then he'd tell Elvis, "I'm not taking any more of your shit!"

"You'll take it if I say so," Elvis would threaten.

"That's it," Lamar would exclaim. "I quit."

"Quit? You can't quit because you're fired."

Then Elvis and Lamar would square off as if they were going to fight, or Lamar would make for the door. In a flash Elvis's mood would change. Elvis would yell, "Lamar, get your fat ass back here." Then they'd look at each other face to face and throw their arms around each other and hug. Jitters? Elvis had them. We all understood that. It wasn't any fun when Elvis exploded, particularly if the explosion was directed toward you, but at the same time each of us wanted to be a part of the growing excitement.

The work of putting the show together began at Graceland and everyone seemed to be involved, particularly Charlie Hodge, Lamar Fike, and Joe Esposito. Of course Charlie would be part of the stage show as would the Imperials, the male vocal group that had backed him on "How Great Thou Art," and the Sweet Inspirations as the female backup group. Guitarist and bandleader James Burton was put in charge of putting a band together in Los Angeles. Elvis told Burton what he wanted in a series of phone calls from Graceland. When Burton had a group assembled that included John Wilkinson (guitar and vocals), Jerry Scheff (bass), Ronny Tutt (drums), and Larry Muhoberac (piano and organ), Elvis and the boys flew out to the West Coast. Although Elvis knew that they would probably use less than twenty songs in the opening show they rehearsed over one hundred. He was booked to do two shows a day for twenty-eight days running and he didn't want to have to do the same songs over and over. With a hundred songs available Elvis could "create" a new show every time he went on stage.

Elvis knew he would need a break and he had scheduled a two-week vacation in Hawaii. Dee, Vernon, Priscilla, my brothers and I flew together to join Elvis at the Hilton Hawaiian Village. We three were excited at being in Hawaii (en route to Las Vegas) and at getting away from Harding Academy and the Church of Christ. But Elvis was not his usual self. In his mind Elvis was working on polishing his act. Back at Graceland he had been practicing his karate kicks and moves as a means to highlight and emphasize his music. The wild gyrating of his performances in the fifties was to be replaced by the athletic grace of his new discipline. Elvis could move like a panther, in a slow deliberate stalk or a sudden powerful spring. Even when he stood still you could feel the power of the "ki," the karate soul-presence. His stage wardrobe would include several black karate "gis" and a karate sash, as well as tailored white jumpsuits inlaid with gold thread and studded with stones.

He practiced karate with us and sat for hours by the pool working on his tan. Once in awhile at the pool or in one of the rooms I'd be walking by and all of a sudden Elvis would leap in front of me and go into a crouch, wearing his classic grin—I've always called it his "shit-eating" grin, but I'm from the south—and I'd do my best to challenge him. But, wham-bam, he'd have me pinned, growling, "Just who do you think you're messin' with?" However, most of the time he seemed bored and edgy. He said he was glad to be away from all the commotion. We tried to interest him in other things, like snorkeling and surfboarding, but Elvis's mind kept drifting back to the preparations for the Las Vegas show. He left Hawaii a week early for final rehearsals with his music director, Joe Guercio, and a thirty-five piece orchestra they'd hired. I later heard that when Colonel, who'd been excluded from the rehearsals, saw the orchestra he almost had a heart attack. Since his split came out of the net after expenses, he was hoping for a backup group of, at most, nine or ten musicians and singers. "What's he need all these people for?" the colonel would exclaim.

Our family, Priscilla included, stayed in Hawaii to enjoy the beach and the surf. When we joined Elvis in Las Vegas a few days before the opening, the town was abuzz with excitement. At the airport, along the main streets, and in almost every shop along the strip there were billboards or posters of Elvis. All the radio stations were announcing his forthcoming engagement and playing Elvis songs. Pretty girls in Elvis T-shirts were roaming the lobbies and halls of the new International Hotel. The Colonel, finally, had been doing his job.

Las Vegas. The place holds little attraction for me now, but then it was magic. The whole city was dazzling white under a hot blue summer sky. The three towers and a metal globe at the front of the International were almost dwarfed by a huge neon sign that sparkled out Elvis's name. For Rick, David, and me, just being in this city of unlimited gambling, shows, and glamour was an adventure in itself. Our previous trips to the West Coast had always taken us to movie sets in Los Angeles, or to more sedate Palm Springs. Now we were older and able to move freely around in the all-or-nothing glitter of this frontier town. Just what promise it held for us or what frontiers we could cross we didn't know. But we were ready to find out. Barbra Streisand had opened the hotel, as scheduled, and had played to steadily dwindling audiences. But Elvis's entire first week was sold out, and calls were coming in from all over the world for tickets that were no longer available. At the moment the Streisand show ended, Colonel had Elvis posters going up everywhere in the International, even setting up a booth in the lobby to sell his "souvenirs." Crowds gathered everywhere. Ricky, David, and I strutted around the International, occasionally turning to a scream of recognition, "Look, there's Elvis's brothers!" Of course we didn't try to hide. We hung out in the main lobby and let all the girls there know that we were Elvis's brothers. We even went over to the Circus Circus and had ourselves paged—as Billy Presley, Rick Presley, and David Presley. That drew some attention. Everywhere we went there were people asking us about Elvis and girls passing us notes that read, "If you can introduce us to your brother I'll do anything!"

Dee couldn't have liked it a bit, but there was nothing she could do. We had a suite next to Elvis's, with an entry, a living room and two master bedrooms, one for Dee and Vernon, and the other for us. But we were never in it. It must have measured up to her worst fears— her three little boys loose in a town of gamblers, prostitutes, hustlers, and propositioning Elvis fans. Even if we'd stayed only within the grounds of the International Hotel as Dee and Vernon kept telling us to, there was no way they could have kept tabs on us. The place was colossal. It had over 1500 rooms, stood thirty stories tall, held the world's largest casino and the massive showroom that Elvis was to play. There were lounge shows, shopping malls, a half-dozen restaurants, and a nine-acre rooftop recreation area with an enormous swimming pool that they called the largest man-made body of water in Nevada after Lake Mead. Next to it were a bar and a nightclub for teenagers where we sipped Pepsis and talked with the better-looking female fans. And, of course, I got lucky. Under those circumstances how could I fail? A pretty blond seemed to like all of us equally, but she and her parents had driven out from Colorado looking for tickets, and there were none available. Being the oldest, I took charge and said I would get them for her. Later, in her room, we got into some heavy petting. I even got her top off—the farthest I'd ever been with a girl. But the next day I faced the problem of actually getting the promised tickets. That required approaching Vernon when Dee wasn't with him, and explaining my predicament. Luckily Vernon laughed, and three third-row tickets were delivered, as promised. After that, I never saw the girl again.

As the time for the show drew near, the air was electric with anticipation. Colonel had been flying the press in from all over the country in Kirk Kerkorian's private jet. Late-arriving fans searched futilely for scalper's tickets. The over-thirty crowd, dressed in leisure suits or formals, mixed with teenyboppers in psychedelic gear, and everyone pushed to get into the showplace early. For a moment we were trapped in the shove of the crowd, and then a blue-uniformed usher showed my parents, Priscilla, and us to our booth at the front and to the left of the stage. As the lights dimmed, my brothers and I squirmed through warm-up acts by the Sweet Inspirations and the comedian, Sammy Shore. I kept looking around that vast multitiered showroom with its huge hanging chandeliers, paintings of Greek ruins, and Cupid statues sticking out from the ceilings and walls. I wanted to see the expressions on the faces in the crowd, but Dee kept nudging me and giving me that stern look that said, "Eyes straight. Keep still." I could feel the crowd behind us grow restless as Sammy Shore concluded his jokes.

Then the giant gold lamé curtain fell. As it rose again the band broke out in an up-tempo rhythm and without a word of introduction Elvis strode confidently from the dim left wing. In his black karate gi, black-dyed hair, and the darkness of the room Elvis looked like a shadow moving across the stage. At first there were gasps, a few squeals, and then a steadily mounting roar. At center stage, in the spotlight, he took his guitar from Charlie Hodge, struck his pose to sing, and stopped. People were standing, many on their chairs, and cheering so wildly that there was no chance he could sing. The vast room that had seemed so empty and quiet when Barbra Streisand had concluded her show now shook like a runaway freight train.

Finally it quieted and Elvis cried, "Well, it's one for the money!" He shook his knees slightly. "Two for the show!" Elvis hit a quick chord on the guitar. "Three to get ready and go, cat, go!" And Elvis was going. Fast and furious. And my brothers and I glowed! He charged through "Blue Suede Shoes," snapping off the lines like karate kicks. And for each vibration of energy Elvis put out, a wave came rolling back to the stage. Afterward, when the applause died down again, Elvis started his second song, "I Got a Woman," and the bedlam continued. When it was finally quiet he said, "Good evening, ladies and gentlemen. Welcome to the big, freaky International Hotel, with those weirdo dolls on the walls, and those funky angels on the ceiling. Man, you ain't seen nothin' till you've seen a funky angel."

The audience ate it up. Elvis felt their acceptance, abandonment, love—you name it, it was simply there. He went into a medley of his early songs: "Jailhouse Rock," "Don't Be Cruel," "Heartbreak Hotel," and "All Shook Up." He'd stop occasionally to get a drink of water or Gatorade or to joke with the audience. He'd hold up the Gatorade jar and say, "This stuff's supposed to act twelve times as fast as water." Then he'd look again at the jar. " 'Cept it looks like it's been used already to me." It was just a wonderful sharing experience for both the performer and the audience. And Elvis was totally in command. Sometimes between songs he'd ramble a little, talking about this or that, teasing the audience. Maybe he was just savoring the moment. His voice was rich, deep, and stronger than any of us had ever heard it. His movements were hypnotic.

He sang "Love Me Tender," stopping to kiss several pretty girls along the edge of the stage (I glanced at Priscilla but she continued to smile). Then he sang "Memories," "My Babe," "I Can't Stop Loving You," and a six-minute version of "Suspicious Minds" that brought everyone to their feet. My brothers and I were mesmerized. We had always loved our big brother. We loved his music, especially his early music—we even loved his movies. But now we were seeing a whole new side of Elvis. I thought of the Beatles, Led Zeppelin, and the Rolling Stones. These were always the big names to us—the groups that could move and shake the world. But Elvis as a live entertainer? That was something that belonged to a different genera-tion. And here we were, completely dazzled. Elvis was as big as any of them. Bigger! Elvis's little brothers were his biggest fans.

In the middle of a song he dropped to one knee as his head bowed and his clenched right fist rose into the night. And again we rose instinctively, but not just in appreciation. My brothers and I felt summoned by his gestures—by his command. I looked to my brothers and saw their sense of wonder. I looked at Vernon, and he stood there with a clenched fist in salute to his son. And I looked at Mom and Priscilla. Priscilla was smiling with her hands clasped together but Dee (my mom!) was jumping up and down with a look of ecstasy and surrender.

Elvis sang two Beatles songs, "Yesterday" and "Hey Jude." Next he went to Chuck Berry's "Johnny B. Goode," and then closed with Ray Charles's "What'd I Say." But with two thousand people on their feet screaming for more, Elvis had to come back, and he did, with the real closer, "Can't Help Falling in Love." Throughout the performance long-haired hippies with dangling coke spoons, and middle-aged women in bouffant hairdos were rising and screaming as one. For Elvis and his music it was a triumph. My brothers and I just looked at each other and laughed. "Did you see that?" we asked each other. "Elvis kicked ass!"

After the show Elvis's dressing room was bedlam. Friends, relatives of band members, celebrities rushed in to tell Elvis how great he'd been. I can't remember all of them, but I was struck by the presence of Cary Grant—to me he was someone you would only see on screen. Elvis was dripping wet, exhausted, and very, very happy. He thanked them all and just sat there with a sly grin on his face. Then the colonel came in and Elvis rose to his feet. I'll never forget what happened next because Colonel and Elvis, to my knowledge, just about never touched. I hadn't seen them as much as shake hands. This time Colonel pushed his way through the crowd saying, "Where's my boy? Where's my boy?" He came up to Elvis, they embraced, and Colonel lifted Elvis off his feet.

"Colonel," Elvis said. "I've been wrong for so long but I was right tonight!"

Then they walked off to one of the colonel's prearranged press conferences where Elvis had to answer such intelligent questions as, "Did you enjoy performing live again?" and "Do you and Priscilla intend to add to your family?"

The backstage crowd continued to grow. People were milling about, stunned and ecstatic about Elvis's performance, and I was beginning to notice a few of the girls who'd offered me "anything" if I could introduce them to my brother. But I was too dazed even to try to speak. I guess I was just trying to take in what I'd just experienced. Of course I hadn't been there when Elvis was driving from town to town in Tennessee, Arkansas, Louisiana, and East Texas introducing rockabilly music and a style of performing that would turn the stodgy, conformist world of the mid-1950s on its ear. I hadn't witnessed Elvis's introduction of rhythmic blues music, black at its roots, to a bland white world. I hadn't seen him inspire a whole generation to bold expression of their inner selves, nor had I seen the efforts of "good citizens" to ban his performances, or the efforts to force disc jockeys to keep Elvis's music off the air, or local school boards' decisions (around the country) to expel any student wearing sideburns or ducktails. Elvis had incited instant hysteria through his live performances, his records, his brief TV appearances, his provocative posters, and, finally, eventually, through the mere mention of his name. More than a decade had been erased in one night's performance; the "rebel king" was back on top of his profession and on top of the world.

Before that night I had always thought of life with Elvis as fun. It had even occurred to me that some day I might like to be involved in his life-style. I hadn't seen how that might come about, since Dee had such very different plans for us. But that night I realized that I'd found the life I wanted and that it was mine to choose. I looked at Rick and knew that he was thinking the same thing.

9

"ALL SHOOK UP"

(September 1969—December 1970)

Back in Memphis Dee enrolled us again at the Harding Academy. I was in my ninth-grade year, and at the time we all thought it was kind of cruel for Mom to take us away from our friends who were all going on to Hillcrest. Maybe she thought the church school would somehow make me a better student (although it hadn't in the seventh grade), or maybe she thought it would make me a better person. It didn't do either. But she had become so afraid that Elvis would steal us away from her that she put us in an environment as different from his as night is from day. Although I was sixteen and could drive, the freedom I'd anticipated was totally thwarted by Dee's determination to control our lives. That meant that the Church of Christ and its activities took precedence. Now I loved my mom then, and still do, and I know in my heart that everything she did was an expression of her love for us. But we'd been to the mountain, as Martin Luther King had said, and we'd seen a new horizon. What could keep us down in the valley of perpetual sin, the life of repentance led by good Christians here on earth, when our hero, Elvis, told us that whatever our actions, we could practically do no wrong? Our mom, that's who.

We were totally in Elvis's world when we were with him, a world without sin, but we belonged to Mom's world when we were with her. I figured out early on that Vernon always sided with Dee until he was confronted by Elvis. So I went to Elvis. I told him we didn't like our school or our church or what they taught us and made us do. Of course Elvis knew our dilemma; how we were torn between our adoration for him and our respect for our mother. His response was heartfelt: "Billy, you must be true to yourself. But you must honor and love your mother."

So where did that put us in the fall of 1969? In Harding Academy. While Elvis, after twenty-eight consecutive days in Las Vegas, took Priscilla to vacation in Hawaii and Nassau and made plans to launch his nationwide tour, we suffocated under the old rules on Dolan Street. While the kids at Hillcrest partied, jammed, and caroused we were in Bible meetings. "How do you keep them down on the farm, after they've seen . . . Las Vegas?" We hadn't just seen Las Vegas, we'd felt a part of it just as we'd always felt a part of Elvis's life.

How far out of it was Harding? You've seen those movies where three or four boys wear plastic pen holders in their shirts and all the other kids call them nerds? At Harding every boy but us wore them in the pockets of their corduroy shirts! At Hillcrest and in high schools around the country girls were wearing miniskirts; in the big cities and at colleges (and in Las Vegas) some wore microminis. At Harding a girl once wore a "maximini." She was sent home and told never to show her knees again.

There was only one thing that I liked about that Christian school—their football team. Not that it was any good. It was lousy. But they saw my abilities as a freshman halfback and quickly moved me up to the varsity. In the third game, already two touchdowns behind, they put me in and I made several successful runs, the last over thirty yards. That took us down to the opponents' one-yard line. We had already lined up for an easy touchdown, with my number called, when the coach called a time-out. He pulled me out in favor of a senior, who took the ball into the end zone on the next play. I was so angry that I went up to the coach and demanded an explanation. "Why did you take me out?"

He said, "Because the guy who made the touchdown is the team captain, and the guys wanted him to score."

I said, "Well then the heck with you guys!" and walked out.

That did little for my popularity at school, and my grades continued to suffer. It was a bleak fall.

As always, things livened up around Christmas time. As soon as Elvis got back to Graceland we were there most of the time. Dee would start calling over about ten in the evening telling us she was going to bed. "That's nice," we'd say. Then she'd call at eleven telling us it was getting late and we still had a few days of school left before vacation. Then she'd call at midnight, telling us to come home. "Why doesn't she just go to sleep?" we'd exclaim. So Elvis would get on the phone with her. "I'll let them come, Dee. Soon as I beat them all in a game of pool I'm sending them home." But we had gotten quite good and Elvis was gone so much his game had slipped considerably. It sometimes took him until two or three in the morning to win a game from each of us.

There were always a lot of presents around when it got close to Christmas. There were wrapped presents that had been sent to Elvis; presents that Elvis had bought that needed to be wrapped; and presents for Lisa Marie (who was almost two) that would fill a room. I was sitting in the den watching TV one afternoon a few days before Christmas when Elvis came in and started rummaging through the boxes. He was looking for something and, unable to find it, was swearing under his breath. He looked as if he had just got up and had had a bad night, so I just kept my eyes on the TV and braced for the explosion.

"Goddammit!" Elvis yelled. "They're gone!"

"What's that, Elvis?" I ventured, cautiously.

"The two goddam TV sets that RCA gave me. I just thought who I wanted to give them to, and they're gone. Someone has ripped me off." Elvis stormed out of the room and although I could hear him going down the hall, swearing and banging things, I figured the storm had passed so I continued watching TV.

"Billy!" Elvis yelled. "Where are my goddam TV sets?"

I sat up and turned around. He was right behind me.

"Uh, Elvis," I said. "I don't know." But I could see that wasn't going to do. Elvis was glaring at me, seething, and almost out of control.

"Maybe someone moved them. Did you ask Gene or Charlie?"

Elvis fixed his gaze on me. "Billy, I want my TVs."

"Elvis, you don't think I took them?"

"You've been in this room all day," he menaced.

I stood up, trying to figure out what to say to defend myself when Lamar, summoned by Elvis's shouts, came into the room. Elvis immediately turned on him.

"What's up, E.?" Lamar asked, looking as if he really didn't want to hear.

"Lamar," Elvis said, "you fat fuck. Did you make a nice profit on those color TVs you stole?" I don't think Elvis really thought Lamar was stealing; he was just letting off steam.

"Me, Elvis?" Lamar took half a step back. "I didn't steal anything."

Elvis made a gesture with his shoulders, just a suggestion of a karate stance, and poor Lamar retreated another step.

"Don't you back away from me!" Elvis growled. Lamar stood still. "Someone's ripped me off. My guys are always ripping me off! Here, this is Elvis's. Take it. That asshole will never know it's missing. Fuck him!"

"Not me, Elvis," Lamar pleaded. "I never saw any TVs."

By this time the room was filling up. Elvis was in one of his tempers, and though it might seem the best response would be to hide, Elvis somehow always knew who was around. If you didn't show up for the confrontation you were either "chicken shit" or guilty. It was much better to appear and give an account of yourself.

To the full room, Elvis repeated his accusations: Someone was ripping him off and someone there had either done it or knew who had. He started going back through his private list of offenses—how they'd sold the Rancheros he had bought them at the Circle G, and how they'd taken his other gifts and turned them into cash. He wasn't going to put up with it any longer. Everyone was standing around with a "Who me?" look on their faces when Priscilla came into the room and asked what was going on.

"What's going on?" Elvis mimicked sarcastically. "Nothin' special, little one. Just the usual Elvis rip-off, that's all!" Elvis's eyes continued to burn holes into anything they encountered.

"Someone made off with Elvis's TVs," Lamar explained.

"Elvis!" Priscilla scolded. "I sent those TVs off to my parents. I asked you about it and you said I could. The shipper came and got them yesterday."

For a second Elvis looked as if he had a bone caught in his throat. Then he started laughing. "Then what am I doing throwing a fit?"

We all shook our heads and smiled.

"Over a couple crummy RCA portables," Elvis continued between fits of laughter. "Lamar, can you believe it?"

"I don't know. Sometimes, E. Sometimes I believe it." Lamar was spreading his arms and laughing himself now.

Soon everyone was laughing and Elvis was on the floor, banging his hands above his head the way he always did when he had a laughing fit and couldn't stop. It was contagious. When you see someone laughing like that you start chuckling. You stop but then you start again and pretty soon you're laughing harder. You don't know why you're laughing, but the guy on the floor (Elvis) is laughing and pointing his finger at the fat guy (Lamar), who's laughing so hard he looks like he'll fall over backward. Then he does fall over and everyone is howling and trying not to fall over themselves.

When it was over and everyone had stood up, wiped the tears from their eyes, and left the room, I turned the TV back up and sat down, arms folded, where I'd been before. I tried to pick up the movie from where I'd had to leave off but my eyes were still teary and I couldn't help but chuckle from time to time. What had it all been about? It was just Elvis. Elvis was like southern weather in the summer, all warmth and soft breezes and then, when you least expected it, a gathering storm. When it was over, the storm never came back to say, "Sorry I got you wet," or "Sorry I blew your barn door off." It had always been that way and the guys who'd been with him a long time like Lamar and Charlie and Alan Fortas knew you just had to weather it. Elvis never apologized and no one expected him to, except Priscilla. Happily, for the rest of the Christmas season Elvis was sublime.

Because of school, we had missed Elvis's month in Las Vegas, his second engagement at the International Hotel. But then Mom and Vernon told us that they were taking us out of school for a few days at the end of February so that we could fly to Houston to see Elvis perform at the Astrodome. While Las Vegas was out of the question, Houston apparently was all right for a couple of reasons. First, it wasn't Las Vegas. And second, Dee had a plan.

I had been dating a girl named Carol Cooper. Carol, like all the girls at Harding, was very straight. But, since I was now driving and Dee couldn't account for my every movement, she must have had apprehensions. After the announcement that we would be taken to the Astrodome, Dee took me aside and told me that she had arranged for Suzanne Daly to go with us as my date. This didn't disturb me at all since Suzanne was probably the prettiest girl at Harding, but she was also Reverend Daly's daughter, and he was the preacher at the Church of Christ. You could sense the wheels grinding in Mom's lovely head. She was about to chaperon and manipulate me into the best match possible, with visions of wedding me to her beloved church.

But I didn't resent it. I remembered Elvis's third rule: Always treat women in a special way. Suzanne was bright, friendly, and carried herself with grace and self-confidence even in the chaos in Elvis's dressing room after the show. I just tried to do the same.

The performance itself was wild enough, with Elvis riding out in a red jeep with white seats and over forty thousand people screaming and yelling as he mounted the stage. And there was nothing wrong with Elvis, and his band was great—I think. There was no way of really knowing because the acoustics at the Astrodome were about as bad as they could possibly be. Since August in Las Vegas Elvis had added Neil Diamond's "Sweet Caroline" and Tony Joe White's "Polk Salad Annie," which had been a huge hit in Las Vegas. In the Astrodome, when Elvis sang, "That's polk" (bump hip and pause), "salad" (pause), three echoes of "polk" obscured the "salad." It was almost embarrassing. But Elvis wasn't embarrassed. He put on a great show and the audience reacted as if it was a great show, even though they couldn't hear it the way he sang it.

Afterward I heard Glen D. Harding, who played piano and organ, being asked, "What's it like working with Elvis?" He grinned from ear to ear and said, "It's the greatest. The man just loves music." And how did he like playing the Astrodome? "Well, Elvis told us, 'This is going to be rather atrocious, so don't fight it. Go ahead and play your music.' " I asked Elvis what he thought of it and he said, "When does the balloon go up?" meaning "when will something real happen?" or "when can I get out of here?"

Colonel had booked the Astrodome with an eye to profits. The huge crowds would gross Elvis over a million for three nights of performing. He was making up for the money Elvis had lost (by his reckoning) by hiring so large a band in Las Vegas.

Meanwhile, I had it in my mind that I was going to kiss Suzanne some time during the trip. Somehow the time never seemed quite right.

I don't remember the rest of that spring very well. Probably there was little to remember. Mostly, we went to school, went to our church prayer meetings, and looked for a way out. If we were obnoxious it was with a purpose. Rick and I skipped school a few times and were reprimanded. I've mentioned the problem I had on the football team. But there was more to come. David, big and strong and very independent for his age, got into a fight with the assistant principal. We saw it outside my classroom window. He also hit his math teacher, a woman. David was expelled immediately. Rick and I got into some other trouble too, once shooting off "bottlerockets" on the school bus. By the end of the school year the school's administrators met with Vernon and Dee and recommended they find another school for all three of us. It wasn't exactly a fun transition but finally we were all out of Harding and destined to go back to Hillcrest.

Summer at last meant an end to school, and a chance for freedom, travel, and jobs. The summer before I had found a job bagging groceries at the Big Star supermarket. I don't remember what the pay was but it wasn't very much. The real pay was supposed to be the tips you got when you carried the bags out to the cars. Aunt Delta, who did most of the grocery shopping for Graceland, always smiled and gave me a two-dollar tip. It's a good thing she shopped often (they went through a lot of food at Graceland), because everyone else gave me a nickel or a dime or sometimes a cold "Thank you."

Then Elvis put me in charge of washing his cars at a salary of $150 a week. And it was on payroll. Vernon wrote me out the paycheck. Elvis never did anything that wasn't accounted for. No money under the table—even for family. He always wanted everything to be on the up and up for the IRS. But that was a lot of money for a kid my age and I had almost no way to spend it. I did wear nice clothes, but Dee wanted to pay for them. I had to sneak off to spend the money Elvis paid me.

In the summer of 1970 we went to work full time for Uncle Earl. I still had my duties washing the cars, but our major project that summer was to rebuild the fence that surrounded Graceland. The old one was rotting and falling apart at some places and they'd decided to replace the whole thing. Now, we're talking about a fence that stands seven feet high and encompasses fourteen acres, and our early enthusiasm was soon replaced with the realization that this was a big job. Of course, the days got longer, hotter, and muggier. Rick and David and I were out there every morning, trying to show that we could work as long and as hard as any man there, but every day it got a little harder. Pretty soon I learned how to pace myself.

We finished that fence just before we went back out to Las Vegas for Elvis's second appearance there. We were there for a full week, catching every show, flirting with Elvis's fans, checking out all the action. We felt pretty good about ourselves.

That fall, 1970, we were back at Hillcrest where the girls wore real miniskirts and being Elvis's brother meant something. But being the brother of someone famous won't do much for you in high school unless you've got something going for you on your own. We had that something, Elvis had given it to us: confidence.

All three of us made the football team. I became a split end, Rick was the second-team quarterback, and David, big and strong with my father's build, was the tight end. By this time, Rick and I were in the same class—changing schools so much hadn't helped the progress of our educations. David was only a year behind. He was already bigger than either of us. For the first time since Breezy Point Farms, we started making separate friends in school. We still wore nice clothes— Dee wanted us in ties and sports coats every day and Elvis forbade wearing jeans. When he was in school he had nothing to wear but jeans, mostly overalls, and he detested blue jeans all his life. Socially, we were making up for lost time. Soon Rick, with his blond hair and natural good looks, was a hit with the monied clique, the country club crowd. I was right in there with him. Rick and I rushed and soon joined the Tau Beta Sigma fraternity. Within a few weeks we were at the center of its social activities. In fact, I made history by becoming its president as a sophomore. Until that time only seniors were considered eligible to become fraternity president. David joined the Delta Pi Omega fraternity, which, like the Sigmas, was made up of rich kids and jocks, like David. He became the center of a gang of big, rowdy athletes who dominated the drive-ins with their presence alone even before any of them had cars.

The Tau Beta Sigs were pretty much hell-raisers and ours was the only fraternity in high school that had its own house. It was a furnished split-level on Winchester Road and within days of renting it we'd moved in a stereo and a pool table, stocked the refrigerator full of beer, and were throwing the first of many, many parties. A lot of the girls who came to the parties were from the Beta Beta sorority, the female equivalent of Tau Beta Sigma, but occasionally a girl from the upper class Sigma Sigma sorority would show up to . . . well, to slum it, I guess.

When Elvis got back from his West Coast tour in late November Rick and I presented him with a fraternity jersey with "Elvis" on the back. We'd voted him in as an honorary member. Rick and I begged him to come to see our fraternity house and accept his membership. "Ah, Nub," Elvis said, "I'd love to do it. I'd love to do it for you. But as soon as one of your buddies knows I'm coming and he puts the word out you'd have a riot on your hands and the cops would come and you'd be without a fraternity house. Paul Shafer's got the Memphian lined up for tonight. Let's all go have a night at the movies instead." So we ended up going to a lot of all-night movies with Elvis and the gang, and never got him to see our fraternity.

I'll never forget the night my brothers took me home from "hell night." Dee was up to greet me. I couldn't even stand up and I couldn't stop giggling and falling over. Dee gave me a hard look as if to say, "What hath God wrought?" But she didn't make us quit the fraternity. I think she realized she was losing control over her sons. It must have made her sad.

I wanted to have my own identity, to belong to something outside of Vernon's and Dee's careful plan. The fraternity helped me do that. Elvis had broken loose, and he'd done it in a big way. But it was harder for me. I felt I had never been anywhere or done anything on my own. I was the little brother of the man who was once again taking the rock world by storm. I identified with Elvis and I felt that others of my age looked to me to exhibit some of his flash and daring. I knew my parents could never accept that. So, when I wasn't at the fraternity, I turned to a world where acceptance was easy. I fell in with a faster crowd. Marijuana, alcohol, and late-night cruising were our bag. You didn't have to do the boring stuff—all you had to do was smoke dope, listen to the latest music, and talk about how the adult world was fucked up.

We had this spot, the Tree, directly across the street from McDonald's, about two miles south of Graceland, and anything could happen there. There were joints being passed, "hippie chicks" you'd never date but might try to pick up once you got high, and freaks who'd take acid and then wander out into the traffic.

Rick and I hung out with the freaks, but we also hung out with the more socially acceptable crowd that still came to Dena's. Although both Rick and I had cars by then it was still necessary to wait for Dee to go to bed and then negotiate the awning leap to the garage and the descent to the pavement before we could fire them up. Free of the Church of Christ and its meetings, we became hot stuff, Elvis's little brothers on the loose. Rick and I even got into a dating contest. I don't know who was ahead, but it ended when I met Kathy Hannah.

Kathy was my first love, but shortly after we had started dating we were confronted by one big problem. The year before she'd been going steady with a guy who was a big star on rival Whitehaven High's football team. He'd been both a tackle and a tight end at Whitehaven and now he was on scholarship at the University of Tennessee, playing tackle. Needless to say he was considerably bigger than the Nub. When he came back on weekends to see Kathy and learned she was going out with me he started following us. One night we saw him at McDonald's and we sped off before he could get to my car. Now he knew who I was, and he put out the word that I'd better stay away from his girl. I was tempted to tell Elvis, but I felt embarrassed to say that I didn't think I could handle the situation. But I was also scared. I even told my mom about it.

Elvis came home for Christmas about the third week in December. The second night he was back he and I were shooting pool together and Elvis asked me about my new girlfriend. I said, "Elvis, you met her in November. Kathy. She's terrific."

Elvis said, "What's this I hear about some old boyfriend of hers who's threatening you?"

Dee had told Elvis! When I recovered from my surprise I told him it was true, that the guy was not only big and strong but he had been following us and had a lot of friends who were promising to kick my ass.

Elvis asked, "Where is he?"

I said, "I hear he's in town this weekend. His college is off for Christmas."

Elvis said, "C'mon. Let's go talk to the guy."

Within minutes Elvis and I were in my '57 Chevy with me driving, with Sonny and Red West following us in a limo. I knew they were all armed—I saw Elvis slip a gun into his boot before we left—and I was nervous. I took Elvis to McDonald's and the other hangouts where I expected my rival to be, but we didn't see him. Then Elvis asked me if I knew where he lived. I didn't but we made the rounds, talking to some guys who knew him. Pretty soon we had an address.

I didn't feel comfortable with any of it. It was OK for Elvis and Sonny and Red to be tough guys, but I wondered what would happen and how I'd be thought of after they left.

When we got to the guy's house Elvis told me to go to the door, so I went up to press the buzzer. By the time his mom was there to answer it Elvis was by my side saying, "Billy, go back to the car." I stayed within earshot, hearing Elvis introduce himself and ask, politely, if her son was at home. His mother was shocked. Elvis didn't need to say, "I'm Elvis Presley." She sure knew that. The woman was astonished to see him at her front door.

A few seconds later the son appeared; he was in deeper shock than his mother. Elvis was wearing a typical white shirt and black pants, but he also had on sunglasses, a black cape, and he carried a cane (in addition to the hidden gun). He was quite an imposing figure. From my distance I couldn't hear what was being said at first, but at one point I heard Elvis raise his voice and say, "If you ever follow my brother again, I'm coming to get you. If *anyone* follows my brother again, I'm holding you responsible. Do you understand that?"

Well, I never saw him again, and when I saw his friends they went out of their way to avoid me.

Elvis had resumed his city-to-city tours in the fall of 1970 with a six-city tour that began in Phoenix in September. That was followed by a second tour that touched down in eight West Coast cities in eight days beginning in Oakland in November. Outside of the long engagements in Las Vegas and the three-night affair at the Astrodome, these had been Elvis's first true tours in fifteen years and he was excited. In the spring of '71 Ricky and I were sitting in the den at Graceland when Elvis and the guys started planning another tour for the coming fall. To us, listening to his tales of the completed tours and to his plans for future tours was almost as exciting as being there. Afterward, Rick said, "Man, I'd give anything to go on tour with Elvis." I nodded my agreement. But I knew that Dee would never let us go to anything more than a special event, certainly not an organized tour and not during the school year. When I added it all up there was no reason to dream of tours to far-off cities. And I had things going pretty much my way right there in Memphis.

10

"ARE YOU LONESOME TONIGHT?"

(Christmas 1970 ■ June 1971)

A few days after the incident with Kathy's boyfriend I overheard the biggest fight ever between Elvis and Vernon. I actually saw very little of it because I was down in the den watching TV and they were up in the front foyer. I heard the arguing, and after I realized who was arguing I expected it to quiet down quickly. Elvis could argue for hours with one of the colonel's men or with one of his own, doing most or all of the shouting himself. But for Elvis to continue in a raised voice to his father was rare, and for Vernon to respond in kind was rarer. I went to the stairs to try to discover what it was all about. I saw Vernon waving some bills and yelling, "Over thirty thousand dollars in guns! And all those expensive cars!"

"They're presents," Elvis yelled.

"Presents? Where's the money coming from?"

"It's my money," Elvis shot back.

"This is too much!" Vernon yelled.

I went back into the den and turned the TV up. I couldn't figure it. Normally Vernon would bitch or complain about Elvis's bills and Elvis would say, "Daddy, it's only money." And that would be the end of it. If Vernon went on, Elvis would placate him with, "Well, Daddy. I've spent a lot of money and now I'll just have to go out and make some more." If Vernon kept after him then, Elvis would get mad and Vernon would quietly withdraw. They were too close to argue. They loved and respected each other too much. Vernon had had a troubled childhood, beaten repeatedly by a drunken and abusive father, I was told. I think he was determined never to be that way with his son.

Even above the increased volume on the TV I could hear their battle raging on. Father and son were not cursing each other, but they were cursing everything else.

"It's my fucking money," Elvis yelled.

"Goddammit, it ain't right what you're doing," Vernon countered.

Vernon brought up the subject of the colonel and Elvis said, "Fuck Colonel. He can't tell me where or how to spend my money. I'm terminating his contract! I'll hire John Fisher, he's not so damn pushy."

And then there was a third voice, shrill, bitter, and just as determined. That was Priscilla taking Vernon's side, not out of sympathy with Vernon, but rather to get at Elvis. "You don't know what you're doing. You haven't a clue. What are you doing? Buying people so that your own family can go without? You don't ever look beyond where you are right now."

I gave up on the TV and went back to the stairs. Vernon and Priscilla were standing in the foyer and Elvis was halfway up the stairs to his room. Vernon's head was bowed; I could sense that the argument had already gone further than he'd expected and he was weary of it. But Priscilla pressed on with the accusation that Elvis was so busy looking after his guys he'd forgotten his family.

Then Elvis disappeared into his room. Minutes later he came back out wearing his purple velvet suit, a cape, and sunglasses. He brushed past Vernon and Priscilla.

"Sonny, you can't leave," Vernon wailed.

"Don't you dare leave," Priscilla commanded.

Elvis turned and his lips trembled. "No one tells me what to do."

"Sonny, where are you going? You don't need to go," Vernon pleaded.

"Don't go," Priscilla said. "Elvis, please don't go."

But Elvis was out the door and gone. Which car he took, what arrangements he made, what his destination was, we didn't know. I went back to the TV room feeling deeply disturbed, not just by the unprecedented argument between Elvis and Vernon, but by the way Priscilla had made that rare and ugly confrontation her own. I thought about her attacks on him and about his explanations. "The guns are for my friends and the people who work for me. They're gifts but they're also practical. In this world, and with what we come up against, they're necessary. The Mercedeses are gifts too. One's for you, Priscilla, and another is for Sheriff Bill Morris, who's done more—" But Priscilla had cut him off. I'd liked her and I certainly loved Lisa Marie, who was often left at our house when Elvis and Priscilla went out. No one who worked for Elvis liked Priscilla—no one from Memphis—and it dawned on me that I'd only pretended to like her, out of family loyalty. To Vernon, Dee, Rick, and David, she was family and above criticism. I wasn't even sure she was family. Since Lisa Marie's birth she'd lived in L.A. most of the time. She came to Graceland as seldom as possible and never unless Elvis brought her. She criticized Elvis, his tastes, his friends, and everyone around him. She was pleasant and polite with Vernon and Dee and my brothers but there never seemed to be any real warmth or spontaneity behind it. At Graceland the only people she seemed truly comfortable with were Joe and Joanie Esposito, a couple of West-Coasters who themselves didn't like Memphis and only came when it was so ordered by Elvis. And from what I'd just seen, Priscilla really didn't seem to like or even respect Elvis. I don't know if he realized it yet. But I certainly did.

For the next three days the interior of Graceland resembled a funeral home. There must have been a thousand lights strung from the Music Gates to the front door and a thousand more in the windows and on the huge Christmas tree. There were presents everywhere, people everywhere, a kitchen full of food, but no Elvis. Vernon shuffled forlornly about the house repeating, "Sonny's never done this before." And he never had. It was a family rule, first established by Gladys and Vernon, that you always called to say where you were. If you left home you called as soon as you got where you were going. If you were on the road you called when you left, told your family where you were going, and called when you got there. Elvis never forgot it once, even when he was on the road performing as the voice of the country's rebellious youth. He never forgot in Germany, nor thereafter. But now Elvis was breaking the rule. Dee was wringing her hands and trying to be cheerful; Priscilla was distraught. I forgot my sudden anger for her. I was sorry. I was mad at Elvis one moment and worried about him the next.

When Elvis returned, two days before Christmas, he offered no apologies or immediate explanations. Jerry Schilling, who'd flown from Los Angeles to join Elvis in his adventure, had called Vernon the day before to say that Elvis was safe and would soon be home. But Elvis still wasn't talking. Then after a formal dinner and much strained small talk he pulled a federal narcotics badge out of his pocket and cleared his throat. "I've been to Washington, to see the president," he announced. "President Nixon. He presented me with this here badge and appointed me a special federal narcotics agent." Elvis glanced around to see if everyone understood the importance of what he was saying. "With this authority I mean to work effectively with law enforcement across the country to curtail the rising wave of crime and street drugs and to work as a positive influence on the youth of our nation."

Pretty heavy stuff. Everyone nodded at the importance of what he was saying but no one said anything. Unbeknownst to the rest of us, Sonny West had joined Elvis in Washington. He said, "Tell 'em about Finlator, E. And the letter." So Elvis told us that a Drug Enforcement Agency boss, John Finlator, had turned down his request for a DEA badge, so he sent a personal letter to Nixon. Nixon dropped everything and granted Elvis a personal audience. Then Elvis added, "The Secret Service wouldn't let Sonny or Jerry into the Oval Office. But I had a word with the president and we got them both in."

Sonny blurted out, "The president said to us, 'You guys are big. Bet you were football players—' " but Elvis raised an imperial eyebrow and Sonny shut up (for once).

Now Vernon was smiling that "Look at my Sonny—even when you think he's doing wrong he's doing right" smile. And the rest of us were impressed. Still no one was forgiving him (except Rick, David, and me—to us Elvis could do no wrong). Not yet. But then Sonny said, "E., tell them about Washington's portrait."

Elvis relaxed his high and mighty air and laughed. "Well I walked up to this portrait of George Washington and I looked at his powdered hair and the frills on his shirt and cuffs and I said to Nixon, 'This dude dressed kind of funny.' And the president looked at my velvet suit and cape and said, 'Uh, Elvis, I could say the same thing about you.' And I said, 'Mr. President. You've got your show to run and I've got mine.' "

At last everyone laughed. The ice was broken, Elvis was back home, and Christmas could proceed as usual.

As usual there was a lot of playing and watching football that Christmas season. After the University of Tennessee beat Arkansas in the Liberty Bowl, Elvis invited the team to Graceland. Practically the whole team (I don't remember seeing Kathy's old boyfriend among them) showed up a few days later.

But Elvis was after even bigger game. With the NFL-AFL merger and the emergence of first the New York Jets and then the Kansas City Chiefs as Super Bowl champs, Elvis started working with local officials to try to bring an NFL team to Memphis. Because of this and the many other things Elvis had done for the community, most of them behind the scenes, the National Junior Chamber of Commerce named Elvis one of the seven recipients of the "Young Man of the Year" award for 1970. At the awards, held in Memphis that year, I sat between Sheriff Bill Morris and Charlie Hodge (next to Charlie was Elvis, then Priscilla and Vernon). I was never so proud of my brother.

The only problem was that he was taking his DEA badge so seriously. He called Rick and me up to his room one day in the winter of 1971 and told us that we could become narcotics agents. He told us we were the right age to begin and that we were probably just then being exposed to the worst elements in our society. We could in turn expose them and become heroes in our culture. I pointed out that I had turned eighteen only a few days before and Rick was a year younger (David was young enough to be spared this initial confrontation.) Elvis's response was, "Nub, when I was your age I was making a million dollars a year!," which wasn't totally true. He was off by a year and a half at least. He meant when he was our age he had that independent drive to achieve that he felt we were ready to acquire. Now he had a goal that could be expressed through us. But we simply weren't ready for that. How could we do what he asked? Sure, we knew a few minor dope dealers who hung out at the Tree and other spots, but what was that worth? To nail a few minor characters we'd jeopardize our newfound popularity. We still had to go to high school and we had our fraternity. In any frat a little marijuana-smoking might occur. Not only would we have to give up our friends; if our fingering got too vehement there could be serious problems.

Elvis was less than satisfied with our response. (We didn't mention that we'd tried dope ourselves.) He called in a guy named John O'Grady, an ex-narcotics agent with a good reputation as Elvis's top security man. He'd first been hired to investigate a paternity suit. Since Red had helped raise us, Rick and I already hated the guy before he said one word to us. Elvis repeated the importance of our mission, and then we said our piece. O'Grady turned to Elvis and said, "Maybe you shouldn't put all this on them. They've got to live in this community and they're just kids. What you can achieve is a national commitment."

Rick and I looked at each other. O'Grady, the DEA man, was getting us off the hook. Elvis waited until he'd left and then narrowed his eyes at us. Finally he relaxed and said, "I still want you two to consider it. That's all. Just consider it. Maybe when you get out of high school you'll be ready." So he put the idea away for a time.

You just can't see this sort of thing when you're eighteen. But looking back, I think Elvis was right and O'Grady was wrong. It's at that age, and younger, that drug abuse begins. If you mean to fight street (as opposed to prescription) drugs as these two did, we were the perfect age to enlist. Looking back at that day from the perspective of seventeen years later, with Elvis dead, with my memories of him alive, and looking back at my own eleven years of drug abuse, one has to wonder. What if we had risked our popularity and security and accepted Elvis's challenge? Would it have made any difference in our lives, or later on, *in his?*

Elvis was home at Graceland a lot in the spring of '71. There was a paternity suit in Los Angeles that occupied some of his time (Elvis, Priscilla, and Lisa would fly off to the house in Bel Air—Elvis would be back a few days later, alone), and a couple of recording sessions in Nashville. But there were no tours that spring because Elvis had a problem with his eyes, glaucoma, so that he was required to wear a patch over one eye. That didn't slow him down much. I'd been looking after Elvis's cars for a couple of years by then, including: the '55 pink Caddy he'd bought for his mother, the '56 Mark II, the '61 black Rolls Royce, the '66 El Dorado convertible, the '66 white Cadillac with a black vinyl top, and the '68 black Lincoln limousine (the famous Stutz Blackhawk coupe didn't arrive until that September, and the Trikes, Ferrari, and Pantera came later). In addition there were go-carts, snowmobiles, Hondas, Triumphs, and Harleys. Everything had to be washed once a week and cranked up and run twice a week except for the Harleys. For them my instruction was to start but not drive them. That spring Elvis and I took them all out. And his interest didn't end with his cars. He was just as interested in mine. Vernon had bought me a '62 Starfire, red with a white top, with a 425-cubic-inch engine. When we showed it to Elvis, he said to Vernon, "Damn after us. Daddy. It's just like you or me to buy our kids a car that'll probably end up killing them." Then he turned to me and said, "Looks good. Will it move?" I got in with him and Elvis laid at least fifty feet of rubber down Dolan Street getting us off.

I had a '57 Bel Air that I'd set up for drag racing with race cam, headers, lowered rear end gears, the works. At first it had a 283-cubic-inch engine, then 327, then 350. I eventually blew up all three, one of them at a track and the others out on the road. One day I was changing the plugs on the 350 engine and Elvis came riding over from Graceland on his golf cart. "Where're the keys, Billy?" he asked.

"There're in the ignition, Elvis," I said.

Elvis got in the driver's seat. "You about done with those plugs?" he asked. I nodded and closed the hood. "Then you better get your ass in here," Elvis said, "'cause we're going for a ride."

I jumped in and said, "Dee's in the house, Elvis."

"Don't worry, Nub," he said. "She'll never hear us." He drove the Chevy slowly around the corner and down the highway to Graceland's gates. Once through he brought it to a stop, revved the engine to 7,000 rpm, and popped the clutch. I just held on to my seat. We must have hit a hundred flying past the mansion before Elvis hit the brakes hard and we stopped just a few feet short of a collision with his more expensive cars. "Oooo-son!" Elvis cried. "The only thing that separates this from a G-two rocket is that it has four wheels."

Elvis drove just about every car I ever had, and I drove many of his. We'd take his sports cars out in the country and he'd give me instruction. "When you're coming into a turn," he'd say, "set up for that turn. Negotiate before you actually get there. Always see into the turn. Don't just look straight ahead." Then I'd follow his eyes and his hands as he sped up into a curve. He'd stop the car and we'd go back, with me driving, to check my performance against his.

Elvis didn't like working on them but he loved driving cars. It was one interest we truly shared. If it was anything pertaining to cars, he wanted me to know about it. Even if he was just watching *Bullitt*, when the chase scene came up he'd yell, "Hey, Billy. Watch this!" Later I became one of Elvis's most trusted drivers, sometimes driving point—the car immediately ahead of Elvis's—but more often driving the car immediately behind his, cutting off any vehicle that tried to approach or follow his too closely. It didn't happen often, but one time a few years later we were all leaving the Memphian Theater in the early morning and my date decided she had to go back in and use the ladies' room. Elvis was getting in his car and he saw me just standing there by myself.

"What are you doing?" he asked me.

I just shrugged. "I guess she had to go, Elvis."

As usual Elvis was in a hurry and didn't want to wait for anyone. He got in the back of his limo, rolled the window down, and pointed a finger at me. "You make sure you catch up, Nub."

My date was out within a minute, but even driving at ninety we were halfway to Graceland before I could see Elvis's limo ahead of us on the highway. "Damn," I thought, "Elvis is pissed. He's doing everything he can to make sure I don't catch up." Then I noticed this Challenger pulling up alongside Elvis, and I realized that Elvis was going fast to get away from the other car. Both cars must have been going ninety by then and I had to take my Chevy 409 up over a hundred to catch up. The Challenger was side by side with the limo and only a few feet away, and I could see a hand with a beer bottle waving from its passenger window. I knew I had to do something fast so I passed the last car that separated me from them on the left and then swung immediately to the right. I passed both cars on the right shoulder, swung in front of the limo and hit the brakes softly. When I felt the thump of the Challenger against my back bumper and saw Elvis's limo pull past us I hit the brakes hard. I had the Chevy in a controlled drift and I had that Challenger locked on my right rear bumper. He had nowhere to go except to the right and to a dead stop. Of course the two guys in the Challenger were immediately out their doors and yelling and hurling beer bottles at me, but I laid nothing but rubber and I was away from there fast. I didn't let up on the pedal until we got to Graceland's gates; by that time we'd caught up to Elvis and the rest of them. When we pulled to a stop at the top of Graceland's drive Elvis, Rick, Red, and the others came running back to the Chevy, laughing and whooping it up.

"Way to go, Billy!" Rick yelled. "Way to go! You smoked him!"

Elvis and I embraced. "Oooooo, son!" he howled. "You peeled him off like a ripe banana! Where did you learn how to drive like that?"

"I had this teacher," I said. "Think his name was A. J. Presley." At my reference to the race car driver A. J. Foyt, Elvis laughed.

While we celebrated, my date refused to leave the car. She was angry and probably pretty shaken up. Elvis, sizing up the situation, said, "Rick, why don't you take Nub's date home in your car. It might not be smart for Billy to be on the streets right now. Nub, any damage to your car?"

"I haven't even looked at the back bumper. They did hit me with a bottle or two. Maybe a few dents."

"Let's take a look," Elvis said. He walked me to the back of the car with his arms around my shoulder. "Any damage, you get it fixed and I'll pay for it."

There was surprisingly little in the way of damage. But even if I'd totaled the car in defense of Elvis it would have been worth it. I knew he would have bought me another one anyway.

About this time Kathy Hannah and I broke up. We had a fight, probably about the fraternity, and we both got mad and said, "Well, if that's the way you feel . . . " but I don't think it was the way either of us felt. I saw her in school a few days later and she looked as if she wanted to make up. I know I did. However, instead of taking the initiative to smooth things over I just let it go. Maybe I was influenced by Elvis's attitude toward women, which was getting harder and harder as his relationship with Priscilla cooled. But I wanted to be back with Kathy and probably the reason that I didn't do anything about it was I didn't know how. I'd never had that close a relationship before and I'd never been in that spot. I wanted to ask Elvis what I should do but it didn't seem to be the right time. As I let the opportunity slip away it just got harder and harder till it didn't seem there was any opportunity any more.

Of course I didn't have any trouble finding other girls, and it wasn't long before the police caught me and this girl in the back seat of my '57 Chevy Nomad, both of us with very little clothing on. We thought we were on our way to the police station. But they must have called Vernon from their car because in a minute or two they were back saying, "Your daddy says to put your clothes back on and come straight home." Vernon only laughed when I got my date home and came through the front door. Dee never heard about it.

Besides losing Kathy, the biggest mistake I made that year was signing up for R.O.T.C. I was considered the worst cadet in my

R.O.T.C. class. (I got into R.O.T.C. at the urging of my mom, who pushed it out of respect for my dad, Bill Stanley. I also joined because of Elvis, who had been in R.O.T.C. in high school and *had liked it.*) I tried to get out, but I was told that I couldn't graduate it unless I first got my hair cut. In adulation of the Beatles I had let my hair grow long, and I refused to cut it. So I suffered through the classes, long hair intact, until they cornered me one day, instructors telling me I had to get my hair cut. I was outraged. They got me in late May and it meant I had to look forward to a summer of being a geek when I'd expected a summer of looking cool. When I told Elvis about it he laughed. He was positively delighted. "Nub," he said, "I went through the same thing. They hated my sideburns, what I could grow of them, and they hated my hair. But I loved that uniform [probably his first escape from dungaree jeans], and I loved the idea that I was preparing to serve and defend my country. I didn't care what they said to me. Or who I had to fight to stay in."

One night, shortly thereafter, Vernon sensed my misery. "Son, why have you been staying home so much?" he asked. "Because I won't go out," I answered. He then produced a copy of the Humes High School yearbook for 1953. In it there was a picture of Elvis with sideburns, pompadour hairdo, black coat, and tie, and the following:

Presley, Elvis Aaron
Major: Shop, History, English
Activities: R.O.T.C., Biology Club, English Club, History Club, Speech Club

"Sonny was so proud of being in R.O.T.C.," Vernon said. "It meant just as much to him as when he made the Humes High football team. In fact some years after he started to make money he went back and spent a thousand dollars buying new uniforms for the Humes High drill team." Elvis had quit the team before he went into eleventh grade because the coach didn't like him singing and playing football too. Elvis was told to choose and he stuck by his music.

I guess I was a little surprised at Elvis's dedication to R.O.T.C. But about his dedication to our country I'd never had any doubts. I heard him rail plenty against draft dodgers and protesters over the years, especially Jane Fonda, who he called "that Communist bitch," and against others who demonstrated against our government's foreign policy. But even though I lived with Elvis, my heroes were the Beatles, the Stones, Led Zeppelin, the Jefferson Airplane, and all the other rock groups of the sixties who advocated resistance to the draft and our sorry involvement in Vietnam. This time I knuckled under and I finally got my hair cut and graduated from R.O.T.C. the way Elvis and Mom and Vernon wanted me to. I spent a miserable summer with a "military cut," when everyone cool had long hair. But I still thought of myself as a longhair, and my political views matched that attitude, so there did come a day when I had to confront Elvis with my beliefs.

The occasion was my notification of request for a draft physical in June of 1971. Elvis found out that under some category (religion, I believe) I'd put down "conscientious objector." The only reason he even found out was that I'd made the grave mistake of asking Vernon how to spell it. Within a few hours Vernon told me that Elvis wanted to see me. Now I knew what was going to happen, how Elvis felt, what was expected of me because of my natural father. I knew Elvis was going to be angry. Vernon took me up to his room and although minutes before I'd thought I knew what to say, as we climbed the stairs I was scared. I thought, "Here I go." Just as we got to the top of the stairs Elvis opened the door. He'd been watching us on his monitor. And his appearance was dramatic. Elvis was wearing a black cape, white shirt and black pants, and he was holding his silver cane. He stuck the cane up into my chest and pinned me against the wall. "Chicken shit!" he said. His famous blue eyes were riveted on mine. "Are you afraid to stand up for your country?"

"No, Elvis," I said.

"Then how come you didn't volunteer?"

"Because I don't believe in what's going on."

"Billy!" Elvis shouted. "What would your real daddy think?"

"Elvis, I don't know," I said. "But he fought a war to save Europe and America. What are we saving in Vietnam?"

Elvis relaxed the pressure on the cane. "If they call you to go, you'd better go." he said. "You'll be a soldier."

"If they call me, Elvis. If they need me, I'll go. I swear. But I'm not going to volunteer."

"OK, Billy," he said. "You'll go if they need you. That's all I want to hear." Elvis pulled the cane back and went back into his room. Vernon and I walked back down the stairs and across the grounds to our house, saying nothing to each other.

11

"CAN'T HELP FALLING IN LOVE"

(July — September 1971)

When Elvis left for Lake Tahoe in July of 1971 for two weeks (twenty-eight shows) at the Sahara Tahoe, his entourage had a new name—TCB. TCB meant "taking care of business"; Elvis wanted those closest to him identified in this way. Previously the guys had been called the Memphis Mafia, a term that some writer had hung on them when he saw them all in Las Vegas one day wearing suits and sunglasses. The expression never really was to Elvis's liking. So Elvis designed a logo, the letters TCB with a gold thunderbolt crashing through, that symbolized the message he wanted to convey. You took care of business and you did it with lightning speed. Elvis had bracelets, jackets, and later, necklaces made with the TCB insignia.

Elvis's intimate group also had a new member—my brother, Rick. Rick was seventeen and he had joined the tour, not as Elvis's younger brother but as full staff member. Elvis had made him his personal aide, a position Richard Davis had held until his recent departure from the tour, and Rick was given the full responsibilities that went with the job.

Rick's admission into Elvis's inner working circle was not as sudden as it appeared to be. The previous November Rick had accompanied Elvis to Washington, D.C., and shortly after Christmas Elvis had asked Rick to join him on a full-time basis. Rick responded, "Elvis. You know that's what I want to do more than anything in the world. But what will Mom say?"

"Better let me handle it," Elvis said. "We'll get her to say it's OK."

But Dee flatly refused. She tried to get Vernon to make Elvis see that Rick was too young and that it was necessary for him to complete his education before entertaining such a notion. By education Mom didn't just mean high school, but college and beyond. She meant for Rick to be a doctor. If he wanted to spoil that dream for her and for himself later, he could. But Elvis wasn't going to spoil it for him now.

Vernon pleaded Dee's case to Elvis. Elvis in turn pleaded his case to Vernon, asking him to make Dee understand that it was what Elvis wanted, what Rick wanted, what would be best for the family, and what would be best for Rick in the long run.

Poor Vernon was the man in the middle, hearing it from both of them, and he couldn't convince either of them to give in. Dee talked to Priscilla about it and Cilla immediately took her side. She argued and then begged Elvis to give the idea up. But Elvis wouldn't. Over several weeks he tried to raise the subject with Dee, but she refused even to discuss it. She had said no and saw no reason to argue further.

Rick had asked me what I thought and I told him, "I think it's great. It's what we've both always wanted."

"Of course you'll be joining us soon. Do you mind that it's me going first?"

"Not at all," I said honestly, "I know it's a lot of responsibility and I'm not sure I'm ready for it just yet. You are, and Elvis sees that."

"Mom's always favored you," Rick said. "Maybe if you talked to her you could get her to see it our way."

"I can try, Ricky," I said. "But I don't think anyone's opinion will change her mind."

It wasn't easy but I tried to bring it up to her. But she looked at me with such sad eyes that I knew I had no chance.

Looking back now that I'm a parent myself, it is easy to understand Dee's position. Rick was very popular in school—he had been president of his class the year before and he had more girls after him than anyone. Although he'd slack off once in a while, he made As and Bs whenever he wanted. He was tall, blond, handsome, and had a winning way with people. It seemed Rick would succeed in whatever he chose to do. He didn't need Elvis.

Then there was the question of moral conduct. Dee had raised us as Christian children and, to her mind, it didn't matter what Elvis called himself or how many books on how many religions he read and could recite. He did not live a Christian life. There were too many parties, too many loose women.

Even Elvis's closest supporters, Joe Esposito and Red West, sided with Dee. And when Rick did eventually go on tour, there was a lot of resentment toward Elvis for having brought him. Joe told Rick, "Rick, we love you. Elvis loves you. We're glad you're here. But you really should be in school. Elvis shouldn't have brought you until you finished school."

To understand why Elvis was so determined you have to understand his background and how it shaped him. We learned much of it from Elvis and from Vernon's mom, Minnie Mae (Elvis's "Dodger") when they'd occasionally talk about the hard times. But they were not just talking about poverty—the kind that had Vernon going shoeless on snowy winter days when he was sixteen, or had Elvis picking through garbage cans on his way home from high school in Memphis, looking for something useful for his family—but poverty was a part of it. In most cases that kind of poverty breaks families apart. In their case, however, it reinforced the concept of family.

My brothers and I were destined to become the young warriors as Elvis's clan grew over the years. Although we'd been born outside the family, we had been fully assimilated into the tribe. Elvis told us more than once that it was destiny that had brought us there, that we had been meant to be with him. Sure, Elvis was glad we did well in school, and happy that Rick was popular and a class president. But this acceptance by peers and the promise of acceptance by conforming society meant little to Elvis. We had a hidden and unspoken pact with our older brother. He'd gain us freedom from the rules that other parents imposed on their children but, in return, he'd expect that we'd be obedient. Dee wanted Rick to go to college, become a doctor, buy cars and houses, and endorse some middle-class values. Elvis's attitude was "What for? We already have cars and houses and doctors. And if we need more, I'll buy them." The choice for my brothers and me was easy to make. Now another job, another purpose, and another promise awaited us all, with Rick as personal aide, Billy as driver, and

David, eventually, as bodyguard. And Rick's position was suddenly available. Elvis was determined that Rick should take it.

So Elvis kept after Vernon until Vernon could no longer resist his son's arguments. Vernon took Elvis's side. Then he kept after Dee until he wore her down and she promised that she would discuss it with Elvis.

One night Elvis came over and everyone else cleared out of the house. As Mom later told me, Elvis tried to break down Dee's many objections. "Dee. This is the family business. If you let Rick come with me I'll make sure he has everything he'll ever need. If Rick doesn't want to stay on the tour he can go to college anytime he wants. All three can. All they have to do is say the word. Education, travel, anything—I'll even get them in the movies. Rick has an opportunity right now that few young men will have. He's going to be right at my side the whole time. I'm not delegating him out to Joe or Red or anyone. He'll be right there with me."

"Elvis! How will he keep up?"

"I'll hire teachers and tutors. Just say yes, Dee, and you won't regret it. You'll see. I won't let you down."

As anyone knows who was ever exposed to Elvis's unblinking blue eyes when he was being his most sincere, it was almost impossible to deny him what he wanted. Dee gave in. "I'm going to trust you, Elvis," she said. "This time. Just don't you let him down. That's all I ask."

"Dee. You know I'll always take care of your boys. You know that."

"Elvis!" Dee exclaimed. "Do you mean to take all three of my boys?" She suddenly realized if one went the other two would eventually follow.

Within a few days we were all at the airport to see them off to Los Angeles. David and I were proud of our brother. Rick was ecstatic. Dee was smiling, proud, tearful, and wringing her hands. "Now don't you forget the teachers," she called after Elvis.

On the chartered jet, just as they cleared the runway, Elvis came back and sat next to Rick. Elvis laughed and put his arm around Rick. "I might as well tell you now," he said. "I'm the teacher."

In June Rick was back in Memphis, full of stories. He'd called me several times while he was on the road but now that he was back, and for the benefit of other friends, we went over everything that happened. David and I were particularly anxious to hear new revelations about life with our favorite person. We'd always known him as big brother, surrogate father, instigator, and counselor. Now Ricky knew him as boss. So Rick told us in detail about the highlights and low spots.

I had been holding my own in Memphis. Fast cars, drag races, hanging out with my buddies, and meeting new chicks probably kept me away from classrooms as much as Rick's commitment to Elvis had. There were always plenty of new girls to meet and Dee, having given in to Elvis on the Rick issue, couldn't keep me at home. Some of the girls' parents were a little leery of me and there was one father who practically threw me out the first time I set foot in his house. I'd taken his daughter out a few times, met the mother, and thought everything was cool. But when I met him he was irate. They had just changed the name of Highway 51 to Elvis Presley Boulevard and he had a shop on the boulevard. It seems he was very upset because he'd just ordered new stationery and now he'd have to change it. I thought he was really stupid. It certainly wasn't going to do his business any harm to have that address.

Some parents would take one look at us and our long hair and say, "I understand you're Elvis Presley's stepbrother." Then they'd just look down their noses and walk away. Didn't make you feel great. But there were others who really got a kick out of it. "What's he really like?" they'd ask. "I mean, you do spend time with him?"

"Sure do," I'd say.

Since Rick's schedule with Elvis that spring was light, he came back to finish the school year without any suspicions on Mom's part that his formal education was lacking in any way. But the time he'd spent on the road with Elvis had only made the day-to-day grind of school seem all the more useless and boring. We both finished out that school year (but just barely), missing as many classes as we attended and often hung over for those we managed to get to.

The late spring had always been party time. As the evenings grew longer and the nights warmed, the parties multiplied. And with Rick's new celebrity status, we were at every one we wanted to go to. If we didn't have one going at the fraternity house we'd throw a couch in the back of a van and go to an outdoor theater. Paul Shafer, who also owned the Memphian, where Elvis had been holding his all-night movie watches for years, owned several drive-ins and would give me handfuls of free passes. We'd load up the van with beer and girls, drive in, and plop the couch down in the front row. No one else did it and

I'm sure we could get pretty loud and obnoxious, but since we were Paul's guests too, no one told us we couldn't do it either.

We had plenty of dates and Rick and I enjoyed, if we deemed them worthy, taking some of them back to Graceland to watch movies or sit by the pool. If Elvis came strolling up it would just blow their minds. But by the time the group left for Lake Tahoe for a two-week engagement in mid-July, Ricky was more than raring to go.

The night before they left we had a party out at McKellar Lake (which is actually a branch of the Mississippi River) and I took a date out to the back end of the lake to park. She wasn't just a date, she was a girl to whom Rick had introduced me and I was smitten, struck, enraptured. Her name was Annie and she would become my constant date for the remainder of the summer. But that night I just wanted to get her away from the crowd. You weren't really supposed to drive out there and I soon discovered why. Here I was, thinking I was the hero of *Vanishing Point*, not to mention all the racing movies Elvis had made, sitting in my '70 midnight-blue Challenger—unstoppable, uncatchable, undefeatable—with the best-looking chick at my side. And I was definitely stuck in the Mississippi mud.

After a long walk to a phone I called Graceland praying that Elvis would answer and that he would get me out of the jam. To my great regret Vernon answered.

"Is Elvis there?" I asked, trying to disguise my voice.

"No he's out," Vernon gruffly answered. Then, after a pause, he said, "Billy?"

"Yeah, Daddy, it's me. I just wanted to check in with him. To see when he'd be back."

"Billy, they all went to the Memphian. They won't be back for hours."

"Daddy," I said, "I'm stuck."

"Where are you, son?"

So Vernon came with a tow truck and we were rescued. I got Annie home. When I got home Vernon was still up, and he seemed oddly amused by the incident. "At least we got the car back this time," he said.

"This time?" I asked.

"You don't know the story? I guess it was a few years back. Even before you came here. Maybe it was even before Sonny went to Germany. He and a bunch of his friends went on the back side of the lake pretty close to where you got stuck. I don't know what got into them but they started digging this big pit in the sand, digging deeper and deeper until the hole was so big that Elvis jumped in his car and drove it right in." Vernon was laughing so hard by this time that he could hardly go on.

"Then what happened?" I asked.

"Nothing. Elvis got out and they buried that car. Buried it in the sand. Something about the car had displeased him and he just buried it and walked away from it."

"Guess that's why they call him crazy," I said, laughing with him. I forgot for the moment that Vernon brooked no criticism or disparaging of Elvis, even if it was in jest.

But he wiped his eyes and went on laughing. "I guess so, son," he said. "I guess it is." Vernon was in a laughing jag now, the kind Elvis would get into. For Vernon, a man who wrung his hands and wrinkled his brow at Elvis's every extravagance and who'd visibly sweat every time he pulled five dollars out of his wallet, this was rare.

After two sold-out weeks in Tahoe, Elvis and the TCB group went straight to Las Vegas to prepare for four weeks at the International Hotel. David and I went out with Vernon and Dee and met up with the group on opening night, August 9, 1971. In between his duties to the show and to Elvis, Rick introduced me to every good-looking girl he could find in Las Vegas—and he always seemed to have one on either arm.

When he got a chance Rick took me aside for a private talk. "Elvis needs more help, man. We all do. Jerry Schilling's taken a job with a movie production company in L.A. Red's working with a sound studio in Nashville. He only comes out to join us for the big events. And Joe likes the life in L.A. and is getting tired of touring."

"I know you've got your hands full."

"You don't know," Rick said. He filled me in on the rest. Alan Fortas and Richard Davis were gone. Priscilla and Vernon had argued against Elvis's replacing either of them—to save money. And although they'd also argued against Rick becoming part of TCB, there were now, including Rick, only four close hands to assist Elvis. "And we've got a big schedule this fall," Rick concluded. I knew he was leading up to something, so I just smiled and waited.

"Billy, I'm talking about you joining the tour. I know you've wanted to take your time about it but we need you out here now. Just let me say the word to Elvis, that you want to come on. You've never told him that, but you know the door is wide open."

I still didn't answer him, and he could see I had something else on my mind. "How are things going for you in Memphis, anyway? I haven't thought to ask."

"Great," I told him. "I've met a girl that I've gotten pretty involved with."

"Well, don't get too involved," Rick said. "The girls in Memphis are OK but you should see what we come across out here. And I mean every day."

"This is pretty serious, Rick."

"Who is it? Anyone I know?"

"Yeah. It's Annie."

"Annie! Billy, she's not the right girl for you!"

"Rick. I am involved."

"With Annie? Billy, I know her. I introduced you to her. Do me a favor. Do yourself a favor. Forget her!"

I let it drop. Ricky thought he knew her first but I'd had a thing for Annie since we were together in the eighth grade. I'd just never told her. She didn't even seem to remember that we were in that grade together at Hillcrest. That was fine with me. I'd changed—I was more confident, more in control, and, as it turned out, more headstrong.

"Rick. I don't know about that."

"Now is the time to think about joining the tour, Billy," Rick urged. "Elvis always meant that you'd be the first anyway. Think about it. Forget Annie."

I thought about it. The rest I already knew, but the part about Joe Esposito being "tired of the tour" was news to me. Joe Esposito was the main man, the guy who made it all work. Anger, misunderstandings, riots, threats—anything you could think of—could happen and Joe was there to handle it coolly so that no one got too mad. If he left, the operation was in serious trouble. I knew that if Elvis asked me I'd be right there—and that I would probably lose Annie. But Elvis hadn't asked me, not yet. So I went looking for a phone, to call Annie. Then I realized that it was three in the morning in Memphis, too late to call.

The next afternoon I was sitting with David near the pool, listening to the line he was giving some girls, when Rick came up. "Elvis wants to see you," Rick said. "He's in his room." I went there with a feeling of apprehension, but also of self-importance. As I'd told Rick, and

Elvis before, if called, I'd go. I just wasn't sure I was ready to be called.

It was a little after three in the afternoon when I walked into his room; Elvis was still in his pajamas. He was sitting on the edge of his bed sipping orange juice. "Nub," he said. "I've got a job for you. Can you do something for my neck?" I went behind him and started massaging, waiting to hear what the job was. "Ooh, that's good. Man, I do work up some kinks out there. Oooh, son! Billy, you are good at this. Am I paying you for this?"

"No, Elvis. You only pay me to wash your cars."

"Shows how dumb I am."

I'd been massaging Elvis's neck for a couple of years and this was the tightest I'd ever felt it. But his neck muscles began to relax and he finally got to the point. "Did you know Cilla's in town?" he asked.

"We all had dinner together last night."

"Nub, I didn't think she'd be here. You know wives are only welcome opening and closing nights. But she's here. And I've got this girl that I've been getting friendly with. I want you to take care of her, man. Pick her up, take her out, let her gamble. Take the money out of my box. But don't bring her to my show. And don't bring her around me while Priscilla's here."

"Got you, Elvis."

"She's a little feisty."

"I can handle it."

"'Course you can."

So that was it. A baby-sitting job. I don't know whether I felt relieved or disappointed. But I went to the girl's room at eight that evening and was greeted with a curled lip. "I'm Billy, Elvis's brother," I said.

"Yeah. He called," she said. She went back into the room without inviting me in and came back moments later with a mink scarf around her neck. I'd always liked most of Elvis's ladies but I took an immediate dislike to this one, and from her expression I knew the feeling was mutual. "Where are we going?" she asked. I told her I was taking her to meet Tom Jones, who was headlining another club in Vegas.

"What about Elvis?" she asked.

"He's meeting us later. Soon as he gets rid of Priscilla and my mother. Don't worry, Elvis and Tom are buddies and when they get together things happen."

We were walking out of the casino when I saw the colonel. Naturally, I tried to slip past him. "What about enlisting the colonel?" I had asked Rick. We had both laughed. If anyone still thinks that Colonel Parker took charge of any of the actual shows, let me now forever correct them. Colonel's job was advance. He had nothing to do with the tour or the performance. He had his buddies at RCA and before that at MGM and he had his standing deals with the Hilton International, but with the show itself he was an unwelcome outsider. Before Elvis arrived he'd do his bit by bullying hotel management, disc jockeys, and street vendors, but when Elvis appeared the colonel's job was done. At Vegas that meant he was free to hit the roulette tables, where she and I encountered him. He caught me by the neck and pulled me over. "Billy, my boy," he boomed, "you're here to bring me luck. Pick a number."

"I don't gamble," I said.

"You don't need to!" he bellowed. "Pick a number for the colonel."

Elvis's girl was impatient. But by then Colonel had a sweaty armpit wrapped around my shoulder. "Pick a number!" he commanded, winking at the girl. She had no idea who he was.

"Twenty-three."

"Twenty-three it is," Colonel said, pushing ten thousand dollars in chips to that number. The wheel spun and the ball finally rested on the three.

"Bad luck," Colonel barked. "Pick another."

Elvis's date, having been around Vegas awhile, recognized the value of his chips and the enormity of his bet. After having backed away from this balding fat man, she now pressed in close to my side.

"Pick a number, Billy," she echoed.

"Thirty-seven," I said.

Colonel put another ten thousand down. The wheel spun and the girl, who a few seconds before had been bored out of her skull, pressed her torso against Colonel and me. "Thirty-seven!" she yelled. But again Colonel missed.

"Oh, no," she cried, rubbing her breasts excitedly between Colonel and me. "That was so close!"

Somehow her breasts, with an ability of their own, were pressing up above her dress, white and full, and the colonel, not known as a womanizer, was impelled to look directly at them.

Colonel laughed. He said, "Have your friend pick a number. If she gets it right the first five thou are hers!"

Now she was breathless. "Twenty-one," she whispered. "That was my birthday last month. No, twenty-three. That's my target year. God, make it twenty–twenty-three!"

Colonel nodded and pushed another ten thousand to the number twenty-three. The wheel spun and the ball settled on nine.

I grabbed the girl's arm. "C'mon," I said. "We're going to see Tom Jones."

In less than ten minutes I'd seen Colonel blow thirty thousand dollars. And when we left he was laughing. She was laughing too, in delight that she had, in her opinion, been responsible for extravagance. I was disgusted. I'd just spent half the summer working in the Memphis heat with Uncle Earl for one hundred and fifty a week. It was all Elvis's money either way, but this guy was out of control. Colonel was sick.

I took the girl to wherever it was Tom Jones was playing that night, and we caught part of the show. There were women screaming, but no one had to worry about this one wetting her pants at his performance. She'd already done that watching the colonel gambling. I think she didn't much want to stay with me anyway. Since I didn't speak another word to her after leaving the colonel's side, she might have gotten the idea that I didn't like her. (Some people have told me that I set my jaw and won't speak when I'm upset. I believe I probably set my jaw and wouldn't speak that evening.) She spotted some friends and asked if she could join them for a minute.

"Sure," I said.

"You won't disappear?" she asked, torn between the desire to get away from me and the knowledge that I was her link to Elvis.

"I'll be here."

I was gone in a flash. This was not one Elvis would ask about, particularly with Priscilla in town.

I didn't see her again. In any case, Priscilla, despite daily threats that she'd go back to L.A., hung on. So Elvis had other dates in waiting whom he entrusted to my care. But he never mentioned a full-time tour position.

Near the end of our two-week stay Rick confronted me. "Billy, what have you decided?"

"Nothing. Elvis hasn't asked me anything yet. Maybe he doesn't want me."

"He does. You've got to ask him! What about Annie? Have you thought about her? About what I told you?"

"Yeah. I've thought about her a lot. She's mostly what I think about. When I get back to Memphis I'm going to ask her to marry me."

"Billy!" Rick wailed. "Don't do this. Listen to what I'm saying. I *know her*. I don't like her. I don't think you should marry her."

"I do. I will. If she'll have me."

"You'd be making a big mistake."

Rick raged on. He was upset, angry, and finally tearful. My mind was set.

"I'm going to tell Elvis about this," Rick concluded. "He'll do something about it."

"You can tell Elvis," I replied calmly, "but I don't think there's anything he can do."

As I said my mind was set. I was in love.

12

"BLUE CHRISTMAS"

(September 1971 — January 1972)

Annie said yes. I waited for several days, riding on a cloud, and then told my parents. Dee's reaction was to be expected. She was angry. Vernon just looked confused. To make a pronouncement he would somehow have to be able to relate the situation to money, and he hadn't figured that part out yet. Then they gathered their forces.

"We forbid it," Dee said.

"We're both eighteen," I answered. "We don't need your consent."

"Well, we won't have it. Billy, you're too young and we don't know enough about this girl."

"Then we'll elope."

"Elope!" Vernon thundered, picking up his cue. "Then how will you survive? Where will your paycheck come from? Your cars and your shelter?"

"I'll have to get a job."

They tried reasoning but I was having none of it, and after a couple of hours Dee developed a headache and announced that we'd discuss the whole thing the next day. Then Elvis called. They had just closed

Las Vegas and were down in Palm Springs for a spell of rest and recuperation.

"Billy," Elvis intoned deeply. "What's this I hear about your planning to get married?"

"It's true, Elvis."

"What?" Elvis said as if he had trouble hearing me.

"Elvis. It's true. I've found a girl that I want to marry."

"Uh, Nub," Elvis said. "We've . . . uh, we've got other plans for you. Big plans. You should be with us now. We're having a good time out here."

But from his voice I could tell otherwise. Elvis had just done twenty-eight performances in fourteen days in Tahoe and followed it with fifty-seven performances in twenty-nine days in Las Vegas. He'd given his all in almost every one. He was exhausted beyond the ability to sleep and he was obviously on downers. All musicians used them—uppers to get going when you felt you couldn't, and downers to help when the performance was over but your body continued to race in high gear. Elvis, despite his repeated pronouncements against drugs, was not immune to that problem. And, as I was soon to learn, he had serious problems of his own, with Priscilla. He said something else but I couldn't hear it clearly and then his voice trailed off. I think he was close to falling asleep.

Then he was back. "Billy, do you hear what I'm saying?"

"I do, Elvis. But I've found a girl I love and I mean to marry her. She wants it and so do I."

"Aw, Nub! I told you you'd marry the first girl you slept with!"

"Elvis, she isn't the first. I know what I'm doing."

"Billy, I'm going to turn you over to Rick. He's standing right here. I want you to consider what I'm saying. I've been around the block a few times. You hear?"

"I hear you, Elvis. Thanks for calling."

Elvis said something else but I couldn't understand it. Then Rick was on the phone. "You hear what Elvis said?" Rick asked.

"I heard," I said. Rick understood my tone.

"Billy. You are making a big mistake. There are people who want to help you and stand by you and *they are your family.* Don't turn on your family."

"I'm not turning on anyone," I laughed. "I'm getting married."

Rick hung up. Of course he called back. But neither his arguments nor Elvis's nor Dee's nor anyone else's made any difference. Unexpectedly, Dee gave in first. Once she saw that we were determined she asked us when we wanted to be married. I said within a month. That was about the second week of September and on November twenty-first, at our house on Dolan Street, Annie and I were married. Elvis, after a tour engagement in Salt Lake City, chartered a plane and flew back to congratulate me, but he didn't stay for the wedding itself. Rick stayed on the tour. Vernon was my best man.

Looking back after all these years, I think I understand Dee's compliance with my demands. Rick must have told her about the possibility I'd join the tour. So she saw me as being caught between two forces—Annie and Elvis. I think my mother chose to accept the lesser of two threats.

That fall Annie and I lived with my parents. We both went back to school at Hillcrest and life seemed pretty normal. I liked being married, didn't like school, liked living at home, and I liked working on the cars at Graceland. Rick called me a few days after the wedding to say he couldn't have made it, and that now that we were married he wished us both the best.

In December Elvis and Rick came home after an exhausting tour that took them to Minneapolis, Cleveland, Louisville, Philadelphia, Baltimore, Boston, Cincinnati, Houston, Dallas, Tuscaloosa, Kansas City, and Salt Lake City for fourteen shows in twelve cities in twelve days. When he got home Elvis stayed in bed for three days, as usual, but Rick was too excited and too busy filling in David and me and his other friends on what they had been doing.

As always, Rick and I went off in my car so we could have a private talk. Then I learned the full story of the night that Elvis had called from Palm Springs to urge me not to rush into marriage. "If Elvis sounded wiped out," Rick told me, "it's because he was. We had all the people who'd worked Vegas down. And there were lots of chicks. We were having some parties and it got pretty wild, particularly after Elvis retired to his room. You know Elvis wouldn't permit it but after he left no one seemed to care if they wore clothes or not. That afternoon, Priscilla and Joanie Esposito drove over, unannounced, from L.A. and found a party in full swing. When Priscilla walked in there were girls in bikinis everywhere. Cilla was storming and everyone was running for cover. Elvis just sat there looking at me as if to say, 'Do something, Rick.' "

I laughed. "Sounds bad," I said.

"I tried to smooth it over," Rick said. "I told her none of the women were with Elvis. That we'd just invited a few people over and it got out of hand.

"Cilla said, 'Ricky I know this isn't your fault. Stop defending him.' She walked away from me.

"Elvis came over and asked, 'Rick, is she buying it?'

"I shook my head. 'Keep talking,' Elvis said. 'You keep talking 'cause right now you're the only one she'll listen to.'

"Just then Priscilla turned and caught us both in an icy stare. Elvis said, 'I'm nailed, Rick. This time I'm nailed.' "

"Sounds real bad," I laughed. But I hadn't heard anything yet to merit Rick's serious concern.

"You haven't heard the bad part," Rick told me. "Cilla and Joanie went back to L.A. and Elvis cleaned up the act at the Springs. But she'd ruffled some feathers. The day after she left, Red told me she was having an affair with Mike Stone. You know him, Ed Parker's friend."

"The Hawaiian?"

"That's the guy."

"Bullshit," I said. "She wouldn't have the balls." But it was true.

On another occasion, I walked in on Rick and "Hamburger" James just as James was walking out of the room. " 'Hamburger' just told me something really heavy," Rick said. I gave 'Hamburger' a look. "He says Lisa Marie said, 'Mike took us camping. I saw Mommy and Mike wrestling in their sleeping bag on the beach. They wrestled all night.' "

"Do you believe it?" I asked.

"Red doesn't lie," Rick answered. "Even the Brow knows it."

"The Brow," I laughed. The Brow was a guy named James Cowley. He'd always hung out at the Graceland front gate or at the Memphian theater when Elvis went there. He never stopped asking Elvis for a job and one day Elvis hired him. Of course, the starting job is always that of gofer. One day Elvis said, "I need a hamburger, James." As James rushed out the others called after him, "Hamburger, James!" The name stuck and everyone just called him Hamburger James. Rick and I had a different name for him. He had very thick, dark eyebrows that rose up when Elvis or Joe gave him a command and narrowed down when he spoke to either of us. We called him the Brow.

"How does the Brow know anything?" I asked.

"Henrietta [the Holmby Hills maid] told him. Billy, everyone knows but Elvis. But no one wants to say a word. Imagine saying, 'Uh, now, Elvis. I want you to be aware that your wife is sleeping around.' It's out of the question."

"So it's true?"

"I'm afraid so. And you know Elvis. In his mind he was always true and loyal to Priscilla. To be caught like he was in Palm Springs, was bad news, man. Billy, he was ashamed. In his mind the family must always be kept intact. Elvis still feels that he can make it up to her."

"Let's go home," I said.

"Billy, listen to me. Don't tell Annie."

"She's my wife. Don't you think we can trust her?"

"Out on the tour they know. But no one in Memphis knows except you, me, and Daddy. Elvis is going to be devastated. Don't let it happen through family, or from what someone's heard from family."

"Let's go home," I repeated. When we got home, in the quiet of a sleeping household, Rick and I embraced.

"I love them both," Rick said. "It's so sad."

Rick was upset. But the trouble that Elvis was having with Priscilla didn't surprise me. Problems had been building for some time. Elvis had discouraged Priscilla's modeling career and he put his foot down when she tried to get into acting. Elvis was the breadwinner and he wanted to keep it that way. It was the reason he'd never gotten seriously involved, to the point of matrimony, with any of his costars. He didn't want his wife to have a competing career. Wives belonged at home. But Priscilla had rejected that philosophy and was tired of how Graceland was becoming a gilded cage. Furthermore, she had rejected his philosophical pursuits. When Priscilla expressed interest in learning karate Elvis was delighted. Through Ed Parker and Chuck Norris he set Priscilla up on a training schedule with a Hawaiian instructor named Mike Stone. Elvis had met Mike Stone, liked him, and was more than pleased at the interest and dedication Priscilla took in her lessons. And it gave Elvis a new sense of freedom. Instead of having to take Priscilla off on a vacation to Hawaii or the Bahamas immediately after closing Las Vegas, as he had done in the past, Elvis was able to announce, "C'mon. We're all going to the Springs for R and R. Guys only!"

You could say that Elvis had a double standard. While he loved Priscilla in the traditional sense, and adored Lisa Marie, Elvis had never really stopped dating other women. There was a time, after their marriage in 1967, when you didn't see many women coming around Graceland unless they were wives or steady girlfriends of some of the guys. Even then they fell under Priscilla's close scrutiny. But after a couple of years, Elvis's life returned to normal. And normal for Elvis involved women who were young, attractive, eager and willing. If a girl met his standards, and Priscilla wasn't around, he would no more turn her down than he would a fried peanut butter and banana sandwich.

I don't think you can say Priscilla didn't know what she was getting into. I know my mom has said that, and my brothers too. Poor Priscilla—too young to know what she was really getting into. When she found out what it was all about she tried to change things. And when that failed, sadly, she had to go her own way. Or so the story goes. But I don't buy it. Priscilla may have been young when she met Elvis, but by the time she married him she had known him for over seven years. She had been at Graceland for almost five. She had been trying to inalterably change him for at least four and a half. And he had remained Elvis, a man who found the pursuit of beautiful girls as all-American as Saturday football, and whose allegiance to his extended family was greater than to the conjugal couple. She had been resourceful and strong-willed but she was dealing with a man of boundless energy and determination. Priscilla had tried to change him, to restructure Graceland, to undermine and disband the tribe, and she had failed. If she was a child when she met him she was a woman when she married him. And she was no less a woman when she initiated her affair with Mike Stone. And in both cases, I think she knew exactly what she was getting into. Priscilla had her own double standard, and unlike Elvis's, it didn't include answering to the spouse or making things right or returning to the fold. It was an outright betrayal. Only Elvis didn't know it.

When Elvis was rested, the tractor and go-cart races, all-night movies, and forays all over town to find the perfect Christmas tree began. In a few days thousands of blue lights were strung along the drive, the tree was decorated, the presents and guests started rolling in, and the traditional Graceland Christmas was in full swing.

In addition to the weather, which was uniformly gray and dismal all month—no snow, no sun, just drizzle and dark overhanging clouds—two unrelated events dampened the Christmas spirit that year. The first was the absence of Priscilla, who kept getting delayed in her arrangements to come east. I might not have noticed except I was anxious to see Lisa Marie, to see how she'd grown, to play with her, and to show her off to Annie. Elvis wasn't moping about the house. He carried on with his usual high spirits, games, plans, and orders. But behind the happy mask was a melancholy that we all noticed. Of course a man wants his wife and his child with him at the holiday season, but there seemed to be more to it. He wasn't angry that she was delayed, or impatient, as he normally would be. He just glumly and nervously accepted it as if he had an idea of what was coming and had no idea what to do about it. The second thing was my wife Annie. She'd found she was pregnant, but didn't tell me, and then had a miscarriage. She'd been pretty sick as a result and spent most of the week before Christmas in the hospital. With some buddies, I'd tried to sneak a full-size Christmas tree into her room to cheer her up. But we were turned back and I brought her a small one instead. I was worried. Nothing like this had ever happened to me before, and I spent long nights just sitting with Dee and Vernon at home wondering what was going to happen.

Priscilla's arrival only brought more gloom, although Lisa Marie's brightness more than made up for it. Priscilla was cool and aloof to everyone, especially Elvis. Although she often smiled and made a show of graciousness there was cold ice behind that smile. At one party a few days before Christmas Priscilla was heard to say, "Well, girls, here's to 1971, the year that little Priscilla finally came out." When Elvis tried to introduce her to friends of his she gave them a smile that lasted maybe one-hundredth of a second before it froze. With lifted chin she turned away from them. Elvis grabbed for an egg-nog spiked with rum and downed it as if it were a glass of milk. The man never did learn how to drink!

By Christmas Eve Annie had been home from the hospital for a couple of days and, although weak, said she was feeling fine. We were all dressed for the evening but shortly before we were to go, Annie sat down on the couch and started staring straight ahead. I asked her if she was well enough to walk over to Graceland. She said she'd like to but didn't quite feel up to it. So Dee, Annie, and I sat down and started watching a little TV. I guess I was growing a little edgy—I hadn't missed a Christmas Eve at Graceland since I was at Breezy Point Farms—and I gave Annie a second look. But she seemed to be settling in comfortably on the couch. Then I guess I got more restless, because Dee said, "Billy, why don't you go? You don't want to miss

Christmas with the family and poor Annie just doesn't feel up to it.
I'll stay here with her and we'll be just fine."

"No, Mom," I said. "You've got to be there. Daddy must be pacing
around wondering what's keeping you right now."

"Billy, believe me. This Christmas I don't even want to. I hate to
say it but the air is so thick with tension you could cut it with a knife.
I'll just stay here with Annie. You go and enjoy yourself."

I looked to Annie to see if she concurred, but she only gave me a
slightly irritated look. "The poor boy's been sick with worry," Dee
said to her. "It'll do him good. And we girls can have a good old time
right here. We'll call them if we need them. We'll have them back
here in a jiffy."

"I'll stay if you want me to," I told Annie.

"No," she said. "You go, Billy."

I went. And if it was tense and strained you almost couldn't tell (if
you didn't look at Priscilla)—there was too much going on. I had a
few drinks myself, some good cheer, and now Christmas felt like *Elvis*.
There was one tense moment when Elvis was giving out his presents
and he told Priscilla that he had a new car, a Mercedes, gift-wrapped
for her and sitting in the front drive. "Would you like to see it?" Elvis
asked, rising to his feet.

"No," Priscilla said. "I don't want one of your cars. Give it to
someone else."

Elvis was prepared. He had told her he was buying her a car (he
couldn't keep secrets any better than he could drink), and she told
him she wouldn't accept it. So he reached in his pocket and pulled
out ten one-thousand dollar bills. These Priscilla accepted and they
embraced (sort of) while some pictures were taken and Priscilla
slipped the money into her purse.

Priscilla left the day after Christmas for L.A. Things brightened up
almost immediately. Afternoon football games on the tube were
followed by real games in the yard, usually until well after dark. The
passing game got interesting after dark because, although we had
floodlights galore, all the lighting came from one side. Receivers and
defenders had to congregate on the side the light was coming from in
order to see the ball in flight. The ball was then thrown to the center
of the field with everyone converging at once. Naturally there were a
lot of collisions and cries of foul and interference, but a few balls were
caught. Elvis liked to try to sneak a receiver down the dark side of the
field to catch the defenders off guard. Usually I was the receiver. The

ploy worked perfectly in that I was always alone when Elvis whipped a pass in my direction, but since I never saw any of them, they either whizzed past my head or, once, thumped me in the chest.

"Nub!" Elvis would storm. "I thought you could catch."

13

"NEVER BEEN TO SPAIN"

(January ■ May 1972)

A few weeks later Priscilla was back at Graceland. She only stayed a few days and I don't remember if I even saw her. Certainly I saw a lot of Lisa Marie. She was at our house the whole time, and since we had a new Christmas kitty she was well entertained. Dee loved her, Vernon doted on her, and I cherished my regal little niece, Elvis's heir and his pride and joy!

Though not quite four, Lisa had already learned how to use her exalted position to get what she wanted. "I'm going to have my daddy fire you!" she'd say to threaten a maid or one of the guys. She even said it once to Vernon.

"But I'm your granddaddy," Vernon smiled. "And you can never, ever fire me from that."

For a second Lisa Marie looked confused and then she threw her arms around Vernon's neck. "Oh, granddaddy!" she said. "I'm sorry!"

Vernon laughed and hoisted her up in the air. "Oh, my little darling," he crooned.

I don't know what transpired between Elvis and Priscilla. I only know that she was quickly gone again and that six weeks later she moved out of Elvis's house in Bel Air and into an apartment with Mike Stone. Elvis was devastated. He said nothing of the encounter and no one dared ask him. Whether Red or anyone else finally told Elvis what they knew or whether it was Priscilla alone I still don't know. But Elvis wasn't the same person. If he'd been moody before, the bad moods didn't last long, and then he was soon exuberant, daring, fun-loving, and in control again. If he was angry—well that quickly passed as well. But now he was sad. The people who loved him didn't know how to react, so we all tried to pretend everything was the same.

A few weeks later Elvis and Rick and the rest of the gang left for the winter engagement in Las Vegas. Rick was by Elvis's side virtually twenty-four hours a day, no longer as a rookie younger brother but as Elvis's confidant and sometimes, protector. Elvis's performances, like his life, became uneven. Sloppy and disjointed one night, tight and exhilarating the next. Not that the fans noticed. They thought it was all great. But the critics, always on the lookout for a downbeat performance, had their openings.

But even a down Elvis was more than most entertainers could handle. Tom Jones could come to his shows and there'd be oohs and ahhs when Elvis introduced him, but Elvis would go to Tom Jones's shows and after introducing Elvis, Tom would have to work half the night to get the audience's attention back on him. One biographer claims Elvis stole his techniques from Tom Jones! That's like saying Sinatra stole his phrasing of a song or Julius Caesar stole his courage in battle. This is not to put down Tom Jones. The guy was great. Elvis liked him and I'm sure he learned a lot from watching him. Elvis learned from other performers as well. He loved to watch Paul McCartney, Roy Orbison, Chuck Berry, and his friend, Jerry Lee Lewis. Elvis learned from a lot of people from Carl Perkins to B.B. King. Did Joe Namath ever watch Johnny Unitas? Did Joe Montana ever watch Namath? Today's musicians and singers are still learning from Elvis. And most of what they learn is that he can't be duplicated.

But Elvis was starting to get into prescription drugs as a way to get himself out of a funk and into a performance. He'd been using speed or "trucker's bennies" for years. It dated back to guard duty in Germany and later, getting moving on mornings when you just didn't feel like it. He used these when he was making the movies that he no longer cared about or recording songs the colonel had set up that he felt were not worth recording. Once, when we were younger and unable to stay awake at the amusement park in Memphis, he'd given Rick, David, and me speed so that we could enjoy the night's adventures without nodding off. He'd used speed to curtail his appetite and help him lose weight. He'd given it to Priscilla when he wanted her to stay up with him and he'd given her sleeping pills when he wanted her to relax. I'm talking about a few isolated incidents over several years. He used them more for himself, but he kept a close check on all of these through his ever-present *Physician's Desk Reference*. But that spring after Priscilla left, Rick later confided in me, he used prescriptions more and more, often sending Rick out to fill them. It was nothing compared to the drugs reportedly used by the other famous rock 'n rollers of the time. In fact, when I later joined the tour, most of the musicians who worked with Elvis were amazed at how little he used drugs. But it was a problem endemic to the profession.

Elvis didn't know it, but by this time Rick used drugs too. I did too. At Graceland one night Larry Geller came into the TV room while I was lighting up a joint. I tried to hide it, sure that I was in for a bad time. "Could I have a hit of that?" he asked. "Sure," I said, surprised. If it'd been Elvis or Red or Joe or Sonny, let alone Vernon, my ass would have been worse than the grass I was smoking. But Larry Geller, this guy from Elvis's generation, was doing tokes one on one with me. Being cool I said, "You've smoked this weed before." Larry winked. "For a few years now. I guess for several."

"Wow!" I thought. "You mean this guy's been cool all this time and I didn't know it!"

But if you'd asked me about Elvis and drug use, then I'd have said, "No way. The guy's still trying to get me to be a narc." But that February, it would turn out, stung by Priscilla's betrayal—I'm going to say it that way because that's the way I've always felt it, for family the rule always was you stand by Elvis no matter what—Elvis began his romance with prescription drugs. It was meant to be a temporary solution to temporary problems, but it would have a permanent effect on my big brother.

In March, 1972 they came back to Graceland but in April they were off again on a fifteen-city, fifteen-day tour. From that time on this would be the pattern: a few weeks off and then back on the road for a "butt-breakin' " tour. Elvis was a man in motion who could occasionally warn me, "Protect your heart, Nub," but more often would say, "You want to race your go-cart against mine? Let's go!"

By now I was only an occasional visitor to Graceland myself. Annie's parents had moved to Knoxville and she insisted that we join them. That spring we lived with her parents and attended high school in Knoxville. She graduated that June while I, after many transfers and other academic setbacks, was still over a year away from graduation. It was a difficult time for me. I was with the woman I loved, so I thought, but I couldn't account for or deal with her moods. Her mother wasn't any easier to deal with, and I didn't love her! Annie's dad was different. He had run the computers for the air traffic control center at the Memphis airport and when he got the chance, he'd taken a similar position in Knoxville, where he'd grown up. He was a super mechanic and he taught me a lot of things, mostly over the engine of his Volvo sports car, on which we labored incessantly. It had fuel injection just like the Mercedeses that Elvis had taken to buying for Vernon, Priscilla, and himself. Annie's dad showed me how it worked, just as Vernon had taught me the ins and outs of carburetion.

I'd practically decided that auto mechanics would be my career. Vernon had already told Elvis that this was my wish and Elvis had said, "Then we'll send him back to Germany. He'll study with the top Mercedes mechanic and he'll be the best. I'm going to see to it." (A year or so later, when Elvis took my brothers and me to the Pontiac dealership to buy us all TransAms, Elvis, noticing my absence said, "Now where's Billy?" I'd been in the restrooms but I walked back into the showroom just in time to hear Elvis say, "Aw, he's probably got his nose stuck in the grease of the transaxle, working on the car already.")

But being a mechanic on fine cars was just part of my ultimate goal. I wanted to race. This wasn't something I could tell Vernon or Dee (one of them would have a heart attack) or even Annie or her dad. Elvis knew, but he didn't know how far I'd progressed. Within weeks of marrying Annie I'd begun to sneak out to drag races with my '70 Challenger, run a few races on the drag strip (or on county roads— wherever there was a challenge), and come idling home after washing the soap-inscribed race numbers off my windshield. In Knoxville it took me a while to learn the ropes, where everything was, how I could get involved. In Memphis these things had been easy. But Annie's dad helped me. It just all had to be on the sly.

Annie and her mother had different plans for me. They saw Ricky out on tour with Elvis and thought about the fortunes and fame being acquired, and wondered why I wasn't with them. When I told Annie it was because I wanted to be with her, she turned cold. "You could be making a lot of money on the tour," she kept insisting. "You've got an opportunity to make money, connections, everything. And all you want to do is fool around with cars!"

Annie's mother echoed her. "Billy, you've got the world at your feet. Why don't you go out and make your own way?"

Once Annie's dad countered their argument. "The kid's going to be a great mechanic," he said proudly. "He doesn't need a rock 'n roll tour." But the icy stares he got in return silenced him. This was a household run by women and we both knuckled under.

"It's a little strange out there," I warned Annie. "Particularly now with Elvis upset over Priscilla. It's a lot of work and it's a demanding schedule. I wouldn't be able to see you that much."

"It's what we both want. Billy, it will open so many doors. Think of the money you'll be making. And I'll be there whenever you want me."

I had been considering it for some time. Of course I wanted to be with Elvis and had wanted to for years. But I also wanted to make my own living. Dee had wanted that, too, even though she knew I'd never become a doctor as she'd hoped Rick would. I wanted a relationship with my wife that was solid and unbreakable, yet Annie was practically telling me that the only way I could have that was to get out on the road. Maybe it's the best of both worlds, I thought. Maybe I can have what Elvis couldn't.

I called Rick in Palm Springs where they'd all gone at the conclusion of the most recent tour. I told him I wanted to come on. He was ecstatic. "Billy, this is wonderful. Beautiful. This is the mellow hit. Listen! What you've got to do is to call Daddy and tell him. He'll tell Elvis. God, this is great! Elvis will be so stoked."

"Why don't I just tell Elvis?" I asked.

"No. Billy, listen. It all works this way. Daddy's in charge of employment. Tell him you want to do it. He'll tell Elvis. Don't worry. In a few days you'll be with us."

So I called Vernon. "Billy," he said. "What about being a mechanic? You know you'll be a good one and you've got everyone's support."

"No, Daddy. I think it's time I made my mark on the road. Ricky's been out there over a year."

"Son, you could break your mother's heart."

"I think she's been expecting it."

Vernon was silent.

"Daddy, Annie wants it. Her mother wants it. I guess I do too."

"Son. It's rough out there. It's high-powered. You'll have to deal with a lot of people you don't like. And if you're working you'll have to deal with them straight on so Sonny doesn't have to. Rick's on his own cloud now. But you're going to find that there's another side to the job."

"Well, Daddy. I guess it's time I proved my mettle."

"I'll tell Elvis. You tell your mother."

Two days later Vernon called. "Son. You better get back here. Sonny's here and he wants to talk to you."

I went back to Memphis and for the first time ever I walked into Graceland with a sense of fear. Elvis was in the den with some of the guys and he acknowledged my presence with a look that sized me up and considered my qualities. Although he hadn't said a word about wanting me, I no longer regarded him as brother, but as boss.

"Nub," he said. "I've decided it's time you came to work for me. We open at Madison Square Garden in three weeks. You're going to be in charge of my personal things and you'll be security for a portion of the stage. You know how that works?"

"I've seen it, Elvis. I'm ready to handle it."

"Sonny and Rick will train you. It's important. You know there've been threats on my life. And this is New York. The crowd will be tough to handle."

"I'll handle it."

Elvis laughed. "I know you will, Nub."

Elvis playing the piano at home, 1968 or '69. (*photo by Jimmy Velvet*)

Football with Elvis by the sea, in Hawaii. (*photo by Robyn Stanley*)

Karate demonstration.

Elvis on stage, circa 1972–73. (*photo by Jimmy Velvet*)

The King on tour . (*photo by Jimmy Velvet*)

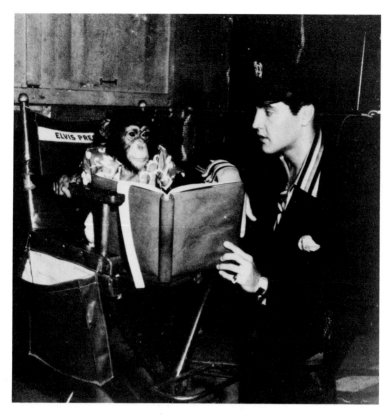

Elvis and Scatter . (*photo by Jimmy Velvet*)

Elvis and Japanese musical comedy star James Shigeta on location in Hawaii.
(*photo by Jimmy Velvet*)

The memorial plaque at Graceland . (*photo by Jimmy Velvet*)

Party days: New Year's Eve 1976. (*photo by David Stanley*)

After Elvis died, my brother Rick became a minister, and was
married. (*courtesy of Rick and Robyn Stanley*)

My brother David. (*courtesy of David Stanley*)

14

"PROMISED LAND"

(June 1972)

I spent the entire week before our departure running back and forth between Graceland and the Lansky Brothers clothing store on Beale Street. Beale Street was the center of the black community in Memphis and the Lansky Brothers' store was only a block away from the statue of W.C. Handy ("Father of the Blues"). As soon as I walked into the store one of the Lansky brothers would be there to see what I needed. "I'm here for Elvis," I said. But they already knew that. They took me around to show what they had in high-collared, V-necked, blousy silk shirts and I picked out several for Elvis. I was careful to choose those that had a strong elastic band at the wrists. I just made sure the jackets had high collars. When I'd chosen the minimum that I thought Elvis would need, they presented me a bill for over five thousand dollars. "Just initial it, Billy," a Lansky brother said. I got on the phone to Vernon. "It's okay son," he said. "You've held it down."

I was nervous about going on tour, and I knew that Elvis was nervous about performing in New York. He knew the people loved him everywhere and he knew that if he gave them a good show in the

Big Apple they'd respond the same way other audiences did. But New
York was also the media center. *Time* magazine had called Elvis the
"hillbilly cat," which he loved—he was a southern boy who moved
with the grace and ferocity of a panther—but they'd also called him
"revolting" and "slimy," and he didn't like that. He knew that they
could put him down, find an opening and turn a phrase against him.
So at the press conference Colonel arranged at the New York Hilton
Elvis answered their questions "Yes, sir," and "No, sir," as Colonel
had taught him when he was first in the spotlight and going on the
Sullivan Show or going off to Germany. But now he wasn't doing it
because the colonel told him to, he was doing it because he was in
control and he saw the whole picture. Elvis never performed for the
press, he performed for the paying audience. For the reporters Elvis
was playing an "oh gosh, you mean I'm a star!" routine. Then
someone asked him if he'd always been that shy. Elvis stood up and
pulled back the flaps of his jacket to reveal the $10,000 gold belt
buckle that had been presented to him by the Las Vegas Hilton
International. He looked slyly at the gathered reporters. "What do
you mean, shy?" Elvis laughed.

If the press conference didn't make Elvis nervous, there was something more foreboding that did. Elvis, like any major entertainer or
politician, had a deep-seated fear of assassination. The Sharon Tate
murders had happened very close to Elvis's Trousdale Estates house in
1969. Afterward Elvis had told me, "Man, that could have been me.
That could have been you. That could have been my family!" He was
obsessed with John F. Kennedy's assassination; he had videotaped the
Zapruder film of the event and watched it for hours and hours,
speculating about what really happened. He was shocked by the
Robert Kennedy and Martin Luther King assassinations, crying, "Oh
man, when is this thing going to end?" The fear that some lone
madman, hidden in crowds of thousands of fans, would find him an
easy target was one that he would have to overcome every time he
walked onto a stage. And New York, still an alien city to this
Mississippi boy, was just the kind of place that Elvis feared the most.
He couldn't shake the image of a Sirhan Sirhan or a James Earl Ray
suddenly stepping forward from the crowd . . .

A few days before we were all to leave for New York Elvis gathered
the TCB group at Graceland. "You're all security," he told us, "and
you're all armed. Billy, did you get your deputies' badges?"

"Got 'em, Elvis." I said.

"We're all legally armed," Elvis continued. "One thing that's been preying on my mind is what would happen if some loony got a good shot at me and took me out. I know you all will do everything you can to prevent that. But if it happens, it happens. The one thing I want to know is that that guy is not going to go around bragging, 'I shot Elvis Presley.' If he gets me, I don't want him to live to talk about it."

"We hear you, Elvis," we all said. And we all meant it.

I flew to New York with Joe Esposito a day ahead of the others. We were there to check out the rooms at the hotel, the hotel security, the limousine service, dates, times, and routes, and to organize the security at Madison Square Garden. It was a lot of work for one day but that's the way the tour was. Everything had to be timed perfectly, everything had to be in place. And then, wham-bam, it was on to the next city with the same demands to be met. Joe knew exactly what he wanted done and how to do it. Casual, good-natured, and efficient, he even found time to smooth out some of the feathers ruffled by the colonel, who was always the first advance man. I just watched and learned how a real pro takes care of business.

Within twenty-four hours Elvis and the rest of the tour would be there looking over the logistics of the whole operation, from checking out the sound equipment onstage to making sure Elvis had the right drinking water, his phones worked, and there was toilet paper in his bathroom.

It was not only my first official day on the tour, it was my first trip to New York. The only thing I knew about New York was what I'd seen in the movies and that usually included gangsters, killings, black and ethnic mobs, and high-speed chases. Chases I felt I could handle, but I wasn't so sure about the rest. When I saw the throngs of hawkers, hippies, winos, hookers, pimps, and freaks milling about outside Madison Square Garden I knew I was now confronting the real thing. I guess my first reaction was, "What are all these people doing here?" Elvis's four appearances had long been sold out and nobody was selling their tickets. My second thought was, "What am I doing here?" I felt the loaded .44 strapped to my chest and suddenly realized that five or six of us were responsible for insulating Elvis from all of this. This crowd didn't look like the concert-goers and fans who congregated outside the hotel in Vegas. I was scared to death.

By the time Elvis and the rest of the group arrived at the hotel I was numb. I hadn't slept much the night before, and from the look of Elvis when he walked in the hotel he hadn't either. I knew he'd been taking a lot of speed to get his weight down. He had ballooned up considerably during his spells of depression after Priscilla left. With the help of the speed, intense karate workouts, and a strict diet, mostly yogurt and greens, Elvis had trimmed down. Now the diet was apparently over. "Billy," he commanded. "Get me some real grub."

I went to the phone and ordered a large sirloin, burnt, with mashed potatoes, collard greens, and a large tumbler of orange juice. "Make that double helpings of everything and make it as fast as you can," I added. "It's for Elvis Presley."

"We've got the room number," came the cold reply. But the food arrived promptly.

After he ate, Elvis took a nap. I sat in the outer room watching the guys come and go, making their various arrangements, and I jumped to the phone every time it rang so that it wouldn't wake Elvis.

Rick came up to me and said, "How's it going, brother?"

"Great."

"I've got some news for you. We're a man short. You're in charge of wardrobe. Can you handle it?"

"Sure."

Rick left and I went over to lend a hand unpacking the forty-odd outfits Elvis carried with him. I knew that opening night he would be wearing the white jumpsuit with the gold sequins and the gold-lined white cape. After that—well, they'd just have to tell me.

In the dressing room in Madison Square Garden we got everything readied and Elvis went off to do his press conference. When he got back he took another nap. I was pacing the floor when I heard a disturbance in the hallway, so I went out. A crowd of fans had somehow made their way into the hallway but were now being restrained by Garden security. At the front were four girls dressed in the fifties style all the way—wool sweaters, long skirts, heaps of petticoats, bobby sox, and saddle oxfords. They had their hair swept back in ponytails and wore thick red lipstick. These girls were lookers. I mean they were beautiful! This was 1972 and these girls were maybe twenty, twenty-one at most but they looked and dressed like teen queens out of some record hop.

I leaned against the wall behind the guards, folded my arms, and smiled. "You girls looking to meet Elvis?" I asked.

"Do you know him?" one asked. "Are you with him?" "Can you do that?" "Who are you?" They were all speaking at once.

"I'm Billy Stanley," I said. "Elvis's brother."

One of them suppressed a squeal while the one in front pressed her ample, sweatered front past the guards. She was close enough now for me to smell her perfume, and she smelled good.

"We'd do anything to meet Elvis. Billy," she emphasized, "I said anything."

"Well, you can't meet him now," I said. "But come by our hotel after the concert and I'll introduce you."

"Really?"

"Guaranteed."

This time they all squealed. I told them the name of the hotel and told them not to tell anyone else. I said that we'd be leaving the concert immediately after the performance so they'd know not to look for us in the dressing room. I said, "Just come to the hotel lobby as quickly as you can after the show and ask for me."

"What's your name?" I called back at the one who'd first spoken to me.

"Paulette," she said.

"Paulette. Ask for Billy!"

Then I went backstage to tell the guys about these four chicks. They just laughed and said, "Welcome to the tour!" and "You'll get used to it," and "How are you gonna handle four women? You're just a rookie," and stuff like that.

"I can take that," I said. Someone said, "I'll give you two weeks. Then you're going to start wanting to go to bed by yourself."

"No way," I said.

By this time the comic, Jackie Kahane, was out on stage doing the warm-up. I hurried back to the dressing room, afraid that Elvis might still be asleep, but when I got there he was awake and sitting up. Ricky and Joe were with him. So were a couple of New York's finest. Elvis always liked to invite a few cops with clout to his dressing room, partly because it made him feel secure, and partly so he could ask them for badges. There must have been a breakdown in security or communication this time, because in a few minutes the room was so crowded with cops we had trouble getting Elvis dressed. And with the door pushed open you could hear the crowd, twenty thousand strong, breaking out into rhythmic clapping in the middle of Jackie Kahane's jokes.

"What's going on out there?" Elvis demanded.

"It's wild," I said.

"Go find Colonel."

But Colonel had already been sent for; he brushed past me into the room. "What's the trouble?" he asked.

"You hear what they're doing to Jackie? They're howling at him." Elvis was livid.

Colonel shrugged. What could he do about it?

Elvis started pacing. Half the people in the room jumped to get out of his way as he moved back and forth. "Well, fuck them. If they can't be polite, just plain fuck 'em! I'm not going to sing for them."

Now he had the colonel agitated. "Hold on Elvis. Calm down. Maybe Jackie needs some new material."

"They're just all riled up about your coming out, Elvis," someone said. "Don't take it personal."

"Somebody better do something!" Elvis yelled. "I won't stand for them treating Jackie like that."

Several people rushed from the room as if they were going to go out in the crowd and explain that they shouldn't make catcalls while Jackie was telling a joke because Elvis wouldn't like it. The colonel looked nervously about the room as if to solicit help, and then he went out. As soon as they were gone Elvis sat calmly down. He was just jumpy and had decided to make a few other people jump.

I was standing next to Elvis, yet he was speaking so softly I almost couldn't hear him. I couldn't tell if he was speaking to me or to himself. Then I heard him say, "Are you nervous, Billy?"

"Nah," I laughed. I must have been sweating bullets. "Are you, Elvis?"

"Not me," he said. Then we both looked down. Elvis had been fidgeting with his rings, something he always did before a big performance, but this time he stopped and just stared at his hands. They were shaking uncontrollably. "Not a bit," Elvis laughed.

We heard Jackie Kahane going off. Then we heard the theme from *2001*. Elvis stood up, clenched his fists, and steadied himself. Then he said, again almost whispering, "I always get this way before I walk out on stage."

We formed a ring around Elvis as we walked him to the curtain. My duty was the right hand side of the stage. I walked on his right, Rick on his left, Red in front, and Sonny behind. Suddenly the band, under the direction of Joe Guercio, broke into a rock version of *2001* and we stopped in our tracks. I don't know about Elvis but I know I had the butterflies going. I had Elvis's right arm hooked in my left arm. At this moment I felt his arm hugging mine. I looked at him and he was smiling at me. I hugged his arm until it went free and I realized that he was on stage.

From my post at the right I looked at the audience but no one was looking at me. All eyes were drawn to center stage as Elvis sang "That's All Right, Mama." The performance was under way! James Burton was driving his guitar, Ronny Tutt rolled the drums, and the audience exploded in applause. Occasionally out of the corner of my eye I would see Elvis with one leg shaking, caressing the mike, or leaping and tossing the guitar, or on one knee with his fist thrust in the air. Then, with the crowd beside themselves, he sang the ballad "You Don't Have to Say You Love Me" while strolling casually toward the front of the stage. It would be his pattern for the night, rock them, get them excited, then croon to them. And when he had them transfixed he would hit them with another hard rockin' song, like "All Shook Up," or "Polk Salad Annie." "This is great!" I said to myself, almost forgetting I was working. Then I'd remember what lay ahead, getting Elvis past all these people on my side of the stage, I'd say, "When is this going to be over? I just want to get through this first night without anything going wrong."

In the middle of "You've Lost That Lovin' Feeling" Elvis was singing, "Baby, baby, I get down on my knees for you," but his next line was "if this suit wasn't too tight!" That turned my head. But Elvis continued with the correct lyrics so I turned my attention back to crowd control. He'd changed the song and no one else seemed to catch it! But I'd dressed him and I had to wonder what hell I'd hear about that suit.

Again the crowd was going nuts. I could see that Elvis had them totally under control. I could feel his music. I was part of it. I realized Rick was right. This is where I belonged. And when I heard Elvis singing "Dixieland" to a New York rock crowd, and watched them eating it up, I knew he could do anything.

At the end of the concert, as Elvis was singing the closing song, "Can't Help Falling in Love," I ran over and stood at the bottom of the steps and held the crowd back with my arms raised head high and a heavy flashlight in one hand. As soon as Elvis took his final bow Rick and Red were with him on either arm, racing him off the stage and down the steps. To my amazement—I could not have held the crowd back if they hadn't wanted to be held back—the three of them passed right through, with me on their tail. The door to Elvis's limo swung open; Elvis, Rick, and Red jumped in. Vernon was waiting inside. I slammed the door behind them, making sure no fan had a hand where it could get caught. Instantly, a second limo was beside me, and Charlie Hodge and I jumped in. Within seconds we were on our way back to the hotel. At that moment I could still hear the echo of a voice on stage saying, "Elvis has left the building. Thank you and goodnight." I was amazed that we'd passed through so easily, like a knife through warm butter. But what if they'd been angry, I thought. What if they had actually tried to stop us?

Back at the hotel, Rick and I went upstairs and helped Elvis change. His outfit, which weighed at least twenty pounds, felt as if it had another twenty pounds of sweat in it. I asked Elvis how he felt.

"Great," he said. Everyone was telling him he should feel great, that the show was dynamite.

"Nub, you did good."

"I did, Elvis?"

"You had it under your thumb."

"Thanks, Elvis," I laughed. "I'm sure you were watching me."

"I was. And you made one mistake. When I sang that line about my pants being too tight, you turned. You shouldn't do that, you're security. Anyway, you handled the crowd. You put fear in them."

"They put fear in me."

"But you didn't show it. You handled them, Nub."

That made me feel great although at the time I really couldn't believe that on a night like that Elvis was grading my performance. Later I would come to appreciate just how much he was aware of while he was performing on stage.

I wanted to ask him about bringing the girls I'd met up to meet him, but as it was my first night I let it go. I finally decided to ask Rick. "Sure, go ahead. Billy, on a night like tonight anything goes."

I went down to the lobby and looked around but didn't see a familiar face. I stood around, paced a bit, and decided they were no-shows. I thought briefly about calling Annie. I was so up, so elated from the concert, that I wanted to share the excitement with some-one. But then I thought I'd probably just wake her up. I'd have to explain it to her. She'd be sleepy, I'd be high and unable to describe my euphoria, and she'd get cross. I wanted someone who'd been there and shared the experience. I was disappointed the girls hadn't shown up.

Just as I was about to get on the elevator I heard some screams at the door and saw the four girls rush into the lobby. They all yelled my name and came running over to me. I loved it. They were jumping up and down and freaking at the prospect of meeting Elvis. We went upstairs, and although the room was crowded with people celebrating Elvis's triumph, the waters seemed to part as I brought them up to him. I mean these girls made an impact. Even Elvis was taken aback. "Now how'd we get so lucky to get you girls in here?" he asked.

The girls surrounded him and asked him questions about his songs, the tour, how he liked New York, all the usual fan questions. Elvis answered every question, sort of mumbling, sort of shy. He was bringing them in closer and closer to look for acne marks, look for personality defects—to check them out in his usual way. While he was doing this he winked at me as if to say, "Not bad, Billy. And on your first night?"

As soon as Elvis said, "You girls are welcome to stay," and turned his attention to some of the more famous guests, the other guys were on them like dogs on a 'coon.

But I had my duties. From the first night one of my jobs was to be bartender at the gatherings after Elvis's shows. Elvis disliked having a bartender supplied by hotels, and although he ordered a full bar for such occasions, he didn't want the hotel's staff to run it. I think he just didn't want outsiders in his private rooms. I loved it. Doling out the usual gin and tonics, rum and cokes, beer and wine, and Elvis's Mountain Valley spring water (I don't think anyone but Elvis drank it—except as a mix), I met and got to talk with a lot of people. Some were celebrities. I think Gregory Peck was there that night, and Art Garfunkel, and George Hamilton. (So many parties followed, and so many guests, that I'm really not totally sure when I met most of them.) John Lennon was reported to be in the crowd but he never showed up at Elvis's party. (Elvis never paraded us in front of outsiders. To the press we didn't exist. But if a George Hamilton or Gregory Peck showed up on our turf, Elvis would always bring them over and introduce them, separately, to Rick, David, and me. He'd say, "These are my brothers," not "These guys are my step-brothers" or "These guys work for me.") George Harrison was there. Elvis brought him over and introduced us, saying, "George, this is my brother, Billy. I told you about him once. He likes you better than me."

I was beside myself. But my favorite Beatle was a very quiet guy. I tried to drag him into a conversation, in part because I thought the world would be watching, but mostly because I just wanted him to talk to me. I told him I loved his "Long and Winding Road," and his "While My Guitar Gently Weeps." Then I panicked, thinking they were both the same song. I flushed, kicked myself, and said, "My brothers and I are trying to get Elvis to do it." Harrison just smiled and said, "That's great." I don't know if he heard anything I was saying, but I kept talking. He had a gin and tonic in his hand but I don't think he ever really took a sip of it. There were so many people coming up to him it was hard to hold his attention for long.

Once in a while I caught sight of the four girls. They were well entertained but they stayed close to the bar and they had a uniform response to all offers. "We're with Billy," they all said coolly.

The party continued for another hour. Elvis was oddly subdued, grateful, and content. After all the name visitors had paid their compliments, Elvis let Rick know that he wanted to go to bed. He was exhausted.

I got his pajamas out, his books—Kahlil Gibran and Hermann Hesse were his favorite reading at that time—got his water, whatever he wanted, and then went back out to party. The room was still jammed and my four bobby-soxed girls were the center of attention. Rick and I figured that it might get too loud for Elvis if we all stayed in his suite so we took the girls down the hall to our room. You should have seen the crowd that followed!

We all knew the concert had been a triumph. But Elvis definitely also cared about what the reviewers would say. I've read that Elvis didn't pay any attention to reviews, didn't even know about them. He knew. Not about all of them, of course. We moved too fast. But he knew about the major ones. If they were unfair he was angry. If they caught him on a bad night and seized the opportunity to put him down he was upset. If they were glowing we never heard a word. Fortunately, this time we all basked in the light of a job well done: "At 9:15 Elvis appeared, *materialized*, in a white suit of lights, shining with golden appliques, the shirt front slashed to show his chest. Around his shoulders was a cape lined in cloth of gold, its collar faced with scarlet. It was anything you wanted to call it, gaudy, vulgar, *magnificent* . . . " (*The New York Times*). *Variety* said, "Presley is now a highly polished, perfectly timed, spectacularly successful show business machine. He performed about twenty numbers with supreme confidence in routines which were better constructed and choreo-graphed than the terping of most Broadway musicals." *Billboard* said, "A stone gas! Elvis has nothing really to do with time. To our everlasting love and envy, he has transcended the exasperating con-strictions of time and place." And on they went.

In our room, actually a duplicate to Elvis's suite, with my bedroom at one end and Rick's at the other, and a large conference room in between, music, jokes, drugs (mostly pot), bragging, celebrating and carrying on followed. "My God!" Paulette exclaimed. "Did you see it when he sent his guitar twirling and flying through the air and bowed to the audience while—who was it? Charlie?—caught it in mid-flight?"

"No I missed that," I said. "I think I was eyeing some weirdo in the third row."

"Did you see it when he raised his guitar mocking James Brown, as if he, Elvis, was really playing the solo? That was funny."

"I missed that too."

"The way he sang "Polk Salad Annie," said another girl. "I thought only Tony Joe White could do it. I resented Elvis singing that song. But Elvis did it better. Like no one could!"

"I could hear," I laughed. "I didn't see much, but I could hear."

As the night wore on my four "finds" continued to be the center of attention—there were other women there, but mine just happened to be the liveliest, best looking, and most sought after. Finally Paulette whispered in my ear, "I want to stay the night. Here." Within minutes I let the guys know that the others were fair game, or maybe Paulette let them know—by this time details were beyond my grasp. I felt like Elvis, having my pick before the others. I hadn't intended for it to turn out that way. I just got lucky. I did think briefly again of Annie, but quickly rationalized that she was the one who sent me out here. And she knew full well about the life on the road. The room soon cleared and Paulette and I spent an unforgettable night. By noon the next day she was gone and two days later we were on the road to Fort Wayne, Evansville, Milwaukee, Chicago, Fort Worth, Wichita, and Tulsa. I gave Paulette a tour schedule and the names of some of the hotels and the number at Graceland. She never called any of them, nor did I see her again. Maybe she was a model on a lark, or had a rich husband or even children. You never really knew anything about the people you met on the tour. Even if they told you, usually it was a make-believe story. Ships that pass in the night. Only we didn't exactly pass. In a way it all seemed like make-believe.

15

"LONG-LEGGED GIRL (WITH THE SHORT DRESS ON)"

(June — August 1972)

On the road with Elvis life took on a whole new dimension. It was glamorous, fast-paced, and seductive, but it could also be a grind. You not only worked for him twenty-four hours a day, you lived with him twenty-four hours a day, and you lived like him. It was a big adjustment for someone who had grown up with Elvis as a big brother, and it wasn't easy. "It's your baby," he would say when he gave one of us a job. "Now rock it!" For guys like Lamar Fike and Charlie Hodge it was easy. You do the king's bidding and don't ask why. But for me—well, I had some questions from time to time. Joe Esposito would tell us, "Elvis is thinking about [Priscilla, reviews, schedules, performances, whatever] today, and it's got him down. So don't mention it to him!" And I'd think, why not mention it? He's my brother. I'll say to him what I want.

But I soon found out differently. When you worked for Elvis you did exactly what was asked. No questions. If you thought you could run it better you ought to go somewhere else.

The job could be exacting and tough, and at times we had to put up with some unusual demands. Getting enough sleep was a problem in itself. If Elvis decided at five in the morning that he wanted a pepperoni pizza, you had to get some place to open and make Elvis his pizza. He didn't want to have to wake us up to get it. That meant one of us had to be awake and on duty at all times. Sometimes the tasks were harder, such as lining up a chartered jet to fly to another city or negotiating rooms and services with hotel management. These might be jobs for Joe or Vernon, but if you were there when Elvis wanted something done, then it was your job.

Looking back, I know that it was a supreme compliment that Elvis expected so much of Rick, David and me. We were still teenagers, but he expected us to act like tour veterans. He really never doubted that we could handle any task he gave us. And I'm not talking about an executive putting his children in charge of some remote company. This was the main act, this was Elvis's life, and he gave us crucial jobs.

There was resentment. We knew we didn't take orders from anyone but Elvis or Joe or Vernon, but some of the others, like Red and Sonny West, who'd helped raise us, didn't like our position within the group. Al Strada, who'd begun as a guard at the Hillcrest house in L.A., not only resented us being on the tour but didn't seem to like us in any context. Rick and I began to call him Al "It's not my job" Strada. Ten years later, after Elvis's death, Rick ran into Al in Memphis. Rick was excited to see him—you know, anyone who was part of the old days was special—but Al gave him one of those, "Oh yeah, I'm cool. Are you cool?" handshakes as he stared off at some distant object.

Amidst all the fears about making mistakes, and despite the rivalries that sometimes caused problems, I felt that when I needed advice I could always go to the same place I'd always gone—to Elvis. One day I told him that I was scared. He was running a high-powered operation, the most successful in show business. I didn't want to screw up and I wasn't sure I was ready for the job.

"Aw, Nub. There ain't nothing out here you can't handle," he told me. "Just go with it. Do it. You'll find it easy. You'll find out you're a nut. Once you find out you're a nut then you'll get along with the world perfectly. 'Cause everybody's nuts. Some of us just see it more clearly."

Well, I had always known Elvis was nuts but this was the first time I'd been exposed to the doctrine of universal insanity. Elvis, the seeker, Elvis, the man at the top of the entertainment world, and

Elvis, the man who could no longer keep his wife on his terms, saw being nuts as an imperative, and, as he repeatedly described it, a gate to pass through on his way to some higher understanding.

To me, Elvis was a hero. We were his crew. With him, we were heroes too. We carried guns. We could right wrongs. We took care of business. And we got the girls.

When we returned home the rewards were shared with family and friends. For Elvis the fairness and necessity of this arrangement was self-evident. It may be that Elvis's special position in the world prevented him from seeing that Priscilla just wanted what most wives would expect, and that he was dead wrong in his infidelities, no matter how he justified them. And it may be that the normal rules just don't apply to those touched by destiny, as Elvis surely was. He had a double standard that rubbed off on some of us who toured with him. Elvis was angry and puzzled when he'd confront Rick or me and ask, "What did Priscilla expect? That I'd lounge around the house in a robe, slippers, and a pipe asking, 'When's dinner, darling?' or 'Who are we meeting at the theater? Should I wear my white tux?' What did she want me to do? Who did she think I'd be? I provided everything for her."

He had given in to Priscilla in the past and he had given in to the colonel and he had given in to movie deadlines and what was expected of him, but he wasn't doing any of that any longer. Now, in 1972, he was giving the greatest performance tour ever seen. *Variety* called his Las Vegas show that year "the Legend at his best." He was carrying on a romance with a great audience.

My job as personal aide was to see to his meals—and his wardrobe, his books, and his privacy. As many people now know, Elvis's diet at Graceland typically consisted of southern home-style pork chops, fried chicken, ham, fried-to-a-crisp bacon (a pound at a time), grits, black-eyed peas, deep-dish apple pie, and banana pudding. On the road it was chopped sirloin, bacon cheeseburgers, Mexican food, and an occasional pizza. He had the chopped sirloin with a baked potato, salad, and iced tea for dinner; I ordered this combination for him every night for months at a time. The only variation was that sometimes he wanted roquefort and sometimes he wanted thousand island dressing. My main task was to convince each hotel's chef that the meat must be burnt, not well done, *burnt*. For breakfast he was more rigid. He'd have a Spanish omelet (made from his Las Vegas recipe, which I'd pass on to each hotel's chef with strict instructions that it couldn't be tampered with), toast, orange juice, and coffee.

An ice bucket with plenty of cold Mountain Valley spring water was always to be at Elvis's bedside. Elvis drank iced tea at dinner, juice for breakfast, Gatorade on stage, but only M.V. the rest of the time. The air-conditioning was always to be at the maximum, with the room as cold as possible the moment Elvis walked into it—or else he walked out. A humidifier always had to be in place and working, the windows had to be lined with aluminum foil so no light could get in, and cotton balls had to be ready for Elvis to insert in his ears when he wanted to close the world out. The phone system had to be set up so that calls were accessible to Elvis's room when we were with him, but could be intercepted in the adjoining room when Elvis wanted to sleep.

Rick did almost all of the talking on the telephone. If you somehow got through to Elvis's rooms, were somehow favored, you still didn't get him—you got Ricky. If it was the colonel or one of the boys, Red, Sonny, Joe Guercio, or J.D. Sumners, or an important member of the band, or Dr. Nick (George Nichopoulos, M.D.), or Priscilla, usually they got immediate access. But not always. Only Vernon and Joe Esposito had immediate access, anywhere, anytime.

Ricky and I and David, when he later joined the tour, were interchangeable. Callers knew they'd reached a "little Presley" and no pleas, cajoling, or threats could get them through without specific instructions. Billy Smith, Elvis's cousin, was one exception. He'd slept with Elvis when they were boys because Elvis would sleepwalk and needed someone there to look after him. Elvis always sought and respected his opinions. If Priscilla called because Lisa Marie wanted to speak to her daddy she'd be connected. But that was rare. Usually Elvis initiated the calls to Lisa Marie.

By the time I joined the tour, Elvis had been officially separated from Priscilla for four months. No wives or girlfriends were allowed at Graceland during this time, nor did Elvis ask us to throw any parties for him where he could look over the qualities of prospective young ladies. Although she was gone, Elvis was playing it by Priscilla's rules, just to prove he could. Of course liaisons were made, dates were kept, and life on the road went on. It just had to be kept out of Elvis's sight.

Not that Elvis had become a prude. A week after the Madison Square Garden opening we were in Chicago for two nights. Since we weren't moving on to the next town immediately after the first night's performance, Elvis had a party in his suite. After the guests had left he held a staff and musicians' meeting. At Elvis's direction we went over everything that we'd done right and the few things that Elvis thought we could improve on. At the end of the meeting Elvis said, "Well, there's only one matter we still haven't resolved. Nub, what's in those notes those women keep passing you? Have you got something going on the side?"

"Uh Elvis," I said. "The notes are for you." I was a little embarrassed at being singled out because the gathering, with both TCBers and musicians, was so large. That night some of the guys did have dates and there were a few lingering guests.

"Could you tell us what they said, Nub," Elvis asked.

I pulled a few crumpled notes from my pocket and was met with a loud roar of approval from the crowd. "He's got them!" someone yelled. "He's saving them up." "Read them, Billy."

Of course everyone on the tour had notes passed to them. But because I was security at the steps to the stage, where Elvis entered the world of the fans and where he exited, I got more than anyone. But now everyone was clamoring for me to reveal their contents. I felt as if I was on stage. But Elvis's eyes were riveted on me and I knew I had to go on. "Well, Elvis, this first one says, 'I'm the best cocksucker in the world. Meet me.' It's signed Sharon, room 1129."

Hoots and howls followed that reading. "All right!" "Encore," and "Read us more, Billy!" followed.

I opened another note, hoping it was tamer. "I'll fuck your brains out till they bleed," it read. Signed by Sweet Mary, room 706.

The celebration in the room intensified. Everyone was laughing and yelling and then they started clapping their hands in unison. "More, Billy. More!"

"Nub, are you blushing?" Elvis cried.

I knew I was. The heat in my cheeks and the tingling in my ears were a clear signal. And I knew it well from my years at the Harding Academy, when I was goofing off and teachers would call on me for answers and I hadn't even heard the questions. I hated it. So I denied it. "No, Elvis. I'm not," I insisted. "Let me read this one. 'I want you up my ass so far that all I'll see is—' " I gave up.

That last attempt was met by boos and derision from the gang. "Oh gross, Billy," "Obscene!," "Burn them!," "Eat them," and "Sit down, Billy."

I sat down, crumpling the notes into tiny balls in my hands. Elvis, again addressing the group, said, "Well, I guess that's wrap." But as everyone stood up to leave he turned to me and said, "Wait a minute! Nub, what *was* the room number on that last note?"

When we returned to Graceland in late June, Elvis was still not ready to date. George Klein, the disc jockey who had a line on almost every attractive young woman in Memphis, would occasionally try to bring young hopefuls to Elvis's attention. Elvis would watch the parade. He enjoyed that. But most of the time he just wasn't up to doing anything about it. Instead he'd call the tour regulars to meet at the pool and either discuss upcoming tours or just relax.

Some of the guys who had long been accustomed to the "no wives" rule on the road couldn't believe that they couldn't take their wives to Graceland. Bringing the wives to Graceland had always been a reward for the weeks they were left behind. But Charlie and Rick got on the phone to all of them. "No wives," they'd say. "No girlfriends. The man is hurting and he just doesn't want to be around them."

I was reunited with Annie, and when we weren't at our apartment or visiting friends, we spent a lot of time at my mom's house. I thought it was convenient because I was on call to Elvis a lot of the time and if he needed me for something it was just through the back gate and across the lawn as always. But for various reasons Dee and Annie weren't getting along. Dee didn't like Annie's attitude or behavior or something, and it was getting a little tense. Part of it was Annie's predilection for short, short skirts, then the hot fashion item with the younger set. Even at my parents' house, despite my objections, she'd always wear a leather or cotton miniskirt so short that when she'd pick up a *TV Guide* or reach for a dropped cigarette, her white underwear was visible. Vernon almost objected one day when Annie presented him with a full view of her backside. "Billy," he said, "I think you might say something to, uh—" But taking another look, he concluded, "Oh, I guess it's all right." I loved this woman but she was wild and she was a tease. That night I confronted her.

"What do you think you're trying to do?" I asked.

"What are you talking about?" she responded.

I threw one of her miniskirts at her. "This is what I'm talking about!"

"Why, Billy! I thought you liked my miniskirts."

"Not the way you strut around in them, in front of my friends and my parents."

"Billy, if your friends have dirty minds, that's on them, not me.

And if your parents don't like it, they just better get used to it because I'm not changing my style for anyone."

So things stayed tense.

One afternoon Elvis called over to the house and said, "Billy, get your ass over here."

"Why, Elvis? What's up?" I asked.

"Nothin's up. I just want you here. You still work for me, don't you?"

"Uh, Elvis. If it's nothing important can I take Annie back to our apartment first?"

"Can't you just leave her?"

"I don't think so."

"Then bring her."

I was surprised, and Annie, whom Elvis had previously excluded, was ecstatic to be allowed to come. She and Elvis hit it off right way. She teased him, he seemed to enjoy it, and for the next several weeks Annie was welcome at Graceland any time she wanted to go. She rode with us on motorcycles, hopping on back with either Elvis or me, and she was even permitted to stay for our tour strategy meetings. Suddenly she was accepted as part of the inner group. Even when nothing was planned, Elvis would call us up and say, "Nub, why don't you and Annie come over. We'll just lay out by the pool and take it easy." If I showed up without her, Elvis would ask, "Where's Annie?"

It was a source of pride to me. And it was a hope. Our personal relationship, since I'd gone on tour, had been hurting. I knew she only wanted me out there for the rewards my position might bring us and because she'd felt slighted when no one from the tour came to our wedding. She'd felt we were isolated from the main action yet having me in the main action hadn't done a thing for her. She wanted a taste of it for herself. Elvis's acceptance of her, at a time when women were generally forbidden, provided a considerable spark. She was excited and she was beginning to like and respect me again. You'd think her fickle ways would have begun to wear me down. Instead, I kept hoping we could recover the love we'd had when we were first married.

In late July we left for Los Angeles to spend a week at Elvis's Holmby Hills estate before going to Las Vegas. Memphis was hot and Vegas would be hotter, but from the house on Monovale Road you could see the Pacific and feel its cool breezes. Elvis spent some time with Ed Hookstratten, his Beverly Hills attorney, who was working on the divorce settlement with Priscilla. David and I also spent a lot of time with Ed Parker, working on our karate techniques. I'd studied with Kang Rhee in Memphis shortly after I got my driver's license. Elvis had said, "Nub, I don't know where you're going off to at night but I don't want you coming back here with your butt kicked." And Elvis had been showing me moves for years (I can't remember exactly when it began but I can remember Elvis kicking toy guns out of our hands when we were kids—we were amazed and delighted).

It was an odd thing about Ed Parker. He'd been in charge of Priscilla's education in karate, introduced her to Mike Stone, and turned her instruction over to him. It was obvious that he felt badly that it had led to an affair and the breakup of Elvis's marriage. But Elvis didn't hold it against him in the least. He knew it wasn't Ed Parker's fault. Elvis was perfectly comfortable with Ed around and grateful for his friendship.

Joe Esposito and I left a day early for Vegas to get things set up. Of course the colonel was already there holding press conferences and telling everyone how important he was. He had his crew selling records and photos and dolls and assorted junk. Furthermore he met with hotel and television executives and said things like, "Well, boys, that money sounds all right for my boy, but what have you got for me?" Then he'd slip off and indulge in his true passion, gambling, and let his assistant, Tom Diskin, take care of the details. As a kid, I'd thought he was a big shot as he strutted around with his cane, his cigars, his entourage. By the time I joined the tour, however, I realized Colonel wasn't really involved with what we were doing. He mainly got posters up, he let everyone know that Elvis was coming to town.

Joe and I had everything in order when Elvis and the gang arrived the next day. Elvis wasn't in top form. He was somewhat overweight from the junk food binges that had intensified since Priscilla's departure. But he'd been working on it, dieting, working out, and taking diet pills (speed) to get his weight down. We could see his attitude changing, picking up. Even his meetings with Ed Hookstratten over the divorce didn't seem to be getting him down.

He had even started dating the last week we were in Memphis. George Klein had introduced him to a local beauty named Kathy and he'd taken her out a few times and seemed interested. Two days before Joe and I left for Vegas Sonny took a call and was saying, "I'll tell Elvis," just as Elvis walked into the room. Sonny held his hand over the phone and said, "E, it's about Kathy."

"Kathy!" Elvis moaned. "All of a sudden I've got a flock of women after me. And that Kathy's the worst. Calling every day. I've got a show to do." He was complaining but you could sense he was pleased, and he looked at Sonny as if to say, "Well, are you going to hand me the phone or what?"

Sonny set the receiver down on the phone and said, "E, we just got word. Kathy was killed last night in a car crash. She's dead, E."

Elvis turned on his heel and went back into his room. He stayed there for two days and still hadn't come out when Joe and I left for Vegas. We even had some doubt that he'd make it for the opening. But, as always, he was there and he was ready for the show.

Our security system seemed to be breaking down. Somehow a young woman found her way backstage after a performance and got close to Elvis. She probably was just trying to touch him but she had long fingernails and when she made a grab for him she scratched his face. Elvis wasn't mad. Like most everything that was going on then, he just wished it hadn't happened. We whisked the girl away so fast that Elvis asked, "What happened to her?"

"Don't worry, Elvis. She's gone," I said. But he had this uncertain look as if to say, "I want to talk to her. I want to tell her that she made a mistake. I want to put my arm around her and say, 'That's all right. It was just a mistake.' "

I know that's what he was feeling, that there were a lot of mistakes being made but it would be all right if we all hung together. But that same night another mistake was made. One of the guys got into a fight with some "traildraggers," a group of navy pilots who landed jets on aircraft carriers. Our guy encountered them in a bar at the Hilton. Apparently they made some comment that our guy didn't like. He wasted one of them with a karate kick and a melée ensued. Elvis said, "Well, here's another fight. There's gonna be lawsuits and attorneys and we'll have to pay out some more money." Then he turned his attention to Rick and me. "And that woman shouldn't ever have gotten to me! Is anyone doing their job around here?"

Vernon echoed his complaint. And we had no excuses. Oddly, it was women who always gave us the most trouble. With men we'd just say, "Stand back please." They must have guessed we were armed and ready to deal with trouble, so they stood back. But the women wouldn't pay any attention. Try your deepest voice, Billy, I'd say to myself. Try your meanest look. Wave that flashlight. It meant nothing to them. So we'd get swatted and scratched and pushed and pulled.

Elvis was undaunted. He still gave the fans everything he had to offer and he still accepted their enthusiasm with respect. "These people paid to be here," he repeated to us. "They've got their rights. Just keep them from tearing me into little shreds."

Later that night Elvis's mood mellowed. He had a date with another girl he'd met that last week in Memphis, Linda Thompson. Linda had impressed him with her beauty and her wit. He coaxed her into flying out to Las Vegas. She had been a Miss Tennessee, and had participated in the Miss USA pageant. She'd gone to Memphis State and besides being smart and pretty she shared Elvis's interests: exploration of ideas, thoughts, religions, and means of perception. A lot has been written about how wild the after-show parties got. While much of it is true, a lot is fabricated. But Elvis participated in very little of it. If he was feeling down he went to bed; if he was feeling up he'd follow his onstage singing with hours of gospel singing with J.D. Sumners and the Stamps. That was his release, and Linda shared it. She didn't have to fake it, as many did. She loved it. Although Elvis would, over the years, hold to his belief that you only marry once, and you stick to that commitment, it was with Linda Thompson that he would have the closest and longest-lasting companionship. Elvis was now romancing her, putting so much energy into it that it made everyone feel good just to see some magic come back into his life. Elvis looked at Rick and me in his room one day and said in that innocent, gosh-darn, boyish way of his that he really never did fake, "I'm going to tell you boys something. This one's the real thing. And she's a virgin. I'm not rushing into anything with this one. You respect women like her. And you treat them right. And that's what I'm going to do." And that's what he did. It was his style.

Elvis saw other women but it was Linda's sense of humor and acceptance that made their relationship work for over four years. Elvis was also seeing Cybill Shepherd that summer. She was a young actress from Memphis, and when Linda wasn't around, Elvis had her up to the house several times. Despite her all-American good looks, great body, and self-confidence, she wasn't really Elvis's type. For one thing she dressed like a hippie. And she obviously had her separate row to hoe—her career—which was sure to conflict with Elvis's. Elvis liked Cybill and he'd loved Priscilla, but somewhere between the relaxed Cybill and the stern inquisitor Priscilla was a woman who could appreciate, understand, and stand by her man. That was Linda. And she knew it.

If Elvis's love life was taking a sudden turn for the better, mine was decidedly taking a turn for the worse. Annie came out for our first week in Las Vegas. She loved the activity and the glamour but she was a constant pain in the neck for me. "Billy, I've met these cool people and I want them to meet Elvis," she'd say. "Fix it up!"

"Uh, Annie. I don't know if I can do that."

"Why not? You're with him all the time. You sure don't seem to have time to show me around or do anything for me."

"I can do it. But it's got to be at the right time. When he wants a lot of people around him."

"Hey. You met my friends. They can pick up on any scene."

"Yeah. I met 'em. I thought they were hard-core freaks."

"Billy!"

"I'll do it. But on Elvis's schedule. Not on yours. Elvis just doesn't like people around him he doesn't know or can't read. You know that."

"Why is he so distant?"

"From what?"

"From me?"

"He's got something going."

"That Linda Thompson?"

"Yeah. It's great."

"Oh. Is it?"

"Listen, Annie, I met your friends and they just aren't to Elvis's liking. He noticed them. They look like druggies. A lot of people have noticed."

"Like who? Your mother?"

"Among others."

"Screw you! Screw Dee!"

"Annie. Be careful."

"And screw Elvis. Are you going to try to tell me he doesn't get high? I've been around him. He's a dope fiend. Uppers in the morning to get going. Downers at night to mellow out so he can sleep. Poor teddy bear!"

"Anything Elvis takes is prescribed."

"Prescribed by who? Dr. 'Feelgood'? What's the difference as long as you get it. Do you get it, Billy? Little brother?"

And on it went. I began to get the idea that husbands and wives could say anything to each other. We certainly did. But in between these encounters we also made some furious love. I thought it would all work out eventually. But when a week had passed and Annie was to fly back to Memphis with my mom, I was relieved to have her out of my hair.

Elvis had been having a lot of parties that week. These gatherings were held in the dressing room and in his suite after the shows. Celebrities like Henry Fonda and Rod Steiger (one of Elvis's favorites) were among those who dropped by. Elvis proudly introduced me to them. But because Elvis hadn't wanted Annie coming by, and because she'd have given me a lot of grief if I stayed without her, I hadn't dared stay for more than the first hour of the parties.

The night after Annie left it was different. There was a large gathering that included Raquel Welch. She was a knockout, but she was wearing jeans and cowboy boots, and she kicked her feet up on a table talking and swearing like a sailor. I could sense right away that Elvis didn't like her. He gave me a look that usually meant "Get rid of her." If she had been someone of lesser stature, Rick, David, or I would have shown her out. But as it was, Elvis had to put up with her. He was coolly polite.

When the room finally cleared we all went over to Caesar's Palace and caught the last part of Tom Jones's show. Afterward Elvis took my brothers and me back to Tom's dressing room. They had already popped open some champagne, but the party livened up all the more when Elvis appeared. Tom introduced me to his son, who was about my age, nineteen, and we hit it off real well. After a while the two of us set off and tried to hit every party in town. We finally dragged our tails back to my suite at about six in the morning.

The next day my phone started ringing. I'd really tied one on and I had a considerable hangover, so I just covered my head with a pillow and waited for it to stop ringing. It must have rung twenty times before I reached over and answered.

"Nub?" a voice asked.

"Yeah," I answered.

"Dammit, Nub! Why don't you answer your phone?"

It was Elvis! I looked over at the clock; it was just before noon. What was Elvis doing up at this hour, I wondered. I sat up quick. "Yeah, Elvis. What is it?"

"Nub, Tom Jones just called. His son never got back to the hotel last night. You were with him at Tom's party. Have you got any idea where he might be?"

"Elvis," I answered, relaxing a little, "I've got a real good idea. Right now he's sleeping in the other bed."

Elvis was silent for a moment and then he asked, "Did you guys have a good time?"

"I think so, Elvis. I can't remember. Yeah, we had a great time."

"Then wake that boy and tell him to call his daddy," Elvis growled.

The feeling of relief after Annie's departure lasted for a day. Then I missed her. After another day I missed her more. I called our apartment at odd hours and either there was no answer or the phone was constantly busy, as if it was off the hook. At least a week went by and I'd talked to her only twice. Once there was loud music and background noise that settled quickly when she found out who was calling, and the other time she was too sleepy to make any sense. I was worried and I'm sure I showed it. Sonny West took me into a Las Vegas lounge bar one night and said, "Billy, you look like E's thousand-year-old man."

"Just women problems," I said. "I'll get over it."

"Billy, you think Annie would ever get involved with anyone else?" Sonny asked.

"You mean those freaks she calls friends?"

"I mean someone a lot closer to you. Someone on the tour. Do you think that's possible?"

"No," I said. "Why do you ask that?"

"I just wondered," he said. And then he gave me a funny look but said nothing further.

While that conversation wasn't exactly comforting, I'd learned to accept Elvis's opinion of Sonny—that he was a blowhard, likely to say anything. Still, I was troubled. What was Sonny trying to say—that he'd had an affair with Annie? I couldn't believe that. Sonny had always been my friend. I wanted to ask Rick, the only person I could really trust with so delicate a question. But Rick had been opposed to our marriage, though he now seemed resigned to it and was even friendly to Annie, accepting her as part of the family. I didn't want to rock that boat.

Then I thought of my friend, Alan, back in Memphis. Alan's sister was one of Annie's best friends. I called him. "What's happening?" I asked.

"With Annie? Billy, I hate to be the one to tell you this but it isn't good. Man, it just isn't right. She's got some motorcycle gang from

Texas over at your apartment. They've got their bikes and they've got some black limousine parked right outside."

"Is she balling them?"

"That I don't know. They're living there. Make what you want from that. And Billy, they're doing drugs. It's really bad."

"I'm coming out."

"Billy! Hold on. You could get yourself in trouble."

"Someone's in trouble. I'm coming back there."

"I don't know."

"I'm going to be on the next flight. You let those fuckers know. I'm coming to get them."

16

"YOU'VE LOST THAT LOVIN' FEELIN' "

(August━November 1972)

I went to Elvis immediately. He was in his room singing with Linda and J. D. Sumners and the Stamps. I waited until they'd finished their song and said, "Elvis, I've got to talk to you. It's something that can't wait."

We went in his bedroom and I told him the whole story. I laid it on the line.

"This is heavy," he said. He slumped on the bed. "Aw Nub, this is bad."

A few minutes before, he'd been singing "Amazing Grace," and now he was hearing something he didn't want to hear. "I didn't want to bring you down, Elvis. But I've got to leave the tour for a few days, maybe a week. I've got to go back there and I've got to do it now."

"Let me take care of this," Elvis said.

"I've got to take care of it myself, Elvis. It's my wife, my home."

"You could be stepping into something. This is heavy shit. You could get hurt. Let me make some calls first."

"I can handle it," I insisted.

Elvis got up, walked to a dresser, and pulled out a .44. "Maybe we should all go back," he said. "Teach those Texas dopers they can't come into Memphis and pull this kind of thing."

"Elvis, you can't leave. But I've got to. I'm OK. Really. Let me handle it."

"You want Red or Sonny?"

"I'm leaving you shorthanded already."

"You armed?"

"You know I am."

"You don't want to pull anything unless you mean to use it. Unless you got to use it. You know that?"

"I know that."

"Nub, I don't want you going."

"I'm going."

"I can at least see that. I'll tell daddy to get you booked on the next flight out and to give you whatever you need. 'Course he'll be short on the money. You got any?"

"I'm a little short myself."

"I'll give you all I've got," Elvis said. Then he started looking around. I had to laugh. Elvis didn't know where his money was. He almost never knew. Rick had previously carried his briefcase but when I joined the tour it was my job. The briefcase that held his thick wallet, stuffed with cash, credit cards, badges, and IDs, was in a valise that also held his favorite books, some prescription drugs, and a fully loaded .45. It was sitting in the closet where I'd put it.

"Where's my money, Billy?" Elvis asked.

"I don't need it."

"Where's my damn money?"

I showed him. "How much have I got?" he asked.

"I don't know," I said. "I never counted it. There are a bunch of twenties."

"Take it."

"I don't need it."

"Damn you. Take it!"

I took half—about six hundred dollars. We woke Vernon up and the next morning I took the first flight out of Vegas. I didn't know it, but Elvis had hired a private investigator to follow me. He got him up in the middle of the night and the dick was on the plane with me. And Vernon had called Dee who'd hired another private cop to meet my flight—again to remain in the background unless it appeared that I would have trouble. Who knows who else Elvis had called among his friends with the sheriff and the Memphis police. But I thought I was walking in cold—angry and scared, but determined.

When I got to the apartment Annie was alone. She said she was surprised to see me, but I knew she'd been tipped off, which was probably lucky for me. Those Texas bikers would never have fled from me alone, but they had gotten the word and they thought they were dealing with Elvis.

Annie denied everything. "What are you talking about? This is crazy. Who told you these things?" she asked.

"We're getting out of this apartment," I said. "Right now."

"Where are we going?"

"To my parents'."

"Fuck you. I'm not going to your parents' house. If I go anywhere it's to my parents' house."

"You tell me," I said. "One or the other. You aren't staying here."

"I'm not?"

"You're not."

Annie had at least enough sense not to challenge me. The next morning I rented a U-Haul and we were on our way to Knoxville. She was silent most of the way, later warmed up before we arrived at her parent's home, and then was nice for a couple of days. But that couldn't last. "When are you going back to Elvis?" she asked.

"I called last night. They want me back as soon as possible."

"Take me with you."

"I can't. This whole thing's got to cool out first. This is the last week in Vegas, and everyone there knows you've been hanging out with bikers."

"What if I told you I was sleeping with Elvis? What would you say to that?"

"Sonny West said you were sleeping with someone. Was it Sonny?"

"Maybe. But what would you say if it was Elvis?"

"I'd say bullshit. And I'd say if you ever did I'd leave you so fast your head would spin."

Annie had this imperious, snot-nosed, smile. "But Billy, what if I said it was Elvis I slept with," she persisted.

"Did you?"

"No."

"I'm going," I said. And in a few hours I was back on the road to Memphis and a flight to Vegas.

When the four weeks of the Hilton engagement were over, Elvis didn't want to leave. That was unusual, but he was having a good time with Linda. He was also enjoying the attention he got from other celebrities like Leon Russell, Vikki Carr, Ann-Margret, Barbra Streisand, Wayne Newton, and Robert Conrad, all of whom regularly came by after Elvis's performances. Glen Campbell, Liza Minnelli, Gregory Peck, Kirk Douglas, Rod Steiger, and Muhammad Ali came too. Alice Cooper, George Harrison, or even Linda Lovelace (to Elvis's chagrin) might show up in the dressing room after the show. In the past Elvis had not quite known how to behave when celebrities and performers offered their compliments, but he was beginning to like it and feel comfortable with it.

We'd get the arrangements set and sneak Elvis into the theater where Tom Jones was appearing just after the house lights went down so that no one would notice him. Elvis would get to catch the whole show. He loved it. He was having fun in Las Vegas, just like a tourist. And he liked the people around him. He'd been taking Dr. Nick (George Nichopoulos) with him regularly. Dr. Nick was subsequently tried for his role in supplying prescription drugs to Elvis. He admitted prescribing drugs for Elvis but defended the charges by saying that he was trying to keep Elvis's drug use under control. He said he used the maintenance theory, prescribing one type of drug to wean Elvis from another, and substituting placebos for the drugs Elvis wanted. Dr. Nick was acquitted of all criminal charges arising from his supplying of drugs to Elvis.

On one night Dr. Nick brought along another physician, Dr. Wayne Flowers (not his real name).

Elvis came to like Dr. Flowers, and he decided to fix him up with a woman. That was easy. In addition to female fans and groupies, as they were then called, sometimes some of the guys in the entourage would line up a few of the best-looking hookers in town. They weren't just out there for the money, they wanted to be part of the Elvis scene too. And although Elvis would never touch them—he didn't need to and he didn't want to—he knew this was the best, or only, solution for some of his new acquaintances—those who were too timid or dignified or comatose to score off the abundance of nonprofessional followers available.

So late one night (which always meant sometime in the early morning wherever Elvis was) when they were all partying in Elvis's suite, Elvis told me, "Nub, get Dr. Flowers a lady. Exotic and willing. I want this guy to have a good time."

I got her, got the key to his room with the swift move of an amateur pickpocket, got her in place, told her to wait, and went back up to the party to report to Elvis.

The girl had a sweet smile on her face when we walked in. After a few moments, Dr. Flowers had stripped down to his underwear. He looked at the girl, and started jumping up and down on the bed singing "Love Me Tender." And all he had on was his skivvies. The girl didn't know what to make of him. Elvis and a few of the guys were laughing so hard that we fell on the floor. When we finally got out of there the good doctor was profusely thanking Elvis for his gift and boasting that he'd make good use of her. The whole episode was wild. Some of these doctors Elvis had were as berserk as anything I'd seen.

It was within a few days of my return to Vegas from Knoxville and Annie that Elvis had his "moment" with Ann-Margret. Of course they'd had a thing going for a long time, dating back to the movie *Viva Las Vegas* eight years before. Priscilla's jealousy and the demands of Ann-Margret's career had effectively squelched that. After Elvis's last performances that year I could sense they were making significant eye contact, subtle enough that Roger Smith, Ann-Margret's husband-manager and an actor himself ("77 Sunset Strip"), wouldn't notice though I, for one, could read Elvis's behavior. This was one time when Elvis did smile a lot. Ann-Margret wasn't even talking to Elvis. She was talking with me about Harleys and how much fun it would be for us to go out riding together just as she'd done with Elvis and Priscilla years before. But Elvis's ears were alert. He knew her words to me were meant for him. After only a few private words with her a rendezvous was set.

When they left, Elvis told Joe Esposito and me about it and asked our help in arranging it. Elvis said it was going to be tricky with Roger, who was known for his jealousy and was particularly suspicious of Elvis, but that it could be done. Roger was going to have to spend a lot of time arranging the stage, sound, and backup for a show that Ann-Margret was opening. She was going to try to slip free. Joe was to organize the logistics. My job was to entertain Linda Thompson during Elvis's absence.

The next day Ann-Margret showed up at Elvis's room. I answered her knock and told Elvis there was someone important to see him. Elvis slipped out with a word to Linda that he had some business to take care of. I spent the afternoon with Linda. If she suspected anything she didn't show it but I figured she had to know something was up—she was certainly no dummy. She was just a happy, accepting person, totally unlike most women I had known including Priscilla and Annie!

Afterward Elvis told me, "Billy, we just wanted to spend a few hours together. For old times' sake." A while later he fell asleep.

On some occasions Elvis would go into detail about his lovers. He said of one, "Man, did we have a time! She likes to be titty-fucked. She was begging for me to come in her face!"

Elvis was expansive and elated so I asked him which of his leading ladies from the movies he hadn't slept with.

"I slept with a lot of them," Elvis said. "I especially liked the dancers. Those bodies! I remember one who liked to make love under a baby grand. That way she could put her feet at the bottom of the piano and move her hips any way she wanted to."

Later that night marked the first time Elvis spoke openly to me of his drug use. "Dr. Nick's sedatives aren't working," Elvis complained. "Go wake him up. I need something more."

"Elvis. It's four in the morning."

"Wake him! That's what he's here for. That's why I pay him!"

Was I shocked by any of this? Maybe a little. Troubled? Not at all. Life on the road with the number one rock star had its own life-style and its own code of behavior. It was just what any teenager would fantasize—Elvis was living out the fantasies of his own deprived adolescence. What should he have done? Slept alone? When fairy-tale actresses and goddesses were at his beck and call? Elvis would have had to be a special kind of wimp to turn all that down. And wimp he wasn't.

After Vegas we went to Palm Springs to unwind. Certainly the pace slowed down, and the emphasis went from nighttime endeavors to racing dune buggies and motorcycles in the desert and lounging by the pool in the hot afternoon sun. Elvis usually didn't get out until the sun was well into its decline and he always had a book, on Buddhism, Taoism, Hinduism, or the Bible, in his hands.

In the quiet desert air I began to think of Annie in a gentler way. You know, absence makes the heart grow fonder, and all that. But it was true. Two days together and she drove me out of my mind. Two weeks apart and I couldn't remember anything really bad between us. Just a longing to be together again and make things right. So I finally called her in Knoxville to see how she was. "You okay?" I asked.

"I'm fine. Sorry 'bout those last days in Memphis. I miss you. Are you with Elvis? Where are you?"

"Palm Springs."

"Can I come out? I want to make it up to you."

"Palm Springs is off limits to wives and girlfriends. You know that."

"Can you ask?"

"I'll ask."

Actually, general rules were being broken and, although Elvis had sent Linda back to Memphis, a few of the guys had had their wives over for short stays. I asked Elvis if Annie could come out.

"No. No wives," was his reply.

I mentioned Joe's wife, and told Elvis that we'd almost resolved our problems in Memphis. This was an opportunity to straighten things out for good.

"No," he said. "No wives."

I didn't press it any further. Annie's response, when I got the nerve to call her with the news, was outrage. I tried to calm her down but only ended up getting angry myself. "Annie, If you're going to act like this I'm just not going to call you anymore."

"Don't," she said, and hung up.

David had stayed on after Las Vegas, refusing to fly back with Vernon and Dee. One day David and I got bored with the slow pace around the pool in Palm Springs and took off in Elvis's dune buggy. We roared through various local subdivisions and thought we were having a good time until we got back to the house and found the police waiting for us. Elvis smoothed them out, but when they had gone he lit into us. "Dammit," he said, "if you want to race that thing get out into the desert!"

That was all we needed to hear. We took Elvis's buggy out into the first open stretch of wilderness we could find and started attacking the sand dunes. Within an hour we saw Elvis coming out in another buggy.

He pulled up beside us, kicking up as much sand as possible. "What are you guys doing?" he asked.

"Racing."

"You got a track?"

"Out here?"

"You've gotta have a track."

"Elvis, we make a new track every time we go out."

"Wait here," he said. Elvis took his buggy out and ran a course, then went back and repeated it precisely. "See those tire tracks?" he asked. "That's our course. Nub, have you got a watch?"

"No."

"No? With all I pay you, you don't even have a watch?"

"I got one, Elvis," David said.

"Call it off, David," Elvis said. "Let's race."

Elvis took off with us right behind him. As soon as I got the hang of it, we were in front of him whenever I really wanted to be. But the object wasn't to beat Elvis, it was to have fun, so when I'd shown what I could do I pulled back and let Elvis take the lead. When we got our times down to the minimum for the course, we started trying to see how many variations we could do—dune jumps and spinouts— and still hit the established times. Then we went after jackrabbits. Elvis saw the first one, near twilight, and chased it. Then I saw another and took off in fast pursuit. We leapt a hill, came down on all fours, saw the rabbit darting to the right, and pursued. What I didn't see was a mound of sand surrounding a desert tumbleweed; when I hit that the buggy went up on the two left tires, almost flipped over, and came down to earth with a thud. The engine quit. Before I could get it started Elvis was beside us.

"You gotta watch out for those mounds," Elvis called.

"Elvis, I didn't see that thing," I explained.

"Nub, you're a great driver," Elvis said. "Good as any I've seen. But you haven't learned what I've been trying to teach you. You haven't learned to look out for the unexpected. It almost got you that time."

"Let's run the course again, Elvis," I said. "One last time."

"No. Let's head in. The sun's gone and it gets dangerous out here at night. We'll do it again tomorrow."

But we never got Elvis out on the desert course again.

David, after the two weeks in Palm Springs, dropped out of school to run Elvis's karate school in Memphis, and a few months later Elvis brought David on, first as a personal aide but shortly thereafter as his personal bodyguard. David could handle it. He was the youngest Stanley brother, but he was also the biggest, the toughest, and in many ways the most dedicated.

A few weeks later we were back in Memphis. I was staying with

Vernon and Dee, but since I was part of the tour they had a hotel room for me at the Howard Johnson's on Elvis Presley Boulevard where Joe and the others stayed, just in case I wanted to use it. I called Annie and told her I was in town and that I wanted her to come down. She was in Memphis for only a few days. The encounter was typical. We made up, made love, languished in each other's arms. Then I got a call from Graceland that Elvis wanted me. Annie wanted to come along. I asked, permission was turned down, and had to tell her she couldn't come. The next afternoon I told her I had a plan. She should go with me to my parents', where we'd be together when Elvis called to say that he wanted me at Graceland, or we were all going to the movies, or whatever plan he had. When I went she would go with me. That way she wouldn't be excluded, which I now believed was the real problem in our relationship.

We were sitting in my house watching TV and talking with Vernon late that afternoon when a convertible pulled up out front and honked its horn. Annie, recognizing some friends, ran out and started talking to them. I stayed in the house with Vernon. After Annie had been out with them a long time I went to the window to see who they were. She was laughing with a group of what I considered to be a bunch of low lifes. She turned and saw me at the window, so I went back to the sofa. Then Annie came in and grabbed her purse, saying, "Billy, I'll just be a minute. I've got to show them something." She grabbed her jacket and ran. Suspicious, I got up and ran after her. But when I got to the door I saw them backing the car out of the drive; Annie was just waving to them. So I stayed at the door. Then Annie looked at me and made a run for the car. They were waiting for her. It was all planned. Now I ran after them, as much out of anger as hurt, but they were already squealing off by the time I got out there. I chased the car for about a block, enough to hear laughter and a mocking, "Good-bye, Billy."

When I got back to the driveway Vernon was there. I bowed my head as I walked toward the house because I didn't want him to see the tears welling in my eyes. Vernon, who'd never showed us much affection, wouldn't let me pass. He threw his arms around me, holding me even though I didn't want to be held. "Take it easy, son," he said.

I just sobbed and tried to break free. Why hadn't he ever held me like this before when I was growing up, when Elvis was the only one I could really look to for affection and reassurance? "Take it easy, son," Vernon said soothingly. "Come back in the house. She isn't any good anyway. Your mother was right. She just isn't any good." I went back in the house and watched TV with Vernon. No call from Elvis ever came.

Within a week we were back on the road. This time the tour started in Lubbock, Texas, on November 8, 1972, and then went to Tucson, El Paso, Oakland, San Bernardino, Long Beach, and concluded in Honolulu with three performances over November 17 and 18. I couldn't believe El Paso could be so cold. The ground was frozen, and light snow blown by a high wind stung my face and hands. I wandered out of the hotel and took a long walk that brought me to the banks of the Rio Grande. I'd been thinking about Annie and how she was only happy with me when we were having sex or doing drugs, or having drug induced sex, or when I could get her access to Elvis. And I finally realized that that was all there was to it. I delivered Elvis or she got moody, angry, or went and got high with her friends. And that just wasn't good enough for me. She had used me, but my anger, I realized, made no difference to her. "Get angry, Billy. Play the fool," she seemed to be saying. "Then get me in with Elvis." I pulled the gold wedding ring from my finger and hurled it into the shallow river. Some Mexican kids playing on the other side noticed, and then looked away. I hoped that one of them would remember and look for it. The ring might do him more good than it had done me.

17

"I'M SO LONESOME
I COULD CRY"

(December 1972 ━ May 1974)

Back at Graceland for Christmas I had a lonely time. I guess I was moping around the mansion a lot and Elvis got down on me about it a couple days before Christmas, when I was just sitting in the den, watching TV with my feet propped up on the coffee table. Elvis walked into the room, took one look at me, and said, "Billy, get with it."

"With what, Elvis?"

"Don't give me any smart lip. You're bringing everyone down. Get with it or move on somewhere else," he yelled.

I got up slowly, turned off the TV, and walked back to my parents' house. About a week later there were a bunch of us in the living room at Graceland and I heard Elvis say, "Yeah, that'd be great. If some of us can get over our attitude problems." I realized he was staring at me. This time I stormed out of the room.

The day after Elvis's birthday January 8, we all flew to Honolulu to prepare for the "Aloha from Hawaii" special. It's amazing what the gentle shock of the tropics in winter can do for an attitude problem. For my brothers and me it was a week of high jinks, surfboards on

Waikiki, paddle-boat fights, football games by day, and cruising the beach strip at night. Elvis was dedicated to preparations for the special, and with the help of amphetamines, he had his weight down and his spirits up. He wanted so much to show Priscilla, his critics, and his fans that he was still the king. Elvis played to a sellout crowd at the Honolulu Convention Center, where my brothers and I handled security. In addition, satellites beamed Elvis's performance to fans in over thirty countries for a total audience, I later read, of a billion people. Ironically, fans in America had to wait until April 4 to see it; the show wasn't broadcast in the U.S. till then. When he sang the final number, "I Can't Help Falling in Love with You," and raised his clenched fist in the air, I said to myself, "This is the greatest performance ever." But I'd said that before. I'd felt it before. I felt it each time!

We unwound in Los Angeles. This gave Elvis an opportunity to spend more time with Lisa Marie before the February opening in Las Vegas. And it gave us all some time for karate practice. Elvis enrolled David, Rick, and me in Ed Parker's karate school. That first night Ed brought his friend, actor Chuck Norris, up to the house in Bel Air, Elvis introduced us.

"Nice to meet you, Chuck," I said. Elvis shot me a look.

Minutes later, in the bathroom, Elvis said, "Now, Billy. You're a white belt [a novice]. Chuck Norris is a black belt. When you meet a black belt you call him master."

Elvis had everyone don gis and he got me out on the mat with Ed Parker. Elvis said, "Go ahead, Nub. Show him what you've got." At that time, most of the training I'd received had been from Elvis, and in most of that I was just a prop for his demonstrations. I wasn't really even convinced the slow and deliberate karate moves I'd seen were really all that effective. So I decided to challenge Ed Parker as if I were a boxer. I tried five or six short, quick punches, all of which missed, and then felt my body slam down hard on the mat. Ed Parker had easily avoided my punches, and with a sweep of his leg had quickly taken my legs out from under me. The fall knocked my breath out. Elvis was standing there laughing. "Billy," he said. "That's what happens when you try to fool the master."

Over the next two weeks my brothers and I learned quickly. On the night before we were to leave for Vegas, Elvis suggested I invite the whole class from Ed Parker's school back to Elvis's house. We showed up, eighteen strong, all in our white gis, and started a tournament on the lawn. Elvis loved it. He took over as the head official and became the "instructor" himself, showing everyone his moves. When it became dark, Elvis invited everyone in and the class ended up sitting in formation, with legs crossed, listening to Elvis's ideas about a new form of karate that he was developing.

When it came time for a demonstration, Elvis said, "Billy, why don't you come out here?" Elvis and I formally addressed each other— arms extended with an open hand above a closed fist—and bowed. Then we went through some of the attack positions and standard defenses. "Try something different, Nub," Elvis whispered. This time I felt a little better prepared and I tried a quick leg feint and arm sweep that I thought he might not know. Naturally, I was immediately on my back on the mat again. "Ah, young one," Elvis announced. "I've taught you everything you know. But I haven't taught you everything I know."

Then Elvis brought David out and I was excused. David was a better student than I—one of the best in the class—and Elvis liked having him out there because it made Elvis look good to demonstrate his methods on someone even bigger than he. The students were more than impressed, not just with his skills, but by the fact that it was Elvis Presley patiently showing them. They were still going at it when I left to take Lisa Marie back to her mother's.

When Elvis had started sending me to pick Lisa Marie up at Priscilla's apartment in Marina del Rey, he asked, "Nub, are you armed?"

"You know I am, Elvis," I replied.

"What happens if you see some danger to Lisa Marie?"

"I shoot first and ask questions later."

"Can you do it?"

"Don't worry, Elvis. I'll do it."

But Elvis did worry. A kidnapping of his daughter, or worse, something grotesque like a Manson ritual killing, preyed on his mind. It bothered me too. Los Angeles was really the only place where I packed a handgun. If someone was going to make a kidnapping attempt, it was likely to be an organized affair with more than a couple of people involved. The logical time to do it was when Lisa Marie was with me. I was twenty years old, alone with a four-year-old child, and scared. Who knew what was out there, and how many bullets did I have in my gun anyway? My hands shook. But what I said to Elvis was the truth. I'd go down firing before anyone touched Lisa Marie.

Priscilla and I barely spoke when I picked Lisa up—just "Hello," and "Here she is." But in the car with Lisa Marie it was constant chatter, mostly Lisa's.

"Billy, can I help steer?"

"No."

"Why not?"

"You're too young."

"You let me steer at Graceland."

"That's on a golf cart. It's different."

"Why? Billy, it's my birthday on Thursday. Are you coming to my party?"

"We'll be in Las Vegas."

"My daddy too?"

"Yep. I think you'll be coming to see him there."

"When are we going to Graceland?"

"I don't know."

"Why not?" Every question and answer was followed by a "why?" or a "why not?," including her favorite: "Billy, who's your girlfriend?"

"I don't have one."

"Where's Annie?"

"She lives with her parents now in Knoxville, Tennessee."

"Don't you have a new girlfriend?"

One night Lisa had a more thoughtful question. "What does my daddy do for a living?" she asked.

"He's an entertainer. Why?" I asked.

"Because I've never seen my daddy work."

I laughed. "He works very hard. It's just that he does his work late at night."

But that piece of information didn't seem to hold her interest long, because when we got to Elvis's house Lisa skipped in singing, "Billy don't have a girlfriend."

Priscilla brought Lisa Marie to Las Vegas for her fifth birthday party on February 1, 1973. She brought Joanie Esposito with her, and both women sat coolly at one end of the table while Lisa Marie sat between Elvis and Linda Thompson at the other end. The encounter was a disaster. Priscilla quickly had Lisa on a flight back to L.A. No one had even touched the birthday cake. A few days later Elvis got word from Priscilla that she and Mike Stone decided it might be a good idea if Elvis didn't see Lisa Marie for awhile. She said she was concerned about the drugs Elvis was taking and how they affected him. She was beginning to feel it might not be safe for Lisa Marie to be around him. Elvis was stunned. He told us what Priscilla had said and then went into his bedroom. Rick, Lamar, Joe, and I sat in the next room wondering when the explosion would come. The door flew open and Elvis yelled at Lamar, then slammed the door. Then he came out again and asked, of no one in particular, "Where's Dr. Nick?"

"He's back in Memphis," Joe answered.

"Why the hell isn't anyone here when I need them?" Elvis demanded. Then he yelled at Lamar again and told him to get out. Lamar knew better. He stayed just in case Elvis wanted to yell at him again. Elvis raged and fumed and even Linda Thompson couldn't calm him down. Finally the house doctor was found and gave Elvis a shot. Elvis apologized to us. "I only yelled at you guys because you were here," he said. "But Priscilla! I gave her everything she could have wanted. And now she's taking my little girl and handing her over to that Mike Stone."

The situation helped lead Elvis into two obsessions that would dog him for the rest of his life: prescription drugs and overeating. Of course he'd already been using drugs and he'd had weight problems. But they were nothing compared to what was to come.

Elvis had another reported obsession. It's been written about enough, principally in Red and Sonny West's book, *Elvis, What Happened?* It was Elvis's threat to kill Priscilla's lover, Mike Stone. The notion was born of anguish and despair—and drugs, the prescription drugs that various doctors prescribed for him. And it was fueled by his love for Lisa Marie and the pain that separated parents was bound to cause her. For weeks Elvis was in a constant rage, quieted only by the soothing and comforting Linda Thompson and regular shots from the doctors. He would mull things over in his mind, brood, agonize, and often overeat. As soon as the shots wore off the rage returned. Did Elvis ever blow his top? Sure he did. Everyone does sometimes. But with him it was always an act. If he really wanted something done to Mike Stone he could easily have paid someone to do it.

"Boys, tonight we're going to drive to L.A. and kill Mike Stone," he'd announce. Then he would get out his arsenal, and discuss his plan of attack and his motives for revenge. We'd all strap on guns, get in the car with him, and drive out into the desert. Then one of us, usually Rick, would say, "All of this is OK for you, Elvis. You need your revenge. But think about Lisa Marie."

"What're you talking about?"

"What's she going to go through if her daddy is thrown into prison for murder? How's Lisa Marie going to deal with that?"

"Okay. Turn this car around," Elvis would say. The show was over for the night.

When Elvis thought about the dramas he was staging he was aghast. If you knew him, you knew he could never harm anyone. I was with him after he struck an employee who'd stolen from him. And I was with him another time when he accidentally hurt someone with a misplaced karate kick. In both cases Elvis was beside himself with guilt. He couldn't stand the idea that he'd physically hurt someone. He meant only love for his followers. He gave it. He received it back a hundredfold. That was the lesson my brothers and I learned. Today, Rick is a Baptist minister, David a speaker to youth assemblies. But they're just carrying on Elvis's word. It wasn't violence, it was love. It was respect. It was the triumph of care over indifference.

That February Elvis's rage subsided into depression and he got down on everyone. At times it seemed I was his main target. One day he walked out of his bedroom saying something about long hair. I didn't pay much attention at first, but he raised his voice and said, "I don't pay anyone working for me to look like some hippie off the street." I turned to see him glaring at me. "Nub, I'm talking to you!" he said.

"What's his problem?" I wondered.

Then I realized that he was treating others the same way. Elvis was down on Sonny West for being too loud at times and too moody at others. After a while Elvis wouldn't come out from his bedroom if he knew Sonny was in the adjoining room. And one thing about Sonny—if he was there, you could hear him. Later, Elvis practically had him barred from Graceland. Elvis said, "That's the one guy I gotta pay to stay away from me." Elvis was down on Red West as well. Elvis often said, "Red is anger." For a long time he admired the quality. But he was beginning to realize that eventually he'd have to let both Red and Sonny, and their anger, go.

Elvis didn't fire either Red or Sonny just then. Instead, he fired me. He had Joe Esposito tell me. It was the last week in February and Elvis had only a few more days to play Las Vegas anyway. So it didn't really make any sense, except that the group was going on to Palm Springs and L.A. before returning to Memphis and I guess Elvis didn't want me there. Why not just say that? Joe told me it was necessary to cut back on the tour group. Since I was the member with the least seniority . . . and so on. I called Vernon and said, "Daddy, I can't believe it."

"I'm sorry, son," he said. "You know it's probably just temporary, until we get things worked out. It's the expenses of the tour and the other money Elvis is spending. It's not your fault. But that's the way it is now."

I flew back to Memphis and Dee was glad to have me home. When we were all younger Vernon had never gone anywhere without her. Now he spent most of his time on the tour with Elvis, and I began to get the idea that things were not right between them. I found I was still on the payroll, and at exactly the same wage—so much for Vernon's monetary considerations—except that I was again working for Uncle Earl, which I could do or not do depending on my mood. Why was I fired? Rick explained it over the phone. I was bringing Elvis down. Everyone else treated him like a deity, jumped at his every command. Since the Aloha special he'd been eating his way to obesity on junk food. And I'd called him on it. "Billy, get me a pizza," he'd command. "Where are you going to put it?" I'd ask. "Not much room under your belt."

But it was more than that, I knew. The day before Joe gave me my walking papers I'd gone to Elvis, in my despair, and said, "Elvis, Annie and I are getting a divorce. I can't relate to her anymore. I don't want it. I love her. But it seems the only thing we can do."

Elvis said, "Well, Billy. That sounds like the best thing for all concerned."

"Elvis?" I asked. "Isn't there something you can do?"

Elvis shook his head and walked out of the room. Cold? I thought so. I'd always expected more from my big brother. I'd always received more. But our relationship had been running hot and cold since he'd said I had an attitude problem at Christmas. I realized that he had his own problems and didn't want to hear mine. He had his own grief and wanted to see bright faces, not my long and dreary one. What I didn't know was that every time Elvis saw my face he was looking at his own guilt.

I had only been back at Graceland for a few weeks when Dee decided to reveal to me our true father's address. I called Bill Stanley, Sr., immediately. I told him I wanted to see him, and he said, "Son, you don't know how much I'd like to see you." Within a few days Jackie Stovall and I had made plans to drive down to see my dad at his home in Jacksonville, Florida. Since we were driving my car, and passing close to Knoxville, and because I was a fool, I called Annie. I had this notion that if the two of us could get away from Tennessee, Graceland, Knoxville, her friends, and all that, maybe we could find a new life together.

She sounded all for it. She even said, "Billy, we could live in Florida!" as if it was her dream. The day before we were to leave, Elvis, Rick, and the whole group got back. I told Rick what we were up to and he said, "I'm going with you." Soon the four of us were wheeling down old U.S. 41 to Jacksonville.

Bill, Sr. was very happy to see us after all those years. We felt strange calling him "Daddy." Vernon had been our daddy for thirteen years! We embraced and soon we were all in tears. I know I was the first to mist up. Then Bill Sr. said, "You boys need a haircut." But he almost choked on the words. (If his new wife was less than ecstatic to see four of us camping out in her house she didn't show it.) Bill wanted to know everything about us. What we had been doing over the years, what it was like living and working with Elvis, everything. So the stories went on and on. He told a few of his own: about World War II, the battles he was in, his medals and how he won them, and his years with General Patton. As little kids we'd just known him as daddy. We were too young to have formed any notions as to his personality or character. Dee had later portrayed him as a hard-drinking, hard-fighting serviceman and war hero who never seemed to grasp that the war was over and, as a result, hadn't been much of a husband or a father. He didn't deny these things. "I did a lot of foolish things. I just couldn't keep out of fights," he said. "That's why for all those medals and all those years of service with Patton I never made more than sergeant. That's why Vernon Presley, of all people, had more pull with my C.O. than I did. 'Course you kids didn't know anything about all this. You were pulled away from me and I was pulled away from you and there wasn't anything any of us could have done. But for years I've thought, 'I just wanted the chance to spend more time with my sons.' Well, I guess I'm finally getting a little of that now."

Bill was good to us but he always referred to both Elvis and Vernon as "Presley." "What's Presley doing now?" he'd ask. "Has he still got the world buffaloed?" He called Vernon a "chicken-shit," and said, "He wasn't much of a man." That didn't set well with me. He also told us how he'd been trying to cut down on the drinking over the years, but we didn't see any sign of that. Bill drank heavily, but Rick, Jackie, and I were right in there with him.

Annie drank, too, but preferred coaxing uppers and downers out of me. I had some left over from the tour. We had been in Florida for three days when she told me she was going to take the opportunity to visit an aunt and a cousin across the state line in Georgia. She said she'd be back in a few days.

After about a week Rick and Jackie decided it was time they got back to Memphis. That night I got a call from Annie. I asked her where she was and she said, "Knoxville. Billy, I'm just calling to let you know that our divorce has come through. It's final."

"That's great," I said. I hung up. It was just like Annie, I thought. Devious. She couldn't say she was leaving Florida and going home. She hadn't even told me she'd filed for a divorce. But nothing she could do would surprise me anymore. Nor hurt me. That, at least, was over. I made my way back to Memphis.

From mid-April to mid-July I worked at Graceland with Uncle Earl, enthusiastically at times, lackadaisically at others, more or less as I always had, but always with the expectation that Elvis would soon return, or that I'd be called to rejoin the group. But the months went by. Spring turned to hot summer, and outside of the staff, the mansion was deserted. The Fourth of July went by without the customary fireworks display and fights. Finally Elvis returned on July 21.

Now he had a recording gig for RCA, not in the hated Nashville but at Graceland. The sessions did not go well. There were musicians and soundmen and RCA executives all over the house, but Elvis, at least thirty pounds overweight by this time, stayed in his room. When he came down to the impromptu studio the recording engineers set up he was unprepared at best, and usually belligerent. Somehow they made an album of it. Elvis was still Elvis. RCA was still happy with what they could get from him, musically, and I was still happy just being with him.

That summer Jackie Stovall and I got involved in fast bikes. First I got a Honda 750 and then Jackie got a Kawasaki 900, the first we knew about in all of Memphis. We'd go riding with Elvis with him astride one of those heavy Harleys, and even though we knew how much he'd hate it, we'd pull out of the pack and blast past him. Jackie and I just poured down the highway and none of those guys on their Harleys and Triumphs could keep up with us. We'd cut back and Elvis would glare at us. He'd say, "Now you two settle down and stay back there." We knew "the wild one" couldn't stand for us to break ranks so we'd move back in the pack—for awhile. But we had too much power going for us; we'd turn the throttle again and in seconds we'd be right up with Elvis. Elvis would turn to look at us and say, "What the hell are you doing here?" and wave us back again.

Elvis got to hate those Japanese bikes. They were just too fast, but he hated to admit it. He liked the image of the Harley. (In the movie *Roustabout*, they had him riding a Honda 350. Elvis couldn't believe they couldn't come up with a bigger bike for the role.) One time Jackie and I were racing our bikes up and down the driveway at Graceland, doing wheelies and just tearing up. We stopped at the front stairs to talk to Al Strada and a couple of the guys but kept the throttles gunning. With open 'headers those bikes could scream! Someone threw open a window on the second floor and started yelling, but with those big engines going we couldn't even hear it at first. Then we looked up and saw Elvis beside himself. "Cut those Jap-f—— bikes off!" he roared. We cut the engines and coasted down to the gate before driving off. A few days later I saw Elvis preparing to go for a ride. I looked at him to ask, am I included? Elvis brushed past me mumbling, "No Jap bikes today."

Elvis was giving me little jobs around like going to the film transit to pick up the films he'd ordered and deliver them to the Memphian theater. One day a local Harley dealer appeared with an all-white Harley that Elvis had specially ordered. I was watching TV with Elvis but I heard them outside so I went to the window and saw them bring the thing up. It was a custom chopper like the kind Peter Fonda had in *Easy Rider*, except that this one was brand new and the chrome just glistened. Vernon met them and signed for it, but I could see that they were waiting for Elvis to come out and inspect it so I went back and told him about it.

"Not now, Nub," Elvis said. "You take care of it."

"Daddy's out there. He'll take care of the paperwork. But don't you want to see it?"

Elvis was watching *Thunder Road*, a favorite movie of his that starred Robert Mitchum, one of Elvis's heroes, as an old-time renegade, butt-kicking, hillbilly rumrunner who was turning his business over to his son. In the movie the part of the son was played by Jim Mitchum, Robert's son. It was a part that Elvis had wanted. He had Lamar try to land it for him, despite the colonel's objections that Elvis should always be the star. But Colonel had somehow managed to prevent it. Now Elvis was more interested in critiquing young Mitchum's performance than his new Harley. I went out to look at it. It wasn't a pure white but rather an off-white snakeskin bordered with a thin red trim. It was beautiful. It had everything. I could just see myself leaning back and riding, experiencing the pure, pure speed. I loved that bike.

The crowd that had gathered for the presentation to Elvis realized that he wasn't going to appear and finally, disappointed, left. I went back in. The movie ended and Elvis mumbled, "I could have had that part. Fucking Colonel!"

"Elvis," I said. "Let's go look at your new bike."

We went out together. Elvis seemed pleased. He started it up and drove it several times around the driveway, checking out its power and handling. God, he looked great on it. Then he let me try it a few times. "How does it compare to your Jap bikes?" Elvis asked.

"Elvis, it's beautiful" was all I could say.

"Then it's yours," he said.

"What?"

"You like it?"

"I love it."

"It's yours. Tell Daddy to sign over the title."

"Elvis, this is the one you've been dreaming about. I can't take it."

"It's yours. I want you to have a real Harley. The best. Now you've got it."

Elvis went back inside to watch TV, and although I was dying to take my new Harley out on the road I followed him in and watched TV with him. It was the first time in months that I didn't get the feeling that Elvis was uncomfortable with me around, or was just barely tolerating me. We spent a quiet afternoon together with no one else around. Hearing Elvis comment on some actor or laugh at some scene in a movie gave me as much pleasure as that big, beautiful Harley ever could. Elvis told me about his close brushes with death, including the time he was sitting in a jeep on guard duty in Germany. "I was freezing my balls off in that jeep," he said. "So I got the idea to start the engine and wrap my poncho over the top to hold the heat in. But I forgot about the carbon monoxide! Man, that is foul stuff! And it made me so dizzy and so sleepy so fast—it almost got me." Another time, Elvis was filming *Easy Come, Easy Go*, in which he played a frogman. After a dive he'd taken off his mask and tank but was still wearing his weight belt. "I got to clowning around on the boat, wrestling with this guy, and I slipped and fell over. Nub, those weights were doing just what they were supposed to do. They were pulling me down. But I didn't have no air to breathe. And that belt wasn't easy to get off. All I could think was, 'This is it!'—nothing intelligent, no flashbacks, just, 'This is it.' I got that damn belt off but it took forever to get back to the surface. When I got there I thought, 'Elvis will live another day. How sweet it is.' "

That day I began to feel that whatever it was that I had done to get in Elvis's doghouse must have finally been forgiven and forgotten. But when they all left for Vegas that August, not a word was said to me. So I didn't ask. I just watched them fly off, wondering why I was no longer a part of it.

That fall Rick and I took an apartment across the street from the high school. I'd already decided to do it because I wanted to be independent and, still on the payroll, I was making more than enough money. Just before they left for Vegas, Rick told me he wanted in too. Elvis had no tours scheduled for the rest of the year, only recording sessions. They were due back to Memphis the first week in September and life at our home on Dolan Street had become a little tense.

Vernon was making an unconscious choice between Dee and Elvis. And his strongest allegiance was to his son. When we were younger Vernon only occasionally went to a movie set or a concert performance, always taking Dee. If it was summer, a holiday, or only a few days off from school, we went too. Now he was on the road every time Elvis was. Dee never went and didn't want to. For the last year or more, when Vernon came home it was to sleep in a separate bedroom. The rest of their relationship varied from cool to icy. Vernon had begun to date on the road and to have regular girlfriends. I knew about it; Rick knew about it. But we worked for Elvis and for Vernon and as TCBers we were bound to a code of mutual protection. We never said a word to Dee. We were loyal to Vernon and the group. But weren't we also being disloyal to our mother? To avoid answering that question we felt more comfortable living in our own apartment.

I leased the apartment while Rick was in Vegas. When I told him over the phone that I'd taken a place directly across from Hillcrest High it broke him up. "This will blow some minds," he exclaimed. "That's our senior class across the street from us. We started high school with those people."

"Seems hard to believe, doesn't it?" I said. Actually, he didn't quite have it right. I was now twenty, had toured with Elvis for seven months, and had been married and divorced. My senior class, and Rick's, had graduated the previous June. However, David's class, and many of the girls we'd all known, were still in school.

"Well, you know what Elvis would say, don't you?"

"Yeah," I answered. "He'd say, 'When I was your age I was a millionaire.' "

When Elvis came home it was only for a few days, so Rick barely had a chance to see the apartment. Then they flew back out to Los Angeles, on to Palm Springs for a couple of weeks, and then back to L.A. where Elvis's divorce became final on October 9, 1973. When Elvis got back to Memphis a few days later he didn't look good. He must have felt as bad as he looked because a few days later he checked himself into Baptist Memorial Hospital. He stayed there for three weeks.

He was there to dry out from abuse of prescription drugs. Of course I didn't know that at the time. I accepted the "exhaustion" story fed to the press. But drugs? No way. Not Elvis. I wasn't naive. I'd been on tour. I'd seen and experienced what drug abuse was all about. I knew he'd had a difficult divorce and that he was getting shots from the tour doctors. However, I associated drug abuse with street drugs, the kind Rick and I and everyone else our age were into, the kind of drugs that Elvis so vehemently opposed. If you'd asked me what Elvis was, in terms of his character, I'd have said, "Great. Wholesome." Nothing at that time could change my image of my older brother. I visited him at the hospital. After a few days there he looked relaxed and handsome, like the Elvis of old. He had Linda Thompson there with him—even made her sleep in the next bed and wear a hospital "nightie" like him. And when he saw me he said, "Hi, Nub. What did you bring me?"

"Uh, Elvis. Was I supposed to bring you something?" Apparently every friend was supposed to bring him something forbidden, from caramel popcorn balls to Valium. But I didn't know that.

Elvis was finally acknowledging his problem with prescription drugs. Rick and I were a different story. We were into street drugs. After a relatively quiet month by myself at the apartment, Rick's arrival ushered in a new age of upheaval. I've heard since that the attendance office at Hillcrest High checked the license plates of the cars parked outside our apartment against the unexcused absences that day. It makes sense. We constantly had one party ending or another starting. Our sound system blared out the Beatles, the Doors, the Rolling Stones, acid rock, even occasionally an Elvis tune. A good friend recently recalled her memories of those parties: "Your 'bong' pipe for pot and hashish, Columbian grass, music, constantly music, and Dee on the phone calling us girls bitches."

During one party I got a call that Elvis wanted me up at Graceland for something. I got on the custom white Harley and had driven about halfway there when I came to a red light. I had been doing Quaaludes and a lot of alcohol. I could see that there was a cop car behind me. So I said to myself, "Now, Billy, just take it slow and easy." So I eased up to this light, pulled to a gentle stop—and toppled over on my side. I'd forgotten to put my foot down! It was something out of "Laugh-In." The cops were all over me. But when I pulled my helmet off one of them recognized me and said, "Oh shit! It's a little Presley." Then they made me walk a line, which I managed, and touch my finger to my nose, and asked me where I was going.

"Graceland," I said.

"We're going to follow you," one of them said. "Just to see if you can get there."

I got there all right, and remembered to put one foot down when I came to a stop at the gate. Uncle Harold, seeing my escort, smiled as he opened the gate for me.

"You guys want to come in?" I called over my shoulder. "Elvis is dying to meet you."

"That's all right, Billy," they called after me. "Another time."

Elvis was waiting as I came through the door. "What was that all about?" he asked. He'd been watching the gate through one of the monitors in his room.

"It was nothing, Elvis. They just wanted to hassle me because of the bike. What did you want me for?"

"Just wait downstairs," Elvis said, seeming to forget he'd called for me. "I'll let you know in awhile."

I went down to the familiar TV room, started to watch a movie, and fell asleep. I didn't hear from Elvis again that night.

Elvis had had TV cameras installed everywhere at Graceland, in all the rooms, at the gate, and at various places on the grounds. All of these fed back to a group of TV monitors in his room. Why Elvis wanted them has always remained a mystery to me. But they were there. There was also a beeper system by which security let Elvis know that something was going on. One night I was watching TV with Elvis in the den when his beeper went off. Apparently there was a ruckus down by the front gate. Elvis said, "C'mon, Nub," and we ran up to his room. On the screen we could see that it was Jerry Lee Lewis. He was drunk, demanding to be let through the gates. Uncle Harold, who'd already signaled us, called up to Graceland on the intercom and Elvis said, "Tell him I'm not here." There was more commotion and I went to a front window to watch it. Jerry Lee Lewis was down at the front gates screaming at the top of his lungs. "Hey, big shot!" he yelled. "I know you're there. Open these goddammed gates! You fucking big shot." Then he got in his car and appeared to leave, only to come driving back at full speed. He rammed his car into the gates, putting quite a dent into them and smashing in the front of his car. He got out and continued yelling for a few minutes. Uncle Harold must have told him that the police were on the way, because he suddenly got back in the car, somehow extricated it from the gate, and went flying down the road with tires squealing and metal dragging.

Elvis and I watched the whole thing on the monitor in his room and then we went back to the den. "That Jerry Lee," Elvis said softly. "The man has so much talent he could do anything he wants to do. Instead he poisons himself with drugs and alcohol. The man just doesn't understand how he's hurting himself. It's such a waste."

The TV monitor system must have been installed so that Elvis could be sure everyone was doing his job and had it under control. Of course some insubordination was unavoidable. One afternoon, Jackie and I were downstairs shooting pool and we just somehow got the feeling that Elvis was up in his room watching us. All of a sudden we both turned and "flipped a bird" at the monitor. Elvis also had this bell in his room. When he wanted something he'd hit it and someone would go up to see what he wanted. No sooner had we given Elvis the bird than that bell started clanging like crazy. We decided to ignore it and went outside in a hurry to ride our bikes.

Weeks went by. Christmas of 1973 was a cold and dreary event at Graceland. No snow—maybe a wet rain. Linda Thompson, a saint in my opinion, was there with Elvis. Lisa Marie was flown in, the trees were decorated, and stockings were hung, but Elvis's heart just wasn't there. Not really. We all waited for him to lead us in Christmas carols, or tell a biblical story about the season, or get angry about something, or get us excited with some unpredictable but typically Elvis act. None of this happened. The New Year's party was worse. Elvis and Linda made a fifteen-minute appearance and then retreated to Elvis's room. At midnight some of the TCBers made toasts to the monitors in hopes Elvis would be watching. And the January eighth birthday party—never a big deal—was eliminated completely.

Elvis was getting into racquetball. As always with Elvis and any new undertaking, it was a total commitment. Soon a racquetball court was under construction at Graceland. He still watched football religiously, and we had a few games in the yard, as well as karate tournaments. But the games lacked the spontaneity and fun they'd had in earlier years, when they could go all day and long after it got dark. "That's it guys," he would say when something went against him. "Game's over." Often he would get hurt—jam a finger, hurt his knee, crash into a fence, or, once, break his wrist. It had always been, "You're hurt. Gut it out. Keep on playing." But now Elvis was getting hurt all the time, and these days that meant the game was over.

The Elvis I knew, the one who had taught me everything I knew, who cut no slack when it came to someone's shortcomings, who'd scold anyone with, "You let yourself get out of shape. You're fat. You're getting old" —that Elvis had changed. Now it was he who was out of shape and fat and getting older. It didn't work to throw his words back at him. Lamar did a few times, and I know I did. Elvis did not take our criticisms gracefully.

At the end of January 1974, Elvis and the group left for two weeks in Las Vegas. Afterward they went to Palm Springs, Los Angeles, back to Memphis for a week, and then they embarked on one of the most strenuous tours Elvis ever did. He started March 1, in Tulsa, went to the Houston Astrodome for two performances, and then went on to Monroe, Louisiana; Auburn, Alabama; Montgomery; Charlotte; Roanoke; Hampton Roads, Virginia; Richmond; Greensboro; Murfreesboro; Knoxville; Memphis; and back to Richmond and Murfreesboro. The tour concluded in Memphis with three appearances on March 20 and 21. I was only with him for the Memphis performances, but Rick and I talked regularly and I knew that there were problems on the tour: Elvis fired Lamar—for a day; Red went back to Nashville, so Elvis fired Rick—for an hour; Elvis fired Marty Lacker (he wanted to make that one stick but he couldn't because he was undermanned), and so it went. Although I could have stepped in to help, I received no call. Finally I got Rick on the phone. I demanded an explanation of what was going on. Rick said he didn't know, but I could sense he did. A few days later they were all back at Graceland and Rick gave me the real reason. "Elvis had an affair with Annie," he said. "It happened that summer in Memphis, almost two years ago. I just heard about it a few months ago from Red and Sonny. I immediately confronted Elvis. He didn't try to deny it. I'd had some suspicions at the time, but I dismissed them. I knew Annie would fuck you up, but I had no idea she'd do it with Elvis. When I asked Elvis about it he couldn't respond, couldn't even mumble an excuse. So I knew it was true. I told him it was the lowest thing I've ever heard. I told him I was ashamed of him. He still said nothing. He feels bad, Billy. Really bad. He's felt that way for some time."

My throat was so dry I didn't know if I was saying the words or just thinking them. "How do you think I feel, Rick?"

"She's a jezebel. She's no good and never was. I tried to tell you that before you married her but you wouldn't listen. She threw herself at Elvis. And you encouraged it."

I remembered the conversation with Sonny West. He'd tried to tell me. Even Vernon, I now realized, had tried to warn me. One day he'd said, "Son, aren't you concerned about the time Elvis is spending with Annie?" I'd responded, "Hey, if you can't trust your brother, who can you trust?" I thought back to how Elvis, that summer, would call over to our house and say, "Nub, we're all laying by the pool. I want you over here." And I'd say, "Can Annie come too?" "Bring her," he'd say. Then he'd have a job for me. Sending me off to Lansky Brothers for new clothes, or to the Memphian, or to a recording studio. But I still didn't believe it.

"Bullshit," I muttered.

"No, it's not," Rick countered. "I told you, I confronted Elvis. Billy, I confronted him with anger. I know you sometimes think I kiss ass and that I don't stand up to him, but this time I did. He couldn't deny it. It's true. It's the God's awful truth. That's why he had you fired. It goes against everything. You've got to understand that for awhile after Priscilla left him he had sworn off women. He tried to live a monk's existence. Immaculate. Then a sexy lady got through the barrier and threw herself at him. He responded."

"She was my wife."

"He was wrong. Dead wrong. He knows it."

"He was more than wrong!" I yelled.

"He was a fool. All this time he's known it. He's kept asking, 'How's Billy?,' 'What does Billy need?,' 'What can I do for him?' I didn't know why he was asking it or why you weren't on the tour until two months ago!"

"Why me?" I cried. Or maybe I didn't even say it. My jaw was numb. I probably did try to strike Rick anyway, but in such an awkward way that he ended up embracing me. I sobbed. I shook. "Why me? I loved him so. It wasn't fair. Why me?"

18

"I GOT STUNG"

(May ■ July 1974)

Had I been a fool? There could be no question. I remembered Annie
sitting laterally in eighth grade, a few desks behind me. By laterally I
mean you could see up her skirt. The kid in front of me turned and
whispered, "Take a look. She isn't even wearing any underwear." So I
used the dropped pencil trick. He was wrong. Annie was wearing
white underwear and I was staring right at it. I gasped—I don't know
what I would have done if she hadn't been wearing anything. The
blood rushed to my head. Finally I looked up at her face and she just
smiled knowingly, and crossed her legs. Her long, soft, tan legs. Her
lean and supple thighs. Her white panties and her easy smile. All
these astonished and thrilled me. What an escape from the stale air
of the Church of Christ. I was smitten.

But why Elvis? Annie was a beauty to me because she represented
freedom, lack of inhibition, the lure of unknown sex, and potential
deliverance from all restrictions. But I was a kid. Many times I
thought that what was happening to me was very similar to what had
happened to Priscilla when Elvis had fooled around, and how I'd had
very little sympathy for her at the time.

Everyone seemed to know about it but me. I had to listen to my mother say, "Annie was just a baby. An innocent lamb. And Elvis took advantage of her. She was just a kid. Yes. I knew about it, Billy. I tried to tell you every way I could. But I could never just come out and say it. I couldn't break your heart."

All I could think was how proud I had been of Annie and how happy I was pushing her and Elvis together, delighted that he took such an interest in my wife.

I later learned that the entire affair lasted one month, roughly the month of July, 1972. It followed Elvis's six-month retreat from women after Priscilla left him, and it ended when Elvis met Linda Thompson. Or maybe it ended when Elvis came to his senses.

Dee was in the hospital the last week of July, receiving treatment for symptoms of stress. When I visited her she'd ask me, "Where's Annie? Is she with Elvis? Did they ride down to the Circle G? Oh Billy, I'm so worried about you." I thought to myself, "Mom is stressed out. What's the big deal about the Circle G? Why is she so worried about Annie being with Elvis?" Dee was trying to tell me but I didn't get it. Now I did. Now I realized what that concerned look she gave me meant. I recognized that Priscilla wasn't dumb, and Annie wasn't and Dee wasn't, but I sure had been.

I was also angry. While Elvis was busy telling singer T.G. Sheppard and his wife that marriage was sacred, something to honor and hold onto no matter what the cost, he was defiling my own marital bond. "I still can't believe it," I told Rick a few weeks later.

"It was almost two years ago, Billy. He was badly screwed up over Priscilla leaving him. I'm not making excuses for him."

"He should have told me. After she split he should have told me."

"Billy. He couldn't. It was hurting him as much as it was hurting you. I didn't know what it was for sure. Not until two months ago. I guess Mom knew. That's probably why she was in the hospital that summer. But she's a woman. They know those things. I didn't. But I knew it was hurting him . . . your not being with us."

"Elvis had you, Linda, Vernon . . . he had the group. I was the one cut off."

"Billy, when I found out for sure I went up to Elvis and I said, 'I'm ashamed of you.' I told him straight off. He hung his head and cried. He loves you, Billy. He's felt so much guilt."

I knew what Ricky was saying was true. I had seen and felt the pain in Elvis's eyes when he had looked at me, but I just didn't know what it was about. And that had made it all the worse for me. Well, let him feel guilty, I thought. It will be good for him. Then later I'd think, I don't want him to feel bad. I don't want to feel bad myself. If Elvis would come to me and tell me. Not even apologize . . . just own up to it like a man. Then I might be able to forgive him.

Over the next several weeks I went through a period of heavy drug and alcohol abuse. To say that Elvis caused it would be a cop-out. I caused it. My anger caused it. Reason pointed in a different direction, but I had no use for reason. I remember reading—and rereading, and saving—a review in *Oui* magazine of Elvis's latest album, "A Legendary Performer, Volume 1," which had been released in January. The album began with Elvis's first single, "That's All Right Mama," his first million-copies single, "Heartbreak Hotel," his all-time best seller, "Don't Be Cruel," and every significant release thereafter. The reviewer said:

> If Elvis's genius is as simple as inborn talent, its result has been as complex as the U.S.A. His goal (if the idea that a hillbilly thinks is still a bit strange, you can call it his instinct) has been to make music that touches, takes, and personalizes virtually every positive side of the American; a completely innocent and mature delight in sex; a love of roots and a respect for the past; a rejection of roots and a demand for novelty . . . a natural affection for symbols of status. . . . There are a lot of contradictions there; Elvis, after all, has become one of those symbols himself. Perhaps that is why one of his earliest critics pronounced him "morally insane."

Whew! Had this guy been on tour with us? Had he grown up at Graceland? He seemed to know what it was all about! I didn't read all the reviews. That was someone else's job, usually Joe's, or someone who worked for Colonel. Elvis saw few of them. But I saw that one. The phrase that first got me was "a completely innocent and mature delight in sex," because that applied to everything Elvis did, not just sex but football, racing, guns (he could never really hurt anyone but he delighted in their power), and competition of all kinds. The phrase that next got me was "if the idea that a hillbilly thinks is a bit strange . . ." Being a hillbilly myself, I can guarantee you that hillbillies sometimes do think. But most of the time they go through life blindly looking for acceptance, material wealth, the good life, and soon, just like everyone else. Two things they remember though, even when they're not thinking, are family and loyalty to family, and the knowledge of good and bad—in others and themselves.

If you accept the idea that hillbillies can think, what could Elvis have been thinking when he got involved with my wife? In so many ways it didn't make sense. It went against family and it was bad. Even Elvis, who seemed to have more of everything than anyone I knew, didn't want to be bad. But this time he stank. I was especially surprised because, though Annie was good-looking by my standards, she wasn't by Elvis's. He usually required beauty-queen looks before even considering a woman. And she wasn't exactly Elvis's type. He liked them wholesome, demure, nonassertive. Annie was aggressive, a flirt, and a loud partier. Annie was everything Elvis didn't like in a woman. And, looking back, she was nothing of what I liked in a human being.

I continued to believe that Elvis should feel guilty, that he should somehow, sometime account for what happened. I now recalled what he had said when I told him Annie and I were getting divorced: "Seems like that's the best thing you could do." Man, I'd thought at the time, that's cold, particularly from a man who's still suffering from his own divorce and doesn't care who sees that he's suffering. Now his cool reaction to the news made more sense.

I also mulled over the phrase "morally insane." Shortly after that review came out I was sitting with Elvis and some TCbers in the den. David was there, and I think Red and Sonny, but I don't remember specifically. Elvis said, "Hey guys, take a look at this!" and tossed this envelope full of photographs out on the table. I could see they had captured the guys' attention so I went over to take a look. The first one I saw was a picture of Priscilla and another woman in a compromising position. I saw some other pictures of Priscilla wearing a cheerleader's outfit with nothing on underneath, pictures from the front and from the back—provocative pictures. I looked at a few of these, and then I looked over at Elvis and gave him a surprised look. Elvis just gave me a nod and a smile. So I looked at a few more. Really, I was shocked. Not that Elvis had taken such pictures—we all like to capture fantasies—but that he would put them on display. The whole thing demeaned Priscilla. I dropped the photos and walked back across the room. The rest of the guys continued to leaf through the photos, making comments like, "All right!" and "Um-hum!" Elvis just sat back enjoying it. I couldn't believe that he would show such pictures to anyone. But to Elvis it seemed natural enough. Why should he withhold secrets from us? We were the inner tribe. Elvis was the chief. This public (to TCBers) exhibition was just one important way he could get back at her.

In fact, though I loved Elvis, I knew he couldn't really keep a secret. If you had a secret, you never told Elvis because pretty soon it could be all over the room. And if it was personally embarrassing to you, that was all the more reason for Elvis to broadcast it—within the group. Here was proof.

At first I tried to steer clear of Graceland when Elvis was in town, but that wasn't easy. I worked on the grounds there and I'd given up the apartment across from the high school to move back into our house on Dolan Street. Luckily Elvis was gone most of the spring. The long tour that ended in late March of 1974 was followed by a short West Coast tour in early May (Fresno, San Bernardino, and the Los Angeles Forum), a short rest in Palm Springs, two weeks at Lake Tahoe, and then his second long tour of the year—one that began with four shows in Fort Worth on June 16–17, 1974, and went on to Baton Rouge, Amarillo, Des Moines, Cleveland, Providence, Phila-delphia, Niagara Falls, Columbus, Louisville, and Bloomington, In-diana, then to Milwaukee, Kansas City, and Omaha. It concluded July 2 in Salt Lake City.

There was trouble along the way, more than the usual amount. A long-drawn-out paternity suit was near trial, with heightening threats on both sides before it was settled. There were death threats. There were fights with fans, or rather, troublemakers posing as fans. There were fights within the group. Elvis had bought big houses for Dr. Nick and Jerry Schilling, and some of the members of the tour, who'd been around much longer, wondered where *their* houses were. Then there was a big fight in Lake Tahoe. Rick told me about it over the phone.

"Man, Billy. It was a bad scene last night," he said.

"What happened, Rick?"

"There was this guy. Seems he bribed someone into getting in to meet Elvis after the show. He showed up at the party afterward and was turned away. So the guy was pissed. He found the fuse box and turned out all the lights on the floor. It was chaos. David caught him first and knew he had the right guy, but Red hit him again and again. Man, it was bad. This guy was handcuffed and Red dealt him such blows, Billy, the guy might die."

Rick was overreacting. The injuries turned out to be minor. But later, in court, this guy charged that several people struck him after he was handcuffed, principally David and Elvis. Everyone was upset. I spoke to Rick again. "He's confused, or else he's just out to get Elvis. David only hit him once," Rick told me. "And that was before he was cuffed. Elvis never touched him. But Billy, Red does have this mean streak and I know Elvis doesn't like it. You should hear Vernon, man. He wants Red gone now. He wants an end to the lawsuits. It's tense."

When Elvis returned from that second tour on July fourth, I forgot my complaints. I was there to meet him. He still couldn't look me in the face but at least now I knew why. There were no fireworks fights that year. Nevertheless, I couldn't stay away. I was still angry, but I loved him and wanted to be with him.

And I felt he needed me. The only job I got at that time was to pick up prescriptions for him at the pharmacy at Baptist Memorial Hospital. This had been Rick's job, and he still did it. But the volume of prescriptions that Dr. Nick wrote required not only one name besides Elvis's. It required several.

Not that I was an angel. I was doing marijuana, barbiturates, Quaaludes, and a lot of alcohol—anything to ease the hurt. At night I was out on the town looking for something to happen. Sometimes I found it. Usually Rick and I did a couple of the Rorer 714 Quaaludes that he'd take from Elvis's stash and we'd set out into the night in Rick's white TransAm. We'd smoke some weed on the way and by the time we got wherever we were going the 'Ludes would have kicked in and we'd be feeling no pain. That's how it was the night of our fight at the airport lounge. Some gap-toothed bikers decided to teach us "candy-assed little Presleys" a lesson. Rick and I put up a good fight but they were too big and there were too many of them. We got beat up pretty bad.

When we got back to Graceland Elvis was livid when he saw our bruised bodies and our swollen and bloodied faces. Rick entered a plea for amnesty. "Elvis, they're just a bunch of dumb bikers who had nothing to do. Probably they've seen us around, resented us, saw their opportunity, and one thing led to another. Elvis, we don't want to stoop to their level."

"Stoop?" Elvis roared. "We aren't going to stoop. Nobody does this to my brothers. We're paying them back."

So Elvis organized a posse with Red in the lead—Elvis wanted that role but we insisted he couldn't be involved—and we found them. Red and the others knocked some heads and set it straight.

It would seem that after so narrow an escape from serious trouble I would have the sense to avoid it for some time to come. But I wasn't that smart. A few weeks later I was still nursing some cracked ribs from a biker's kick when a friend of mine and I picked up two girls at one of the bars I frequented. My friend decided to take us all for a ride and show us some ironwork he'd done on the balconies of an apartment complex. We'd had several beers and a fair amount of weed. When he pulled his car off the street, up on the sidewalk, and drove it into the pool area, it seemed perfectly natural to me. The girls we had picked up sure thought it was funny. But the residents, who were out swimming and barbecueing, didn't like it that much. They started yelling at us. After we'd passed them and saw how angry they were we tried to get out of there, but we had to pass by the pool again to get back to the road. By the time we came back they had formed a human chain and they looked like an angry mob.

"Gun it!" I yelled. People scattered and it looked like we were going to get out of there. But just as we went by some guy threw a brick up against the windshield. The windshield shattered and caved in on us, but somehow we kept going, drove away, and got back to the bar.

My friend was angry, but I was happy to have escaped another mob. His dad was at the bar and we told him the story. I thought he would just tell us to forget it or to call the law (even though we might have started things!). But he came out and took a look at the windshield (which was mostly scattered over the front seat and floor) and went back in the bar to form a posse. Within half an hour the guy's dad had organized a caravan of six cars and had stopped by his house to pick up a pistol. I didn't much like it—I just wanted out of there—but the man had his son and me ride up front with him in the first car.

We drove right back up to the pool. "There's one of them crazy son-of-bitches!" My pal yelled, and we took off running after him. His friends appeared then and almost immediately it was a big brawl. My plan was to hit the guy standing next to me and get the hell out of there. I was already on my way, running across this lawn when an old man came out of the building with a .45 in his hand. He fired a shot in the air and yelled for everyone to stop. Another friend of mine said, "Aw, it's nothing but a fake." As he tried to wrestle the gun out of the guy's hand two more shots were fired into the grass. I could see that the gun was no fake! He finally threw the old man to the ground. When he tried to get up my friend drop-kicked him. The guy went down and he just didn't move. Then someone yelled "Police!" and I started running again. My pal was running right beside me and he wasn't wearing any shoes. It was night now. We were running through this construction area when my pal ran his foot into a high concrete curb that we couldn't see. He went down. I stopped to help him up and all of a sudden we were surrounded by cops yelling for us to freeze.

At the bar Rick had heard everything. He came cruising by just in time to see me being shoved into the back of the police car. He yelled, "Don't worry, Billy. I'll go get Elvis."

They took me to the station and booked me. I was scared.

"Well, Billy," a policeman said, "that old man you guys kicked is at the hospital and he's in bad shape."

It seemed like hours before Sonny West came down to get me. In a few minutes we were out and on our way back to Graceland. "Elvis wants to talk to you, Billy," Sonny said. "But not tonight. He's three sheets to the wind right now and he's upset. Better talk to him tomorrow."

"That's fine," I said. "I'm just happy to get out of there. It took you long enough to get me."

"I'm just coming down off sleeping medication."

"I thought you looked a little funny when you came in."

"You look worse."

The next day I told Elvis the whole story. He just said, "Don't worry about it, Nub. I'll take care of everything."

"I just hope the old guy's OK," I said.

"He's going to make it," Elvis said. "I made some calls. But that must have been some kick your friend laid on him."

"Elvis, it was fierce. It was terrible. But this old man came out there with a gun."

In court I had two legal advisors in addition to Elvis's personal attorney. They told me to just sit there and keep my mouth shut, that they'd do all the talking. My friend was charged with assault and battery and was put on probation.

I pleaded guilty to disorderly conduct, and Elvis paid my small fine a few days before he was due to leave for Las Vegas for his August concert at the Hilton. The day before they left Elvis called me into his room. "Nub," he said, looking me squarely in the eyes for the first time in two years, "you belong on the tour with me. We're leaving for Vegas tomorrow. Do you want to come back to work for me?"

"Want to?" I said. "Thanks, Elvis. Yeah, I want to."

"You know we're going to do this karate film. That's why Jerry Schilling came back. There's probably an action part in it for you, too."

"Sounds great, Elvis."

"You've been getting into too much trouble around here lately, anyway."

So I was back on the tour.

19

"SUSPICIOUS MINDS (WE'RE CAUGHT IN A TRAP)"

(July ▬ November 1974)

So in late July of 1974, two years after Elvis's affair with Annie, I was together again with Elvis and my brothers. Rick and I were Elvis's personal aides, David was his personal bodyguard, and together we were the "wrecking crew," a special division of the TCBers. We put the aluminum foil on Elvis's windows at the hotel so he could sleep during the day but think it was night. We three took turns on twenty-four-hour duty. We attended to Elvis's every personal need and screened phone calls, knowing, sometimes by instinct, which people he wanted to talk to or see, and which ones he didn't. We got him water when he wanted it, and food when he demanded it. We made sure he had the right kind of security and the right kind of toilet paper. We walked with him to the stage and back. We surrounded him. It was our job.

I was again put in charge of Elvis's clothes—carrying them, making sure they were pressed, knowing where everything was so that when Elvis said he wanted something I had it there right away. When I went on tour the first time, it had been simple. Everything was either black or white. A white silk shirt with black linen pants, or white on white, or black on black. But now he was into colors—red, baby blue—and also into sequins, jumpsuits, and jewelry. Some of those jumpsuits weighed forty pounds. I had to carry them, but Elvis had to wear them on stage, performing under bright, hot lights in Las Vegas summers that even the best air-conditioning couldn't ease. Some of those suits could have weighed sixty pounds when Elvis came off stage! Then there were the capes. Whatever you thought of how Elvis dressed, I was the one to go down to Lansky Brothers over the years and pick out Elvis's outfits. Lately it had been a variety of wide-brimmed hats and long coats. I don't know if it was his "pimp" stage or his "gangster" stage, but sometimes he'd ride in the back of a limo in a long coat, shades, a wide-brimmed hat, and he'd be holding a Thompson submachine gun in his lap. He was "Superfly" with a cigar.

Elvis only gave me one instruction when I went shopping for his clothes. That was, "Billy, you know what I like."

"Yeah Shaft," I'd answer. "I know."

Personally I never was too crazy about Elvis's style of dress. It was dramatic and it was his look, but when I chose his clothing I almost never had the feeling, "Wow, I'd love to have that." But once when the Lansky brothers were showing me silk shirts I saw one, a blue paisley, that I just loved. When Elvis saw it he said, "Nub, I don't know if I like this shirt or not. Do you like it?"

"Elvis," I answered, "I love that shirt."

"Then it's yours," he said, tossing it to me.

I got a lot of shirts and some good leather jackets that way. Nothing was ever returned to that store or to any other store. If Elvis didn't want it or didn't like it, he'd give it to someone else. But I never bought anything thinking, "Elvis won't like this, but I do. If I buy it for him I just might end up with it." I wanted praise for the selections I made, not the occasional "Billy, what shade of green is this? It looks like someone threw up."

In those days my brothers and I tried, and sometimes succeeded, to influence his music. It was Lamar Fike's role to find new music for Elvis. When he wasn't on the tour he was working with Hill and Range, the Nashville music publishing company. Lamar always had his ear out for new songs for Elvis, bringing him Credence Clearwater's "Proud Mary" and others such as "Crying in the Chapel," "Unchained Melody," and "You've Lost That Lovin' Feeling." But so did we. When my brothers and I heard James Taylor's "Steamroller," we took it immediately to Elvis. After initially protesting, "Aw, Nub. I don't do your heavy metal," he listened. Lyrics like, "I'm gonna inject your soul with some sweet rock 'n roll and shoot you full of rhythm and blues," won him over. The next day he was rehearsing it and two days later he sang it onstage. Two weeks later it was recorded. I pressed for the hard rock sound, the return to the dynamic Elvis of the fifties. That was the Elvis music I loved best. But Rick and David turned him on to Simon and Garfunkel's "Bridge over Troubled Waters," a song Elvis felt could sway an audience. And it did. They loved it. My musical tastes were more in line with the "original" Elvis, but Elvis rarely heard me on this.

The best time to talk to Elvis was when we were sitting around the Graceland pool, relaxing, and listening to the radio. One day we were listening to Chuck Berry sing, "Hail, Hail, Rock 'n Roll" and I said, "Elvis, you should sing that on tour. It'd blow everyone's minds."

"Aw Nub," he said. "I did that. That was the fifties. I'm doing other stuff now."

The worst time to talk music with Elvis was on tour, particularly just before an appearance. He was always jumpy then. Anything you'd say, like "I think that new arrangement of 'Lovin' You' will work great," or "Elvis, why don't you just drop 'Hound Dog' since you're so tired of singing it?" could bring an angry glance. Once he was on stage Elvis was completely relaxed. One night in Detroit in late September Elvis was going through the planned order of songs when suddenly he switched and started singing, "Hail, Hail, Rock 'n Roll" Chuck Berry style. While the surprised band and backup singers caught up, Elvis shot me one of those grins that said, "Is this good enough for you, Billy?"

On stage he could surprise you in other ways. At the Vegas Hilton I was standing at one end of the stage watching the crowd. In the middle of the performance Elvis, still singing, sneaked up next to the curtain, yanked my arm, and pulled me out on the stage with him. By then he had stopped singing. I just froze out there with all those people looking at me and laughing. I shrugged at them as if to say, "Don't look at me, I just got yanked out here." Elvis said, "I've interrupted this song to introduce you to my brother, Billy. And I just want to say to all you young females out there—watch out for this man. 'Cause he's a fast operator!" Then he pushed me offstage to the laughing crowd's delight and resumed his song.

I stood in my place on the side of the stage with my face burning, but now nobody was looking at me anyway. All eyes were back on

Elvis. This was one of the ways in which Elvis kept us all loose and on our guard at the same time. He still had quick moves. On stage or off, you'd think he'd already walked by you, or you by him, and suddenly he'd grab you and have you in the spotlight.

Elvis loved to do the same thing with Joe Esposito. Joe was a private man. He hated it when Elvis ambushed him and dragged him out before the audience. Of course Elvis praised him, letting the people know that Joe was the glue that held the operation together, all of which embarrassed Joe all the more. But for Elvis it was essential. If Elvis was a hero, so was Joe. He did so much to make it work. And, as a group or tribe, we were frontiersmen in Elvis's mind, the lead team of a new and bold adventure. We were to be known, publicly, as part of the Elvis phenomenon whether we liked it or not. It was one way he could repay our efforts.

Not only had the costumes changed since I'd last been on tour, so had the performances. Interrupting a song had been unheard of. Everything was perfectly timed, choreographed, and performed. But now, in the summer and fall of 1974, Elvis might interrupt a song anytime and start talking about what was on his mind. One night he'd talk about his jewelry, another about the history of his songs, and on another night he might talk about the food served at the hotel. Or he'd talk about J.D. Sumners: "He's the lowest bass singer in the world. He goes down four keys off the piano keyboard." Or he'd talk about karate. "It's an art, not a sport. It has much deeper meaning. It involved the Buddhist monks. They had no way of protecting themselves from robbers. So they studied the different animals. They studied the tiger . . ."

He'd go on and on. I'd say to myself, "What's Elvis doing?" But when he finished one of his long speeches and started to sing, the audience went wild with applause. They loved it. I realized that the fans had a love for Elvis akin to what my brothers and I felt for him. They didn't care when he rambled on about the various degrees of karate belts he'd acquired. They didn't care that he was overweight, didn't move as much on stage, and would rather talk than sing. They just wanted to be in his presence.

Even for adoring brothers, being in Elvis's presence for twenty-four-hour duty got to be tough. The job was much easier in Las Vegas than it was on the multiple-city tours, where there were always lots of arrangements to make with hotels, security, and transportation. In Las Vegas it always followed the same routine. Rick or I would go to his room at three-thirty in the afternoon and start shaking him gently until he began groaning. "Boss? Boss? Hey, Elvis! Man, it's time to get up." He'd groan some more, sit up, drink a glass of orange juice, and then usually he'd roll over and go back to sleep. So we'd repeat the process until he took a second glass of orange juice. Then we'd give him his first cup of coffee. With the third cup of coffee he would take a couple of Dexedrines, and by the fourth he'd be talking.

"Good morning, Elvis," I'd say.

"Yeah, Nub," Elvis would laughingly respond. "What's so good about it?" Sometimes he'd just sneer.

After another cup of coffee he'd either brighten up and ask who was out in the other room and who had called or wanted to see him, or mention the people he wanted to see or talk to. Or his mood would worsen and he'd start complaining about someone. Usually after forty-five minutes he'd be ready to walk out to the adjoining room and get on with the day. We had to be aware of what Elvis was thinking and careful about the people we let into the suite, because if someone was there who Elvis didn't want to see, he'd just spin around and walk back into his room in a rage. And he'd let you know about it.

At that time Elvis was heavily into planning his karate film (which never got made). Jerry Schilling and his friend Rick Husky were handling the production and writing end of it so they were usually the first people Elvis wanted to see. But one afternoon when I woke him he was up and in high spirits almost immediately, which for Elvis was about twenty minutes. He'd met with Barbra Streisand and her hairdresser-boyfriend-manager, Jon Peters, in his dressing room the night before. Streisand told him she was going to do a remake of the film *A Star Is Born*. She wanted Elvis to be her costar.

Elvis was excited that day, laughing, joking, and agitated. "Where's Joe?" he suddenly demanded. "Tell Joe to get the colonel up here. Tell him I want to see the colonel's fat ass on the double. We're going to make a real movie this time. Nub!"

"I'm on the phone, Elvis. I'm getting him."

The usual daytime routine was for Elvis to meet with a few people, tell them what he was thinking, and then settle down to read one of his books or just watch TV. At that time either Rick or I would start rubbing down his shoulders and then his neck to get him loose for the show that night. I was never trained in massage techniques, but I knew his muscles, his tensions, and how to work them loose. Then Elvis would decide which outfit he would wear that night. Again we needed to be in tune with his mood when we presented the alternatives. When he chose one we'd have to make sure that it was pressed, that the collar stood up right, and that no sequins or jewels were missing.

Forty-five minutes before going on stage Elvis always had a large mug of tea laced with gobs of honey, to loosen his vocal chords. Then he'd head for the service elevator with me, Rick, David, Jerry, Joe, Dick Grob, and one of the doctors. Conversation in the backstage dressing room was usually light—jokes, gossip, and more jokes about the gossip. Then, invariably, a rapping on the door, and an anxious voice calling, "Five minutes. Five minutes."

"Jesus," Elvis groaned. "I'm getting tired of that guy every night. I know what time to go on stage. Nub, go tell that asshole not to bother coming round anymore."

We'd escort him onstage, act as security during the show, and escort him off afterward. In Vegas, with two shows every night, it was important we get him out of the sweat-drenched costume he'd worn for the first show quickly, before he cooled down and stiffened. But first we had to treat Elvis's special, resilient voice with aspirin and hot, honeyed tea before it tightened and made a second show impossible. Then, undressed, bathed in sweat, and shivering, he'd have Dr. Nick check his heart, pulse, and blood pressure. Elvis then took his warm shower, changed, and got ready for the second show.

After the second show it was the same routine. After his shower Elvis would let us know if he wanted to be alone with Linda and a few of the TCBers, or if he wanted selected celebrities and friends admitted to the dressing room. He'd also let us know which people he wanted, or specifically didn't want, in his suite. Many nights he wanted J.D. Sumners and the Stamps to join him and Linda for a few hours of gospel singing, but there were nights when he wanted a full-blown party. That wasn't hard to arrange. If Elvis wanted a party there were plenty of people who wanted to party with him. In any event Elvis would take his "sleeping medication" about an hour before going to bed and then everyone could leave except whoever was on twenty-four-hour duty.

The "sleeping medications" included Demerol, codeine, Valium, placidyls, and Diluadid. In Memphis the prescriptions always came from Dr. Nick. But in Las Vegas they came from others. One doctor we called "Flash" because of the speed with which he could get Elvis in and out of the bathroom, presumably for a quick shot of B_{12}. The prescriptions from the other three doctors had always just appeared in my name. But Flash wanted to be more careful. Before he wrote a prescription he had me make an appointment to visit him in his offices in Las Vegas. The first appointment was scheduled for the early morning. I slept through it. A second appointment was made but Elvis had other work for me that afternoon. Finally we had my examination in my suite one night. Dr. "Flash" asked me some questions, in a very professional and fatherly way, took a few notes, and then came to some conclusions. "So, Billy, you're depressed over being fired by Federal Express."

"No. They never hired me. I just applied."

"And you're traumatized by the divorce you went through?"

"Not at all. I can see her for what she was and is."

"And with the other problems it's impossible to deal without deep resentment with an older stepbrother who is rich, famous, and can accomplish everything that is difficult for you?"

I got a little angry. "I can deal with Elvis without help from you. I love him."

"Billy, you're emotionally distraught. Out of focus with reality. I'm going to prescribe Placidyl, in sufficient quantities. There'll be three refills on each prescription. And when those run out just have the pharmacist call me. That way we can avoid any more of these meetings. But if your condition worsens I'm going to recommend you see a psychiatrist."

"Thanks, doctor."

"Uh, sure. Anytime, Billy."

Of course the prescriptions were for Elvis. I just picked them up and gave them to Rick and Rick reimbursed my expenses out of Elvis's wallet. But now I had an insight into how these good doctors made their money, and how Dr. Nick got a loan for his house, the hundred-thousand-dollar investment from Elvis in his racquetball court enterprise, and his keep while touring with Elvis.

After delivering the medication to Elvis I was quite often faced with being his overnight watchdog. That was the lonely job. Sitting outside Elvis's bedroom. Always awake, always alert to his needs, and always on call. Sometimes a novice, sometimes a hanger-on, sometimes a girl would stay with you. If Elvis permitted it. But usually he didn't. If you were on duty he didn't want you romancing some woman or entertaining people he didn't know. If another TCBer volunteered to stay with you that was fine. But who would want to? I know I never did.

Elvis's inspirations came at night, usually from three to five in the morning. That's when he'd call Rick, David, or me, depending who was on duty, and say, "Call Joe Guercio [Elvis's music director]. I want to talk to him."

"Now, Elvis?"

"Right now. I've got an idea for tomorrow's performance."

"What's the idea?" I'd ask.

"Call Joe, man," Elvis would always say. "This is important."

"I'll call him, Elvis. But tell me what it is. I don't want to wake him up in the middle of the night without something to say."

"What time is it?"

"About four in the morning."

"Okay. Write this down. And call him first thing you do. You hear me?"

"I hear you, boss!"

So whichever of us was on duty would quickly write notes on Elvis's thoughts. If Rick was there he usually took over at this point because Elvis's ideas often had no connection with performances anyway—more often they were concerned with his philosophy of life and death. Elvis knew I was the wrong person to speak to. It wasn't that I didn't share his concerns, but I never liked talking about them. However, sometimes I was all Elvis had.

When my twenty-four-hour duty and that night's show were over I was off. Usually I hung out with the musicians. When I was off Rick would be with Elvis, David would be with his new wife, Angie, when she came to Vegas, or with me when she didn't. Donnie Sumners, bass singer J. D. Sumners's stepson, became a friend. Donnie and Sherrill Neilson, who'd been with the Imperials, and Tim Batey, a bass player with a rich voice, had recently become part of a group Elvis formed called "Voice."

Donnie (like his dad J.D.), Tim, and Sherrill were primarily gospel singers. But being Elvis's group at that time they were invited to all the big parties in Las Vegas. Donnie and I often made the rounds together. It was pick and choose. If one party wasn't swinging enough, we'd get out fast. There were others, and they went all night. The summer nights in Las Vegas were aglitter; we sampled a lot of that glitter.

One afternoon, very hung over, David and I got up to Elvis's suite at about four-thirty. I was scared because I was late. "Don't worry," Rick said. "I still can't get him up. He's not depressed or anything. He's stupidly happy. But he won't get up."

I spotted the usual pitcher of iced Mountain Valley spring water and I said, "We can get him up." It was something only we boys could do. No one else would dare. In fact individually we'd be too frightened. But we were all in this together so I dumped the pitcher of water on Elvis's head. He was up in a leap, screaming, "Billy, I'm going to kill you!" As he rose David grabbed his shoulders and Ricky tackled his knees. God, he was strong! He battled the three of us for fifteen minutes, throwing Rick off with a kick, somehow getting out of David's grasp. We wrestled, fought, swore, even bit, sometimes against each other as our allegiances changed, until we were all laughing, huffing, out of breath, and trying to wrestle each other into submission. Elvis pinned Rick, but David drove him off. I jumped David and Elvis got hold of me. Then Ricky and David got Elvis down until he said uncle. It wasn't easy to get him to say it.

"I can't breathe," Elvis said between laughs and gasps for air.

"Say uncle."

"I'm having a heart attack. Let me up."

"Say uncle, Elvis. Then we'll let you up."

So he said it. It was sort of a mumble, but we let him up. Then we all lay down, exhausted and exhilarated on Elvis's huge bed. It was just like when we were kids and "tackle Elvis" was our great game. We all loved it. It was several minutes before Elvis resumed the role of boss, presenting us with his demands for the day.

I cherish that encounter because two weeks later, at an October show in Indianapolis, that newfound feeling of brotherhood ended. We were all gathered in Elvis's suite. He was ranting on about how the behavior of one of the TCBers was getting out of hand. Sonny West was the target this time. Elvis complained that he'd become more concerned with his personal ego than the greater good of the group (meaning Elvis). Now I liked Sonny. Sonny was the one guy, besides Elvis, who had paid special attention to me, taking me for rides on his motorcycle, teaching me how to ride my own, teaching me a lot of other things. Always patient with me, always my buddy. He was the one who tried to warn me about Elvis and Annie. So it hurt to hear Elvis say the things he said about Sonny. There was never a question of my loyalty. It was to Elvis. I'm not sure whether I was always the rebel, like Elvis, or simply obstinate. As Lamar Fike told me later, "David was a Russian bear to everyone but Elvis. And I would stand up to him if he got on me too heavy. But, Billy, you were the one who would snap back at him as if you just didn't give a shit who he was. And Elvis just wasn't used to that."

What Lamar saw as my brave insubordination merely stemmed from my desire to give back some of what Elvis had given me. Some of the spirit. He was my god. But that afternoon he was stumbling heavily around the room, his speech slurred. I could see he was ranting, adrift, and dead wrong. "I'm on to Sonny," Elvis exclaimed.

Somehow Elvis had tapped a vein of resentment in me. Without being asked I piped up, "A number of people here are 'on to' someone else."

"Well, Nub. Who might that be?" Elvis sneered.

"Look to yourself, Elvis," I said.

Elvis turned almost purple. "Billy, you're fired!" he said.

Back in Memphis that fall the scene was just as bad. My mom had absolute proof of Vernon's disloyalty and was set to sue him for a divorce. "I even visited their little love nest," Dee told me. "She didn't even try to deny it." Of course, everyone else had known about Vernon's girlfriend, Sandy Miller, for some time. And we all liked her. She was a nurse and a damned nice woman. But that only made Dee madder. Her own sons had known of Vernon's infidelity and hadn't told her out of an allegiance to Elvis and his TCBer group ethic. It was true. But apart from that how *could* we tell her?

Dee was probably convinced by this time that our allegiance to Elvis verged on devil worship. I couldn't fault her for that, really. She'd had plans for us that included college, medical school, middle-class acceptance, and achievement. And, realizing her worst fears, we'd all dropped out of high school to be with Elvis. Then her husband, Vernon, had dropped out of their marriage to be with Elvis. Everything she'd stood for had crumbled. She just couldn't understand that all that stuff she tried to put us through didn't make any difference to us. Our lives were patterned after Elvis's.

"Billy, I'm so glad, so happy to have you home. You're one of three lost children. But I hope you're now prepared to make a separate life for yourself. Away from Elvis. You've suffered enough."

But I wasn't prepared. Not yet. After a few weeks of thinking it all over I called Rick. Elvis and the gang were in L.A. after closing the tour at the Sahara Tahoe without me. I knew that the unresolved question over Annie had led to my rebellion on the road. I also knew that she no longer made any difference to me, but Elvis did. Rick had always urged me, "Go to Elvis. Tell him you forgive him. He can't come to you. Not on this issue. You've got to go to him." So I got Rick on the phone and told him I wanted to speak to Elvis.

"This is not a good time, Billy," he said.

"I don't care what a good time is," I said. "I need to speak with him now."

"Billy. He's making a last-ditch effort to get back with Priscilla."

"Why?" I asked. "He's got Linda. What could he want with Priscilla?"

"Billy. He wants it. Maybe it's not her, maybe it's just the idea of how it was when she was around. He's not well. He's got this twisted colon. Maybe he thinks he's going to be healthy if he gets her back."

I thought about it for a second. "Linda's better for him," I said. "Elvis ought to start planning for the long run, not some past dream."

"You're right about that."

"I still want to talk to him, Rick. I've got something to say."

"What is it?"

"I forgive him. Annie was my mistake. Not his."

"She was a jezebel!" Rick thundered. "I tried to tell you."

"I know. You were right. But I've got to tell Elvis. Now, when I can."

"Hold on. I'll try to get him."

Rick was off the phone for several minutes. Then he was back. "Billy, he just can't talk with you now."

"Will it be a better time tomorrow?"

"I don't know."

"I mean it, Rick. I've thought it through. I forgive him."

"He knows that, Billy. But I think there's another problem. He can't forgive himself."

What now?, I thought. It must be time to break ranks—to prove my own mettle, and to prove to Elvis that I was whole and unharmed by him. So I set out to do just that.

20

"MY WAY"

(November 1974 ▪ August 1975)

Striking out on my own didn't turn out to be that hard. The first thing I had to do was to stop trying to be Elvis's little brother and stop trying to win acceptance by being bolder and more daring than anyone else. That meant easing up on drug and alcohol use. I found that surprisingly easy. The second thing I had to do was get a good job, something out of Elvis's and Graceland's control. That was tougher. I was a good mechanic but there were plenty of good mechanics in Memphis. And even if I was better or more promising, I didn't have the experience of some other guys. So I didn't get the first job, and I didn't get the next one, so I still didn't have the experience. I tried everything. Even today, driving past the airport or the Federal Express headquarters in Memphis, I'll say to myself, "There's another place I got turned down." After several months, in the spring of '75, I did get a good job with Casino Records. I worked with recording artists like Charlie Daniels and Aerosmith at auditoriums, event centers, and universities around the country. They'd tell me what dates they wanted to fill, what kind of music they wanted, and I'd tell them who was available and at what price. This was a business I knew, and I was good at it. Within eight months they made me a vice-president in charge of bookings and promotion. I'd reached a position where I knew Elvis no longer had to ask Rick, "How's Billy doing? Is there something we can do for him?" I was growing up a little.

But if things were taking an upturn for me they were taking a decided downhill slide for the people I loved. Dee and Vernon separated. The first inkling I'd had that Vernon could be unfaithful to my mom was in El Paso, where I'd thrown my own wedding ring in the river. He took my brothers and me to a cat-house in Juarez, lined up the best hookers, and paid the fare for all of us. At the time we all laughed about it. Later, on the tour, Vernon said, "I just wish I could find a young 'un like that to fall in love with."

"Aw, Daddy," I said, "You're dreaming ancient dreams. But you're a little ancient yourself."

"I guess I am, Nub," he said, slapping me on the shoulder. But I was shocked. When I returned to Memphis, I never said a word about it to Mom. But I could see she was becoming more social. She wasn't having affairs, but she was seeing other people. After a variety of threats, divorce proceedings, temporary reconciliations, and a return to threats, Vernon told Dee that if she kept it up he was going to see that "every bone in her pretty face was broken." I returned home one day to find her sobbing. "How can he speak that way to me?" she said.

About the time Elvis came back from the tour, in the late fall of '74, Linda Thompson walked out on him. Elvis holed up in his room at Graceland for a month. He became a target for his critics. In January 1975 the *National Enquirer*, for the millionth time, had his picture on the cover. On one occasion they said, "Elvis at 40—Paunchy, Depressed & Living in Fear." They didn't have much of a story but they weren't far wrong.

Linda came back to him in late January 1975 after Elvis put himself in Baptist Memorial again for another "rest" and detoxification. While there he was diagnosed as having an enlarged and twisted colon. We all knew that he had been in considerable pain for some time. This was the reason, he told us, why he had to use so many pain-killers. He also learned that his glaucoma had progressed to a critical point, threatening to blind him. He was particularly susceptible to the effects of all those flashcubes that greeted him at each performance. In addition, his liver was degenerating. A liver biopsy showed serious and potentially irreversible damage.

As if that wasn't bad enough, someone got hold of his tax returns and published them in the Memphis newspapers. They reported that although Elvis had earned $7,273,622 (and some odd cents) in 1974 he had, after splitting with the colonel, and splitting again with the IRS, a year-end deficit of over seven hundred thousand dollars. What with jewelers like Lowell Hays selling Elvis hundreds of thousands of dollars' worth of glitter (Lowell became a regular on the tour; in a month he could make more money in Elvis's company than he could at his shop in Memphis in a year), and with doctors like Dr. Nick selling him a combination of prescription drugs and loyal friendship, and hundreds of thousands of dollars in speculative racquetball courts, Elvis was on the verge of going broke.

It was no coincidence that on February 5, 1975, two days after these numbers were published, Vernon, the watchdog of Elvis's money, suffered a major heart attack. Both father and son were in the hospital, both truly scared, not just for themselves but for each other. I went to see Elvis a few days before Vernon's heart attack. Despite his bad health, he was in good spirits. This time he didn't ask what I'd brought him.

"Nub, thanks for coming," he said.

"Thanks for wanting me to come, Elvis," I said. "I guess you had a tough tour."

"Nub, man, they are getting tougher and tougher."

"Looks like this one wore you out."

"That's why I'm here," Elvis said. "Just to get some rest. You know how it is, man."

"You've got to take care of yourself, Elvis."

"I know that now. And I'm going to. Nub, the hard stuff is over. It's all looking up from here."

I called him after Vernon went into intensive care and Elvis was crying. "Nub, this is so bad. And I'm to blame. I've laid all the financial problems on Daddy and now it's killing him. This is not what I meant."

"What do the doctors say?" I asked.

"The doctors. What do they always say?"

"Take it easy, Elvis," I said. "Daddy's too tough to let this get him down."

Later, when they let Vernon accept calls, I talked with him. I didn't see him. It was awkward because Vernon was now living with

Sandy Miller and I was living with Dee. My parents were estranged and I had chosen my side.

"Vernon. Are you okay?" I asked. It was the first time I'd called him Vernon, even though that's how I'd thought of him for the last few years. Up till then it had always been "Daddy."

"I'm fine now, Billy. I've just had too many things on my mind. Sonny's problems. The separation from Dee. But now I've just got to learn to take things easy. How are you, Billy?"

"I'm great," I said. I was waiting for Vernon to say he wanted to see me. I felt he would say it if that was what he wanted. But he didn't. And I respected his privacy just as he had always taught us to respect Elvis's. So I let it drop.

"Are you alone?"

"No, Sandy's with me. And Sonny's getting it set up so that we'll be in the same room. I don't know about that one," he laughed. "I'm supposed to rest."

"If there's anything I can do," I said.

"Well, Billy. There's Sandy's son. You've been through some of the same things he's going through. Maybe you can help."

I had to think about that one. I liked Sandy, and if something happened to Vernon I would be glad to help in any way I could. But her son? He was six or seven years younger than I. I'd had to set him straight on some things, like not acting like a boss to the help at Graceland. He treated them like servants, but they were family to us. Damn, Daddy, I thought. You always did like to give me the toughest jobs.

"Son?" Vernon asked weakly.

"Daddy, that's no problem. I'll help in whatever way you want. You just get well."

"I'm going to do that, son."

After two weeks of detoxification, and with Vernon recovering strongly Elvis left the hospital refreshed and acting like the Elvis of old. And that meant action. He had been leasing the Playboy jet from Hugh Hefner. Now he had another idea. He decided to buy his own plane. He bought a Convair previously the property of Delta Airlines, for a ridiculously low price of $250,000. Even Vernon was ecstatic at the investment for a plane that could carry the whole entourage. Then Elvis had it reoutfitted in Houston so eventually it accommodated twelve passengers and five crew members. The conversion cost

$600,000, but the plane was perfect, the Cadillac of all jets. He christened it *Lisa Marie*.

The layout of the plane conformed to the specifications of Elvis's tour bus: a few passenger seats, tables for dining or games, and a large bedroom with a conference table, queen-sized bed, and makeup room for himself. I mean this was a big bird. Short of a 747 there was nothing bigger in the sky. It cruised at 650 MPH (no commercial jet flew as fast), but it drank gasoline. That's why Elvis could acquire it at such a bargain price. With the oil embargo and the high cost of fuel, the major airlines couldn't keep it in flight.

Another problem was the noise. The Convair's big engines were among the noisiest ever built. Some cities wouldn't allow it to land at all and the Los Angeles airport was always threatening to deny landing rights. Then there was the smoke. When Elvis's old friend, disc jockey George Klein, would announce Elvis was returning to Memphis, the fans crowded the airport to watch one plane after another coming in. With each approaching plane some would shout out, "That's it. Here comes Elvis." But those of us who knew just watched for that long, smoky trail. We knew that was the *Lisa Marie*.

Having bought the Convair didn't satisfy Elvis. While it was being refurbished in Texas Elvis paid another $1 million for a Lockheed Jetstar he named *Hound Dog*. He used the Jetstar to fly friends and family down to watch progress on renovations to the big jet, then let the colonel use it on advance for the tours.

While all this was in the works Elvis opened in March 1975 for two weeks at the Las Vegas Hilton and again, Rick told me, was in top form. Of course it couldn't last. For a man with as many physical problems as Elvis had, plus the added burden of constant and increasing substance abuse, partly to relieve pain, an extended tour was a form of suicide. But Colonel booked Elvis relentlessly. On April 24, 1975 Elvis opened in Macon, Georgia and the tour progressed, consecutively, to Jacksonville, Tampa, Lakeland, Murfreesboro, and Atlanta (six shows in three days), Monroe, Louisiana (two shows), Lake Charles (two shows), Jackson, and back to Murfreesboro. That tour closed May 7.

I was there for the three days in Atlanta. Vernon and Dee, in one of their brief reconciliations, had flown out to Los Angeles in the Jetstar to get Lisa Marie. On their way back across the country to Atlanta they stopped in Memphis to pick me up. Vernon and Dee

seemed comfortable with each other, even glowing. That was the
effect Lisa had on both of them; it didn't last long after the trip. I'd
kept hearing from Rick and David that Elvis's tour performances were
uneven. In Atlanta he wowed them. Sheila Ryan, who later married
James Caan, was Elvis's "date" for that tour. After the concerts I
could sense that Elvis was very interested in her, but that fizzled out
too.

On May 30 Elvis was back on the road again, opening in Huntsville,
Alabama (five shows), and then on to Mobile (two shows), Tuscaloosa, Houston (two shows), Dallas, Shreveport, and back to Jackson
(three shows), and Memphis for the final show on June 10, 1975. As
the heavy spring tour progressed he grew tired and bloated. He'd get
to the point in "Blue Suede Shoes" where he had always gone into a
hip swivel and he'd just stick one leg out. "C'mon, baby," he'd say to
the leg, "shake!"

Elvis behaved badly the last few days of that tour, insulting his
backup singers and musicians, and screaming at his men. When he
came back to Graceland in June he felt guilty, and when he felt guilty
he spent money. He bought fourteen Cadillacs and a variety of other
cars for everyone who had been involved. I showed up at Graceland
with a date the weekend they all returned. When I introduced her to
Elvis he said, "Do you like Camaros?" She was ready to accept one
from him but it was just a casual date and I saw no future with her. I
got her out of there real fast before Elvis could lay a car on her.

That summer Elvis got into snorkeling and scuba diving. He rented
equipment for everyone. Of course there was nowhere to go snorkeling
around Memphis so Elvis just invited a lot of people over and we used
the Graceland pool. The whole entourage got involved and, as usual,
there was a lot of local talent—pretty young girls in scanty bathing
suits, all vying for Elvis's attention. When Elvis got in the water so
did everyone else, but the Graceland pool wasn't that big. It looked
kind of like an underwater fight scene from a James Bond movie with
all of them trying to navigate around in there. Elvis just liked to sit at
the bottom of the pool and watch the girls swimming above him.

However, his mood could easily shift. One day we were all fooling
around in the pool and Elvis wasn't in a playful frame of mind. He
told us to settle down, but we continued to act up, splashing him
while he was trying to read. He walked off in a huff and we forgot
about it. We were still in the pool about half an hour later when we

saw Elvis coming over the hill in the golf cart. He stopped, stood up, and yelled for us to get out of the pool. We just yelled, splashed, and taunted him. So he came driving straight toward the pool with 300-pound Lamar Fike sitting next to him on the cart. We thought he was just trying to scare us but he came busting up and drove right into the pool. Of course we scattered, but Lamar had trouble getting out of the cart. So we all jumped back in to make sure he made it to the surface. Vernon came out yelling at everyone to get out. The cart was electric, powered by batteries, and he was afraid we'd all get electrocuted. Vernon made us drain the pool before pulling the cart out.

Draining the pool had been a regular event for years. Most of the time it was because of all the broken flash cubes at the bottom. Elvis would bring them out in shopping bags and drop them in, where they'd float until we opened fire on them. When we were kids we used BB guns, Elvis used .22s and heavier equipment. They'd sparkle and flash when you hit them and then slowly sink.

I flew advance with Colonel and Joe (or Colonel and Sonny) a couple of times that year, first in the Jetstar and later in the Lear Jet (another $850,000, and dubbed *Little Lisa Marie*) that Elvis bought for the colonel. The trips coincided with my duties at Casino Records. My bosses saw it as a cheap way to get me out in the field, and I'm sure they liked the prestige of saying, "Yeah, Billy's going to be coming out to see you in Elvis's Jetstar." We had a pilot with the wonderful name of Milo High. I just loved getting on the plane and saying, "Hey, Milo. What's our ETA?"

Of course when you traveled with the colonel you had to do some work for him. I went with him to Oklahoma City on July 7, in advance of a two-week tour, and to Las Vegas to prepare for Elvis's August 18 opening. I helped hang posters, organize radio spots, and all the usual stuff. There really wasn't all that much to it, except you had to put up with the carnival atmosphere and Colonel's usual bullshit.

Personally, I'd developed a deep dislike for the colonel. The cigars and bombast no longer impressed me. But his influence over Elvis did. In fact, one day in Oklahoma, it began to scare me. Some reporter or fan asked about Elvis's health. Colonel answered, "He's in fine shape. He works out at karate and racquetball every day."

Another problem surfaced a week before the advance trip to Las Vegas. Rick had fallen off the deep end in drug abuse. He was arrested for forging a counterfeit prescription. He was not only not ready to rejoin the tour, he wasn't ready for life in any meaningful way.

21

"IT'S NOW OR NEVER"

(August 1975 ▬ March 1976)

When I heard about the bust and learned that Rick had been released I hurried to Graceland. "Slick Rick," the smooth operator, the man in control—how could he have succumbed to the fix, the needle? It was the years on the tour, the constant movement, planning, highs, lows, tending to the boss, taking uppers to stay awake for twenty-four-hour duty, downers to sleep when the job was over but your body didn't seem to know it. I knew the constant tension of the tour and the price you paid by being constantly at Elvis's beck and call. It had burned me out too, but then I'd spoken up and Elvis fired me. Rick was fired once too—everyone was fired at one time or another—but it seemed that Rick was the one who was always out there, always tending to Elvis, his eyes and ears and sometimes voice when Elvis was awake, his security while Elvis slept. And Rick's was always the voice of moderation, the one to seek a solution that held something for everyone. That wasn't easy. I'd never tried that approach, but I could appreciate the difficulties involved. I knew Rick had been doing drugs to make it work. I'd done enough drugs myself. Uppers, downers, grass, coke—but needles? I never did that. Needles scared me.

When I went to see Rick he was sitting on a couch in the garden room with his head in his hands. When he looked up his eyes were red and tears streaked his face.

"Rick?"

"Billy, I screwed up."

"Yeah. We all do that."

"Billy. You know the first words he said to me when he came down to the police station to get me?"

"No."

"He said, 'This is going to kill your mom. This is going to wipe her out.' His first thoughts were of Dee."

"Who?"

"Elvis."

"Oh shit. Rick, think of yourself!"

"I am. At least I'm going to. But I got tell you what happened." OK?"

"OK."

"Elvis told the cops to take the cuffs off me. When they were slow to do it he bellowed, 'I said, take those goddamned cuffs off him.' And then they didn't hesitate for an instant."

"Sounds right," I said.

"Then he came up to me and put his arms around me and said, 'I'm going to take care of this. Don't you worry.' He whispered in my ear, 'Rick, why didn't you come to me? If you had a problem why didn't you tell me?' Man, Billy, I needed that hug. I needed Elvis. But I don't know where I am now."

"Rick, is it that bad?" I asked.

"Billy, I've got to look up to see the bottom."

I don't think Rick saw the bottom. He came close. But he had a girlfriend named Robyn (now, and for many years, his wife) who was devoted to him. She was, is, a Christian, with powers of understanding, patience, and forgiveness, and she was always there for him. Rick was beginning to understand and appreciate those qualities. In the fall of 1975 Rick finally did begin to turn his life around.

It was the same with Elvis. His two-week engagement in Las Vegas that August was reduced to two days when it became apparent that he was too ill to perform. Among other things, Rick's arrest and the knowledge that Rick was addicted to heavy drugs bothered Elvis greatly. His immediate response was to increase his own use, but back in the hospital in Memphis he started talking about taking the cure himself. At least he was admitting to those close to him that he could

possibly have a problem. He even followed Dr. Nick's advice and hired
two live-in nurses, Mrs. Marian Cocke and Kathy Seamon, and had
trailers installed for them in back of Graceland. We had a lot of fun
with their names, but they were competent nurses and good people.
Mrs. Cocke, a nutritionist, watched Elvis's diet closely, tacking diet
sheets in the kitchen so the cooks would know what Elvis could and
could not eat. Of course that meant nothing if Elvis wandered into
the kitchen himself and started charming the cooks with, "Now I do
hope I'm going to get some of that good southern cookin' of yours."
Then he'd get what he wanted. They'd been cooking what Elvis
wanted for years. The cooks felt good about it, they loved Elvis, and
they loved to please him.

From a distance it had been easy for me to see that Elvis's health
had declined drastically while I was off the tour. He hadn't just
become fat, he was bloated and very tired. Back at Graceland for the
entire fall, his health and his mood improved with each day he was
off the tour. Again he was full of humor and praise for those around
him. He was even singing, or humming, around the house again. He
made up a little song that started, "Oh, I'm fat, forty, and funky
again," in response to a current *National Enquirer* headline. It was
obviously a time for Elvis to reexamine his priorities. He had been
killing himself on his tours for years. He didn't need to do that, and
he was getting too old for it. Most of the time he was definitely too
sick for it. What kept Elvis on these body-breaking tours? It was part
pride, I knew. It was part finances. It was very much the result of his
love of his audience. But how much of it was the colonel's exploitation
of Elvis? I kept thinking of Colonel's boast about running the winning
horse. To adapt a phrase, they shoot up race horses, don't they? They
run them till they drop. The doctors whom Elvis called friends were
always shooting him up which made it possible for him to perform on
extremely strenuous tours. I began to wonder whose side were they
really on?

One problem we all had, including Elvis—most of all, Elvis—was
our upbringing. To us doctors were the true nobility of society.
Politicians, rich businessmen, even astronauts and rock stars were a
little behind. In our world the integrity of doctors was never questioned. Every drug Elvis took was prescribed by a doctor in response
to a specific problem with his health. Surely they knew what they
were doing, we all believed. But I began to question that notion. I
had talked to Rick about it that summer. One night he was coherent

about it, but on another he said, "Billy, don't say a word to Elvis about this. I mean it. He's heard you put down Colonel and Priscilla. Don't start attacking Dr. Nick. Elvis won't put up with it."

But when Elvis started using prescription drugs again after claiming he was off them for good, we decided to act. After much discussion, we decided to confront Elvis. One night that fall I'd been sent to the Baptist Memorial South pharmacy to pick up a "script." When I delivered it to Elvis's room Rick and David were with me.

"Uh, good to see you boys," Elvis said, sensing an uprising in the tribe. "Nub, you got something for me?"

"I do, Elvis," I said, shaking the paper bag. "But first we want to talk with you."

Elvis was embarrassed and angry but only said, "Okay, little ones. What have you got to say?"

Rick spoke up. "Elvis, what do you need that stuff for?"

"That's prescribed medicine, Rick. You know I've got health problems."

"We know, Elvis. But we're just wondering if that medication isn't causing some of your health problems."

"Rick, I know what I'm doing." Elvis paced the room.

"That's what we're wondering, boss," David said. "We're wondering if your medication is doing things you're not aware of."

"Stand up, David! You want to take me on? Look at me. I'm fit. I play racquetball every day. I practice my karate. Look at me." Elvis had a point. He had lost twenty or thirty pounds since August. The bloated look had almost disappeared.

"It could come back," Rick said.

"It won't," Elvis said. He directed a menacing look at Rick. "I just hope it won't for you either."

"Elvis, we love you!" I said. That was to be my only contribution to the confrontation.

"Then get off my back," Elvis snapped. But instead of following up his command with his usual hard stare, Elvis turned his back to us for an instant and when he faced us again his eyes had welled up with tears. He said, "Boys, I appreciate your concern. I'm concerned too. But I know what I'm doing."

For a time Elvis's physical condition did improve—to the point where we hoped his words might be true. But by mid-November the pressures were again building for him. Colonel, probably knee-deep in gambling debts, guaranteed the Hilton that he would make up for the lost August performances by playing Las Vegas for two straight weeks in December, a very slow month out there. And Elvis, once again financially strapped after spending millions on airplanes, agreed to do it.

In December of 1975, Elvis, David, Rick, and the rest of the crew went back out to Las Vegas. I wasn't there but I heard that Elvis was great. When Elvis was in town there was always an "anything goes" atmosphere in the casinos. Elvis sold out the huge International Showroom every day for the two weeks preceding Christmas. That had never happened before. It has never happened since. After all, there was only one Elvis. And Elvis made enough off those two weeks to tell Vernon at Christmas, "Don't worry, Daddy, we're back in the money. Everything's paid for and it will just roll in from here on."

The overbooked tours should have ended there but they didn't. Colonel had Elvis booked into the new Silverdome in Pontiac, Michigan, for December 31, 1975, a New Year's performance for 1976. Why was Elvis doing it? He hated Michigan, at least what he'd seen of it, and he knew from experiences at the Houston Astrodome that the acoustics would be terrible, the audience far away, and the sound, even with everyone's best efforts, inadequate.

A few weeks earlier Elvis had called me in and asked me how my job with Casino Records was going. I told him that it wasn't going too well, that they had some financial problems and had been trying to get me to go to him to help bail them out. I told him that in fact I'd quit. When I found out they were just trying to use me, and him, I'd just walked away from it.

"Well Nub, I've been thinking," Elvis said. "I want you back on the tour. I've got problems with some of the guys. Everything seems to end up in a lawsuit. I need people that I can trust. And you know the job. Besides, you belong with me."

I went, and I can testify that everything was a disaster and that everyone involved hated it. Was it cold! There were the usual two feet of snow outside—I've never been in Michigan when there weren't—but inside it was supposed to be a balmy sixty-eight degrees. It wasn't even close! The horn players were having trouble getting their lips unfrozen from their instruments and the amplifiers for the guitars broke down constantly. They had Elvis up on a platform where he couldn't hear any of his background music. They had me positioned so far away from him I had no idea how I could get to Elvis if trouble arose. It was about as bad as it could be. On the flight home Elvis seethed and kept mumbling, almost inaudibly, "Fuck that place. Fuck the colonel, I'm not going back to one of those space museums again."

On January 8, 1976, his forty-first birthday, Elvis flew some of the gang out to Vail, Colorado. The trip didn't go well and the group returned early. Something was on Elvis's mind, I could tell. We found out what it was when Elvis gathered a few of us in his bedroom. He had a plot to bust the people who'd gotten Rick on hard drugs. He had the names, courtesy of the Memphis police, whose chiefs Elvis bought cars for and whose staff played softball, with the best uniforms and equipment, courtesy of Elvis. Dick Grob was to act as the man in charge. Elvis had a recording session set up at Graceland and that was to be the alibi for all involved.

We went along with his scheme. Rick eventually said, "We don't really want to mess with these guys. Let's just forget it."

"We can't do that, Rick. They're gonna find other ways to do harm. Someone's gotta stop them. That's our job," Elvis said. The planning continued for a few weeks, but ultimately fizzled out as the recording date grew near.

Was there a contradiction in Elvis's use of one kind of drug and his rejection of another? Of course. But with Elvis you learn to live with contradictions. For example, that summer marked one of the few times when I actually saw Elvis doing cocaine. I walked into the house in Palm Springs and there was this huge rock of Peruvian flake, the pink stuff, sitting in front of him. He was cutting it off with a scalpel from one of his doctor friends and snorting it down with a straw. I sat down next to him and started watching TV, but I couldn't take my eyes off that big chunk of coke. Elvis knew I wanted some. He must have felt like someone eating a T-bone in front of a starving dog. He said, "Nub, you want a little of this?" I did a couple of healthy lines.

"That's good stuff, Elvis," I said, feeling an immediate smooth rush. He pulled the flake back away from me and I leaned back to watch TV, hoping he'd offer me some more. Suddenly I realized he was glaring at me. He not only wasn't going to offer me any more, he was about to give me a lecture.

"Nub, you've done this stuff before?"

"A couple times, Elvis. But nothing as good as that."

"Don't do it again," he said. I got up and went out to the pool.

The album they recorded at Graceland in February was released in May. The album, *From Elvis Presley Boulevard*, featured the songs

"Hurt," "I'll Never Fall in Love Again," "Bigger They Are, Harder They Fall," "Moody Blue," "The Last Farewell," Neil Sedaka's "Solitaire," Willie Nelson's "Blue Eyes Crying in the Rain," and one of Elvis's favorites, "Danny Boy," all reflected his mood of the time. But the "Danny Boy" of that record was nothing like the version I'd heard him sing so many times in his living room and in mine. Elvis's voice was still there.

Elvis went out on tour again in April but the group, particularly the band, was not hitting on all cylinders. First Glenn D. Harding quit, then his replacement, David Briggs left. And then it was Ronny Tutt, Elvis's drummer. Jerry Schilling quit after he and Elvis got in a fight over use of a condo in Vail and then James Burton announced he was leaving. He did for a time, joining Emmylou Harris, but finally Elvis persuaded him to come back at a substantial increase in salary. Elvis had paid them all fairly well but in truth, with Colonel and Vernon pinching pennies, they were all paid less than they could get elsewhere. Loyalty to Elvis had kept them going for years, but when they sensed that Elvis was losing interest in his music they went elsewhere. Elvis seemed to be sliding downhill and they didn't want to take the fall with him.

Everyone was concerned. Dick Grob, Elvis's security chief, took it upon himself to investigate Elvis's use of prescription drugs. Maybe he was acting on Colonel's orders. When he learned the true extent of Elvis's substance abuse—you've got to remember only a few of us, mostly family, had any idea about it—Grob arranged a meeting with Priscilla. Apparently with the blessing of Elvis's attorney, Ed Hookstratten, they made arrangements to dry Elvis out at the Scripps Clinic in San Diego, with a long-range medical plan for Elvis to follow. Once they had worked out every detail Priscilla flew to Graceland and presented the plan to Elvis.

Elvis refused. He refused to admit he had a problem. He told Priscilla that if there was a problem he could handle it. Of course Priscilla was the last person in the world whom Elvis would turn to for help. It was sheer folly to think that she should be consulted in such a scheme, let alone present it. I guess the theory was that Priscilla controlled access to Lisa Marie so she had a special power over him. Or maybe they believed that Elvis secretly wanted to get back with her and would submit to her demands as a step toward reconciliation. To anyone who really knew Elvis, that was ludicrous. If he maintained a relationship with Priscilla it was only so that his access to Lisa Marie went unchallenged. From the time Elvis showed us the pictures of Priscilla I knew what he thought of her.

The problem Priscilla always had was that she wanted Elvis all to herself. She must have had a great sense of power when, as a teenager in Germany, she realized she could influence this famous man. But I think she wanted total control. She didn't realize that we were all a part of her life. She could control Dodger, Elvis's grandmother, with kindness and teenage exuberance. She couldn't really manipulate Vernon but she did adopt his attitudes toward Elvis's finances, and I'm sure she grew to respect him. Rick and David worshiped her (as I did for a time), and the cooks, servants, and close relatives were all susceptible to her young and innocent charms. But she was combative with everyone beyond that. This included Elvis's friends, guards, musicians, and anyone she described as a "bloodsucker" or "hanger-on," people who often were essential parts of Elvis's team. There was a place for everyone and Elvis wanted it that way but Priscilla refused to accept Elvis's concept of how things should be. I think she never understood Elvis's need and love of his fans and his audience. Or the thrill he got performing before them, or the thrill they got in return. That was the essential Elvis. He needed them and he got so much from them and gave back plenty in return. Elvis, when he loved her (and he loved her greatly), decided that separation of conflicting forces was the best route to take. He told her simply, "Cilla, stay at home. A man doesn't take his wife to the office with him." Of course, she was very young when he first laid this rap on her. She could often be charming and gracious. Perhaps Elvis thought she would grow out of her limited, peevish attitude toward his world.

Unlike Linda Thompson, who went with the flow and was part of Elvis's life both at home and on the road, who sang gospel music with him, laughed with him, cried with him, cared for him no matter what he did, Priscilla could only respond to Elvis when things went right for her. Priscilla must have known that Elvis didn't respond to women who tried to wear the pants in the family. But often that's what she was, Miss Bossy Boots. And then she had his child, and then she took his child away. Why was there no attempt to understand the man on his terms?

By this time I realized that Elvis was just a stepping-stone for Priscilla. She may have been only fourteen when they met in Germany but she knew what she was doing. She saw her chance to get away from home, to go on to a bigger and brighter scene. After Priscilla and Elvis separated I never talked much to her when I went to pick up Lisa Marie in Los Angeles. I'd sometimes joke around with Michael Edwards, her boyfriend after she broke up with Mike Stone. It sure didn't help his career to get involved with her. She turned him around and around. He was a hell of a nice guy, too. He did this imitation of the lead guy in the movie *Scarface* that was great. "All you guys care about is focking and socking," he'd say. He was really funny. But I couldn't speak to Priscilla because of what she'd done to Elvis.

Was Elvis unlucky at love? I think so. What if he had met a Linda Thompson when he was younger, someone who was a partner, a friend; someone who understood who he was right from the beginning; someone who shared his interests in religion, not just church-going and the power of reading and singing the gospel, but the philosophical exploration of all religions. Linda was everything Elvis could have asked for and she was loyal. Was Priscilla ever really there? You either loved Elvis or you didn't. If you did you never left him. To me Priscilla violated the first rule—that you stand by Elvis no matter what.

What about my luck with love? Well, I still had some wild times left in me. For example, one night I "borrowed" his custom-built Lincoln Mark IV. I must have been feeling pretty cocky about being back on the tour because that was Elvis's favorite car and you didn't just take it out for a joyride. But I did. I picked up a couple of friends and we cruised Memphis. Then one of them found this blue light. It belonged to the sheriff's department and was used by unmarked patrol cars to pull violators over to the side of the road. All you had to do was plug it into the cigarette lighter. I didn't know it at the time but Elvis had coveted that blue light and the power it represented for years. Actually, the lack of it had never really stopped him. I'd been with him several times when he'd pulled motorists over for speeding or some other offense, producing his badge and a lecture. "Yes sir, Mr. Presley," they'd say after he spoke his piece, and Elvis would send them on their way. But the blue light made it easy to pull cars over with no fear that they might mistake your intentions.

Except my friends and I were pulling girls over. They didn't have to be doing anything wrong. We just pulled them over for the fun of it and to check them out. I know I ought to have acted more responsibly. I was high on this feeling that the good old days had returned, and I guess I was eager to celebrate. One of the cars had two really foxy-looking young women in it; my friends were doing everything they could to impress them and get a telephone number. I just started laughing. I guess they didn't like it and called the police. The officers caught up with us later, pulled us over, and I promised not to use the blue light anymore.

The next day I was walking through the den and Elvis was in there watching TV. He waited until I was all the way past before calling out, "Hey, Billy." I stopped and went back. "What's this I hear about your driving my Mark IV and using my blue light?"

"I was just pulling over some girls and having some fun," I said. I never lied to Elvis.

"Well, the sheriff's department called me on it. And now I have to call you on it," Elvis said. I stood ready to hear the worst. "You can't be doing that. You know that's my car and my light. You don't know what I went through to get that damn thing. I had to threaten the sheriff I'd run against him for his office if he didn't give it to me. And, besides, you could've been hurt. If you'd pulled over the wrong person you could have had your brains blown out."

"Elvis, we only stopped chicks, no guys."

"Meet any good ones?" Elvis asked.

"Yeah," I said. "But I think we only pissed them off."

Elvis laughed. "Well, Nub. I've always taught you not to do anything I wouldn't do."

"Elvis, I didn't."

Elvis laughed again. "OK, Nub," he said.

Whew, I thought. That's it? I half expected Elvis to fly into a rage or at least be sullen toward me for a time, maybe even to threaten my new status on the tour. But none of that happened. I was confronting a new, mellow Elvis.

Maybe I was becoming more mellow too, for not long after this episode I began to date a girl named Debbie. I really cared for her, but by this time I was a little afraid of being used. I didn't tell her I was Elvis's brother for a long time; if I went to Graceland I made some excuse and dropped her off first. But soon I knew I wanted to marry her. That meant I'd have to tell her that I was Elvis's stepbrother, and about what had happened between Elvis and my first wife. In fact, she'd known about my connection with Elvis for some time, and was more than curious as to why I went to pains to hide that part of my identity. So I told her about Elvis and Annie. That shocked her. In March 1976 she married me anyway. But knowing about Annie made her want to stay away from Graceland and Elvis. It made her want me to stay away as well.

We had a big wedding at her family's church and a bigger reception at the Brooks Road Holiday Inn. My brother David had a band that played with him when he was in town and without him when he was touring. David was there for this event. The champagne flowed. I invited Vernon, of course, but he couldn't come because he was going through a bitter divorce with Dee. I didn't invite Elvis, and asked Vernon and everyone else not to mention it to him. Rick was aghast. "Billy, you can't get married and not at least tell Elvis."

"He couldn't come anyway. Not even if he wanted to. It's my wedding. I'll tell him afterward."

But I wanted Elvis's approval. So one afternoon, a few days after the ceremony, I took Debbie up to Graceland. Elvis was still in his room so I got Rick to go up and tell Elvis that I had something important to see him about. I waited with Debbie at the bottom of the stairs. I was scared, I'm not sure what of. After several long minutes Elvis came out of his room and down the stairs. He wore the usual scornful expression with which he had greeted all of us for years, as if to say, "So, you little shit. What kind of trouble have you gotten yourself into now?"

"Uh, Elvis," I said, clearing my throat. "This is Debbie. Debbie, this is Elvis Presley. Elvis, Debbie and I just got married."

Elvis looked at Debbie, then back at me, then he took a long careful look at Debbie. When he looked back at me he had this broad grin on his face that said, "Well, all right, Nub! Look's like you haven't been doing too bad for yourself!" He nodded at me and put his arms around both of us. "Welcome to the family," Elvis told Debbie.

A moment later Elvis said, "Excuse me. I'm going to my room for a minute. Billy, show Debbie around the house," Elvis called back as he climbed the stairs.

I showed Debbie around Graceland and about twenty minutes later both Elvis and Linda Thompson came down. Elvis had changed, looked refreshed, and after he introduced Debbie and Linda he said, "C'mon, let's all take a ride around the grounds."

We got in two golf carts, Debbie and Linda in one, Elvis and I in the other. In the past that would have always meant a race, with the two women trailing, getting both bored and angry, and eventually dropping out and going back to the house. That's the way it always happened with Cilla. But this time he not only allowed the women to keep up, he patiently waited for them when they got involved in casual talk and forgot to follow us. Elvis gave Debbie the grand tour, beginning with his cars, then on to the back grounds, a half hour with the horses in the stables, and ending with the "meditation gardens" where, as always, Elvis said a few words about his mother and how much she'd meant to him. I could see Debbie's attitude toward Elvis softening. Her perception of him as a powerful and perhaps evil force in my life had diminished as our ride progressed. I could see that he was really happy I'd found someone else; it made my spirits shoot up ten feet in the air just to see him smile at me once more. It was as if I was a kid again and the whole thing with Annie had never happened.

22

"YOU DON'T HAVE TO SAY YOU LOVE ME"

(April 1976 ▬ July 1977)

On April 20, we left on the *Lisa Marie* for a West Coast tour that began in Kansas City and went on consecutive nights to Omaha, Denver, San Diego, Long Beach, Seattle, and Spokane. Two days later we were in Tahoe for another ten-day engagement.

The tour was unusual in that there was almost no extracurricular activity. Maybe the scheduling demands of the first several days could explain it, maybe it was Elvis's health. But there were no after-performance parties, no meetings, no reading aloud the notes passed to any of us by fans, no angry scenes, and no joy. We simply pressed on to one engagement after another. Perhaps the tour had become different for me because of my recent marriage to Debbie. I'd taken myself out of the action. And Rick was out of the action because of his determination to kick drugs and his romance with Robyn, in addition to his newly discovered awareness of Christian conduct. Maybe we'd just all grown a little older, just a little more mature, but the craziness was gone, and most of that reflected a basic change in Elvis.

The early shows in Tahoe were often just a conversation between

Elvis and his audience, but while we were there Elvis heard or read that his performances were affected by his use of drugs. He demanded on stage to know who was responsible for "that lie" and proceeded to give a terrific music-only show.

Nevertheless, the effects of drug abuse were becoming more and more evident. Every day he was now taking a combination of several downers in pill form, or getting boosted by a shot. We had to watch him at night while he slept to see that he was breathing freely or that he hadn't fallen asleep with food in his mouth that could choke him during the night. Usually Linda Thompson was there. She played a variety of roles for Elvis: lover, buddy, fellow seeker, and jokester. But at night her role was usually mother or nurse. And by this time, after four years with Elvis, she was asserting her independence. She was gone as often as she was there.

Elvis had had some other flings, but most of his time during this tour was spent trying to catch up on some sleep or with his books. Because I had no interest, by that time, in after-performance parties, I pulled more than my share of overnight duty with Elvis. And Elvis, although he appeared to be sleeping most of the time when he wasn't performing or traveling, slept poorly.

"Who am I?" Elvis asked me in the middle of our first night at Tahoe.

"You're the king of rock 'n roll," I said.

"Billy, you're talking about the performer. Who am I?"

I didn't know whether to take Elvis seriously or not. But since I'd been smoking some pot to while away the hours of night duty I decided to take it all as a joke. I laughed.

"I believe in Jesus Christ," Elvis said.

"I'm at least glad of that."

"Billy, don't mock me," Elvis said, anger rising in his voice. Then he quickly settled down to a sincere tone. "I believe Jesus died for our sins. He died for your sins. He died for my sins. For that reason alone I need to know who I am. Who am I?"

Now sobered, I searched for appropriate words. "You're just Elvis to me," I finally said. "You're my brother. I love you."

"That's a good answer. But it's not a complete answer. I want you to think about it, Billy," Elvis said before going back to his bedroom.

I turned on the TV. I was usually glad when encounters like that ended. Rick and Larry Geller knew the most about this stuff—they talked about the "earth plane" and higher levels of consciousness and being. I carried Elvis's suitcase of books but I've still never read *Siddhartha* or *The Prophet*. I must have tried several times. I just wasn't ready for any of that unorthodox spirituality. I had questions but I did not share Elvis's methodical quest for unconventional revelations.

The questioning continued over several nights. Sometimes it would start with a discussion of performers and their impact. But no matter whose name I mentioned, Elvis always brought up someone who'd died young. "Billy, have you thought about Hank Williams or Jim Croce, and why they died so young?"

"I've thought about it, Elvis. Every music lover has. Sometimes it was airplane crashes. That can't happen to you because you've got the *Lisa Marie* and I think other times it was drugs that cut people short before their time. I guess that's what happened to Jim Morrison (the lead singer of the Doors), and others, like Jimi Hendrix and Janis Joplin."

"So many others," Elvis said. "But Jim Morrison had special abilities."

"Elvis!" I exclaimed, surprised. "I thought you hated the Doors."

"I hated their message. But if Morrison could have kept himself straight he could've been a lot better. He would have grown beyond all that political shit."

"I'm just glad to hear you say you liked him."

"He was the new poet laureate," Elvis said. "But he died before he could understand his power and what he could do with it. That's a tragedy. So much unspoken. Just like James Dean."

Then Elvis was quiet for several minutes. As he sat in a chair across from me I could see his head droop several times as he almost dropped off to sleep. Outside, beyond the foil-covered windows, glittered the lights of Tahoe and the stars above. His eyelids were as heavy as his body. But each time it appeared he'd safely found sleep he'd jerk his body and open his eyes to half-mast. What was happening to my vigorous, handsome brother, I wondered. His breathing was labored and uneven. He had a double or triple chin, and the power seemed to have drained from what had once been a magnificent physique.

Then he awoke fully and tried to sit up. "Why am I Elvis Presley? What do people want from me? All the faces in the crowd. Billy, you saw them tonight. I belong to every one of them! What is expected of me, and who am I?"

I was no more prepared to answer that question this night than I had been previously. I said nothing.

"Billy, do you believe in forgiveness of our sins?"

"I believe I do, Elvis. Do you?"

"I hope so. I know I've sinned. You like to think none of it's intentional. You like to think you're just responding to the situation. And then you think about what Jesus would have done. And you think about what Buddha would have done. You want to do the same. You get to know how they felt, that's the important part. But you want to understand how they acted as they acted. On the spot. They just weren't clouded by thoughts of anger, retribution, or any kind of selfishness. They were so free!"

"You're free, Elvis," I said.

"Nub, I'm just a poor boy from Mississippi," he said. "And I've got the weight of the world on my shoulders." For a moment Elvis gave me an imploring look. Possibly he wanted me to say something that would put his mind at rest. But there was nothing I could say. He continued to sit across from me for several minutes, his head bobbing, his vast body slouching deeper into the chair. Then he shook himself awake, slowly rose, and went back to bed.

Had I missed an opportunity? Looking back, if there was ever a good time for us to discuss Elvis's affair with my first wife, that was as good a moment as any. Away from Elvis, alone with my own thoughts, I'd imagined raising the issue many times. But when Elvis was actually present I always backed down. Most of the time it would have been very difficult. Even though I worked with Elvis on a daily basis many of the conversations would go, "Nub, do this," or "Nub, why hasn't that been done?" But on that spring tour of 1976 Elvis initiated several conversations in which he practically admitted his guilt, or at least his inability to control the events that led to his affair with my wife. I now realized he was inviting judgment, or at least an accusation that required an explanation. He was sincere, caring, and lost. Unable to bring up the question of Annie directly, he was reaching out to me, hoping I could bring it out into the open. I couldn't. I had only been able to question or attack Elvis when he was bombastic, egotistic, and uncaring. Even then I didn't deal with our disputes directly. I just made sarcastic remarks that I knew would get under his skin. That night, after Elvis went to bed, I realized how silly and small I'd been.

It was obvious that the tour was no longer fun for Elvis. He had always said, "When it's no longer fun, I'll quit." Why didn't he? Why was he out here? Why had Elvis done the New Year's Eve date in Pontiac? He had known what domes were all about and he'd always had the Colonel set aside the Christmas season and his birthday, January 8, as unbookable. The answer was obvious. He needed the money. Despite his reassurances to Vernon, his purchase of three jet airliners had tapped him. The one night gross in Pontiac was over $800,000, eclipsing the biggest take the Beatles had ever made. And the gate ranged from 80,000 to 175,000 every night on the West Coast tour. Elvis never dealt on credit, only cash, and lacking the will to get a smart accountant, he'd never used write-offs with the federal government. He had legitimate expenses he never used. Vernon and the colonel just said to pay Uncle Sam his cut and forget it. Elvis did. He let the IRS calculate his taxes. Naturally they were always high. While corporate executives, other entertainers, and even presidents often paid nothing, thanks to clever tax advice, Elvis always paid the limit. He was proud of that. He wanted it that way.

Today I hear people say, "When Elvis died his estate was less than four million dollars. Now they say it's at least seventy million, maybe a lot more. Isn't that amazing? Isn't that a tribute?" Maybe it is a tribute. But my response is always, "It's obvious why the estate has grown. Priscilla and her accountants have gotten smart about the money. Priscilla always was smart about money and Elvis never was. And Elvis isn't around to give it away anymore. Do you have any idea how much money he simply gave away?"

Like anyone, Elvis wanted money so he could do things. But once he had it he felt guilty about having it. So he spent it. It was that simple. Why else would Elvis buy all those cars? Or spend so much on his family and friends, or his pets?

What was it with Elvis? Had he become more mellow, thoughtful, subdued, distracted? Was it the Valium, Demerol, Percodan, Hycodan, Placidyl, or Dilaudid that made him different? Or was it simply that the melancholy that had haunted him ever since his mother's death had finally taken over his spirit?

Whatever the cause, it was obvious Elvis was going through a transformation, and the transformation required changes in his staff. Corporations remove anyone who doesn't contribute to the bottom line. Money decides everything, making sentiment an unnecessary burden. But for Elvis sentiment was everything, money nothing. Elvis could only fire people when he was in an irrational rage. Then later, he'd admit to being irrational, ask forgiveness, and rehire the offender.

The people who worked for him were part of the great experiment—family, warriors, blood brothers. But among Elvis, Vernon, Colonel, Elvis's attorneys, doctors, and advisers a decision was reached. He had to fire Red West, Sonny West, and Dave Hebler. The decision was based on financial considerations. Red, Elvis's "anger personified," had beaten up too many people, and the lawsuits were potentially disastrous. Sonny had participated and had to go with him. Dave Hebler wasn't really guilty of anything except forming a friendship with Priscilla that Elvis always resented. But if the others were to go, so was Dave.

From my viewpoint the decision on Dave Hebler made absolutely no difference. And I knew Elvis didn't like Sonny's loud and demanding presence. He'd said many times that he'd pay Sonny to stay away from him. But the decision on Red was hard for him. Elvis loved Red. Rick, David, and I loved Red. We loved Sonny too. We'd grown up with these guys as our "big brothers," and even if they had been hard on us when we joined the tour, nothing could change our loyalties. The job fell to Vernon, who told them that their jobs with Elvis were over. They took it hard. No one in the entourage knew they'd set out to find a writer and a publisher for the story of their years with Elvis. A writer for Rupert Murdoch's *Star*, Steve Dunleavy, took the job. But we wouldn't hear about that for several months.

Elvis did seven more tours that year. There was no reason for it. In August RCA announced that Elvis's record sales had passed the 400-million mark, far more than any other single performer in history. He was earning millions without moving. He could have done several millions more in one or two performances in Japan or Germany, where fans would have paid anything to see him. Colonel apparently met with representatives from Japan and demanded that they put a million dollars on the table before negotiations could proceed. They put two million in cash before him. Colonel couldn't believe it. But he'd been behind the times since the Chicago World's Fair, as Elvis liked to say. He still turned them down. No one knows why, though there has been a lot of speculation about the colonel's background and his apparent reluctance to travel outside the United States. He was born in Holland and was never naturalized. For whatever reason, he never made the foreign deals that were available, easily the most potentially lucrative of Elvis's career, and instead sent Elvis to Duluth, South Bend, Madison, Cleveland, and Pine Bluff, Arkansas, for less than five percent, per appearance, of what he could have made in Japan.

So Elvis, with steadily worsening health problems, went back on the road with a vengeance. Between August 27, 1976 and November 30, Elvis played in thirty-one cities scattered across the country, giving thirty-six performances in less than three months. And after the November 30 closing in Anaheim, Elvis took one day off and then opened Las Vegas December 2 for fifteen shows in eleven days. Somewhere in the middle of all that there was a changing of the guard.

Elvis was back at Graceland between the October 27 show in Carbondale and the November 24 show in Reno. During his first week back Linda Thompson, after a couple of false exits and returns, finally went her own way for good. Her departure wasn't unexpected, even by Elvis. She had given him everything, and he gave a lot back. But his heart, for whatever reasons, still belonged to Priscilla. Linda probably knew it all along, and she had for a long time hung in there trying to overcome it, long after an ordinary person would have given up. It wasn't just for herself, she truly loved him. But a time came when she decided she had to move on. She ran up some bills that Vernon fumed about, but there was nothing vindictive about her departure. Elvis knew it and accepted it. It was as though he had a beautiful butterfly cupped in his hand and then opened it to watch the creature take flight.

There was a quick substitution. George Klein, always on the spot, paraded several hopefuls past Elvis, who quickly decided on a twenty-year-old Memphis girl named Ginger Alden. She was an odd choice, first because she was so young and second because, although a lot of people thought she looked like Priscilla, Ginger was nowhere near as sophisticated as Priscilla had been at that age. Nonetheless there is more than a little truth in the theory that Ginger was a Priscilla substitute. Not only did she look like her, but Elvis had her wear makeup in the same way Cilla did in the sixties. She was several inches taller but had the same dark hair and large dark eyes. Ginger had two sisters, Terry (a 1976 Miss Tennessee) and Rosemary, who seemed to be much more with it than Ginger. I was surprised by Elvis's choice and others were dumbfounded. "Elvis is going to replace Linda with that bimbo?," one person exclaimed.

Elvis never did anything by committee vote so he moved fast on Ginger. He had her flown out to San Francisco for the shows on November 28 and 29, and then had me fly back to Memphis with her. Two days later I flew out to the December 2 Las Vegas opening with

Ginger's parents. We were using the Jetstar with the affable and highly competent Milo High piloting. Everything went as smoothly as it possibly could, but somehow Ginger's parents found plenty to complain about. Why were we on such a little plane? Why was the ride bumpy? Why were the seats so small? Why hadn't Elvis sent the larger and more luxurious *Lisa Marie*?

After the flight, when Ginger picked us up in a limo, she showed her parents a $50,000 ring that Elvis had given her in San Francisco. Her father's eyes lit up and I saw him smile for the first time. Either he thought I couldn't hear him or he didn't care, because he said to Ginger, "Whatever you do, don't get rid of that one!" The Alden family all laughed in unison at this advice.

I didn't like that. It made me feel that these people were just out for whatever they could get. Later, after Elvis died, I didn't like the fact that they sued the estate over some house that Elvis had said he was going to buy them.

The house in Las Vegas was packed. When Elvis had sold out the year before (after canceling in August with health problems) the big shots at the Hilton were amazed. Logic and past experience told them no one could sell out in December in Las Vegas because everyone was at home trying to handle the pre-Christmas rush. But Elvis was always the exception. They realized it now. The August shows (another slow month, but not as bad as December) were a thing of the past. Colonel negotiated for several Decembers in the future. It made the hotel happy, and it relieved the colonel of millions in gambling debts. The amazing thing was that Elvis agreed to do it.

Elvis was revitalized. He was truly infatuated with Ginger. He took off several pounds and he put on some great shows. But I had a personal snag. My wife Debbie called one night to say that some guy had tried to accost her. It had happened in a phone booth in back of a convenience store. It had upset her. I told Elvis about it immediately and he told me to get Milo to fly me back to Memphis. He called friends on the Memphis police force who met me at the airport, and I was back at our apartment within six hours of Debbie's call.

Gradually, things quieted down at home. When Elvis returned from Las Vegas, dealing with Debbie's incident was one of his primary concerns. In fact he personally directed the investigation, jumping on the police when he thought they were slacking, and making plans to move when the list of suspects narrowed down. But Debbie withdrew from these efforts. She ultimately refused to review a lineup of probable suspects. Her attitude infuriated Elvis; he dropped the investigation.

I'd been with Elvis for only twelve of his thirty-one dates in the fall because of her objections and now I was faced with a real dilemma. Debbie didn't want me to leave her alone again. Elvis, now significantly understaffed, wanted me there all the time. I had always wanted a permanent relationship. Life on the tour was fun and exciting, and we never lacked for women, but I wanted more than that. I grew weary of the demands of the tour, of Elvis's demands, of the one-night stands in new cities with sparkling women. I still felt that I belonged to Elvis and his concept of the "moving tribe," as he called it. I knew he needed me.

The decision was tough, but I went with my heart and quit the tour. This time I wasn't fired, I just left. I told Rick, Vernon, and then Elvis. I told him why. "Well, Nub, if that's what you want," he said. "But this is a bad time. It's just not that Red and Sonny and some of the best musicians are gone. You know, Red and Sonny are up to something. They're calling everyone, asking about dates and stuff. They're writing a book about me. And they can make me look bad. I don't care about myself. But if they tell all they know what's Lisa going to think?"

"I've got to do this, Elvis. I've got to establish my own life. You've got Rick and David and they've always been more capable than me. They've been with you all the time. I'm just a sometimes help. Usually a hindrance, probably."

"You can do this, Nub," Elvis said. "But you know you boys will always be with me in spirit."

So again, and for the last time, I was off. That didn't mean I no longer had duties. When Elvis was in town and driving somewhere in his limo I was still either the point man, driving the car in front, or the tail. Usually, because of my racing and drag car experience I was the tail, the car directly behind Elvis's. It was my duty to make sure that no other vehicle could get to Elvis from behind. There'd been attempts over the years. Whether they were just fans, photographers, or potential troublemakers I'd always been able to speed up, swerve, brake, or simply drive them off the road if they approached Elvis's limo. I'd been doing this, even when I was in Elvis's bad books. Everyone knew I was the best at it.

Elvis left for Nashville in late January for a recording session. He couldn't get Ginger to come with him, and when she didn't show up a few days into the session he called it off and returned to Memphis. Later he left for Miami, to begin a new tour, and I was left behind. I got a job at the Memphis airport, as an assistant jet mechanic. Jet engines are wonderfully simple, less complicated than the engines in most cars. And I'd always been good with engines. I loved this job.

For me it was a smooth, easy spring, and the best time Debbie and I spent together. For Elvis, Rick, David, and the rest it was a "give it your all, then call out the dogs and piss on the fire" tour that went to fifty-one cities between Miami on February 12 and Indianapolis on June 26, 1977. From what I heard from my brothers over the phone, sometimes Elvis was good, and sometimes he was great, including his last show in Indianapolis, but most of the time he just couldn't pull it all together. Not that the fans cared. They never left him. But the critics jumped all over him, harping on his weight problem, his often-slurred speech, the sheets of sweat that poured down his face (they should have tried to perform in those outfits), and his reluctance to hit or even try for the high notes. He certainly was having serious physical problems even while onstage.

Rick and David were with him every day of the tour. I got their reports regularly. When Elvis was in pain, so were they. And even from a distance, so was I.

In late June Elvis returned to Graceland. For several days he and Ginger holed up in his room. Then Rick and I went up to see him. We sat in the nursery off the bedroom for a time, talking about Dee and Vernon and the threatened divorce.

"For some reason they can't seem to get this thing settled," Elvis said. "Probably the attorneys want it to go to court so they can make bigger fees. But boys, I'm just afraid of what's going to happen to all of us if Dee gets up to testify in court that Vernon was dating on the road."

"She won't say anything like that, Elvis," Rick said. "I'm sure she won't."

Elvis looked at me. "What do you think, Nub?"

"I think she'll have to, Elvis. She'll have to say something like that to support her case. But Mom will never say anything publicly against you or any of the others."

"Billy. She won't want to. But if they've got her on the stand, under oath, and one attorney, arguing for Dee, asks if she had reason to know that Vernon was dating other women on the tour and the other attorney, defending Vernon, cross-examines with, 'Wasn't this just normal, innocent tour conduct? Didn't your own sons [David and I] date as well, even though they were married at the time?' Well, how do you think she'll answer? Will she lie?"

"No, Elvis," I said, "she'll never lie."

"You young 'uns haven't been through this. I'm a veteran. I've been in the wars more times than I'd like to remember. I'm always the defendant, and I know how nasty the accusations can get."

Rick shook his head. "This could be bad, Elvis."

"It's going to be bad enough for me with Red and Sonny's book coming out. But this is going to be bad for all of us. The press will sensationalize it. All our private lives will be dragged out like dirty laundry. Daddy's already had one major heart attack. I don't know—" Elvis broke off. There were tears in his eyes.

"What do you want us to do?" Rick asked.

"Ricky, I just want the family to hang together. That's all I've ever wanted. Vernon still loves your mom. And I think Dee still loves Vernon. They'll never get back together. It's too late. But Nub," Elvis turned to me, "you can keep them from hurting everyone further."

"How, Elvis?"

"Just talk to your mom. Tell her we can work things out. She wants the house and Vernon's too tight to give it to her. Tell her I guarantee it. Just ask her what else she wants. You know I've always told Dee that I wanted my brothers with me, and that you'd always be well taken care of. Reassure her of that. Nub, you can be the mediator. You're practically the only one who could."

"Okay, Elvis that's fine with me. But if it ever comes down to choosing sides you know that I would have to take Mom's."

"That's as it should be," Elvis said. "I was always close to my mom like that." Then he motioned for me to follow him into the other room.

"Nub, how's this job of yours?"

"Assistant jet mechanic. I like it, Elvis. I think I'm good at it."

"You know, Nub. I really respect your going out on your own. I really love it. Maybe the life-style of the tour isn't right for you just now. I respect your trying to find a way on your own."

"Maybe I'm just trying to grow up, Elvis," I laughed. It felt great to hear him praise me.

"And you and Debbie?"

"Great, Elvis. Couldn't be better."

"I know you can't be making a whole lot of money."

"We're getting by. We're living with Dee right now. Makes it easier with car payments and all that, but we'll get our own apartment again soon."

Elvis was in his closet getting out his black case. "What kind of a car did you get, Nub?"

"TransAm," I said proudly. "You know I've always been partial to them."

"Billy," Elvis said. He'd grabbed a large bundle of money out of the case. "What're you doing buying your own car? Why didn't you say something to me? I buy cars for people I've never shaken hands with and will never see again. I don't want my brother buying his own car."

"I wanted to buy it on my own," I said.

"Nub. I want you to take this. I don't know what's there but it should be enough to pay the car off and get you into your own apartment. Take it!" After Rick and I left I counted out over $5,000 in the bundle.

Except for watching Elvis play racquetball with David and Dean Nichopoulos, Dr. Nick's son, late one night, I didn't see Elvis again for three weeks. One night he called me and asked if I would try to track his "Gingerbread" down. She had a habit of saying she was going home for a few hours and then disappearing for twenty-four hours or more. So I checked out the clubs, some of her friends that I knew, and so on. But I never found out anything. Never really got a lead.

In late July of 1977 *Elvis, What Happened?* came out. In it Red and Sonny West and Dave Hebler chronicled the dark side of Elvis's life. Every threat, every curse, every display of anger was included. They recounted real events, but nothing of the real Elvis was revealed. I started reading it, flipping from page to page, jumping around in the text. It began with Elvis's threats to kill to Mike Stone and quickly went into a depiction of his extensive drug abuse. But it was sensationalized, one-sided, and unfair. This wasn't the Elvis I knew. And it wasn't the Elvis they knew. They were portraying some monster who really never existed. Elvis didn't care about Dave Hebler's involvement in this travesty. He hadn't been there that long. He wasn't family. But he anguished over Red and Sonny. It was just their expression of their anger at being fired. I understood how they could feel, but not how they could go public with it. And it hurt Elvis badly.

The book wasn't a total surprise. Elvis knew about it, had even managed to get an advance copy of most of it. He had called both Red and Sonny to plead that it shouldn't be released; even, I'm told, offered them their jobs back—and at a substantial bonus. But they refused. And the full revelations of the book drove Elvis into fury and depression.

Joe Esposito called a TCB summit meeting to plan a strategy to deal with the book. They were scheduled to go on a twelve-day tour beginning in Portland, Maine, on August 18, and ending in Memphis on August 30. The meeting was about damage control, really, how to deal with the press and the fans now that they had damning evidence to use against us all.

A few days later Elvis called David and me up to his room. We thought he wanted to discuss *Elvis, What Happened?*, particularly since Elvis and David had been discussing it almost every night for months. David was as angry about the book as Elvis.

"You guys saw it?" Elvis asked meekly.

"It's a cheap shot!" David said.

"It's a Judas act," I concurred.

Elvis just hung his head in a way I'd never seen before.

"Come on, boss," David said. "Don't worry about it. You can't let this thing bring you down. They can't hurt you with shit like that. Nobody's going to believe it."

Elvis looked up at us with tears in his eyes. He shook his head. "At one time I said, 'I'd like to kill those guys for doing this.' Man, I couldn't do that. I loved those guys."

Elvis was breaking up and David and I changed the subject real quick. David started talking about the upcoming tour and the karate movie still in the works. "Remember, I've got a part in that, Elvis," I said.

"Damn right you do, Nub. And David's going to be the number one shit-kicker. He's going to be a star. And Billy, you're going back on the tour with me. You just tell me when you're ready, the sooner the better."

Then Elvis got himself together. "What I really want to talk to you guys about is the trial of this friend of yours who's in trouble." You could have knocked us over with a feather. How did Elvis know about that? If he wanted to discuss any trial wouldn't it be the one coming up between Vernon and Dee? David and I were going to do a favor for a friend who was up for robbery. Elvis had this information, as well as information from other sources that our friend was big into drug distribution. In fact he had a complete police file on him. We sat and listened while Elvis read us facts on where he hung out, who he was seen with, what kind of car he drove, and who else he might be involved with.

All we could do was sit back and say, "Elvis, that's heavy," and "We didn't know about any of that."

"Well, you can't be protecting this guy," Elvis said. "You'll just be making yourselves look bad."

Then he started expounding on his old dream, that we would become undercover agents and expose all the drug dealers in Memphis. David and I went along with it, but reminded him that once you get a reputation as a narc or an informer you had better be prepared to leave town. Elvis replied, "Don't sweat the small change. You guys can hold your own. We'll clean the riffraff out. We can make Memphis a clean town."

So it was Marshal Dillon cleaning up Dodge City. Elvis didn't take it as a joke and neither did we. We just wished we could live up to his expectations. When Elvis gave these speeches, David was ready and so was I. "Remember," Elvis said. "When I'm gone it's you who are going to tell my story."

"Well, boss," David said. "You're not going anywhere without your number one shit-kicker at your side."

"You think you're tough?" Elvis challenged.

"I'm ready," David said.

"You ready, Nub?" Elvis asked. He was getting excited.

"Yeah, boss," I said.

"Billy, hold your hands out like you're going to attack me," Elvis said. He picked up these large karate knives and we both got into our stances. "Now don't move. I've got to demonstrate this." He began to pass the knives over and under my arms. Unfortunately I flinched, which in the old days wouldn't have been a problem. Elvis struck me with the knife. It was the blunt end that got me on the hand but it raised an immediate blood blister. It was an unintentional and clumsy act, my first indication that Elvis's motor skills were deteriorating rapidly. Elvis looked dazed.

"Nub, I'm sorry," he said.

"Elvis. That wasn't your fault. I moved. Let's try it again." But the blood blister was swelling like a small balloon on my thumb.

"Billy, let's get some cold water on that," Elvis said. He led me into his bathroom, holding my arm, and I could feel how unsteady he was on his feet as we moved. This was Elvis, the man who could prance like a tiger. But walking was tough and uncertain.

We stumbled together, Elvis trying to support the thumb he'd bloodied, me trying to support all 250 pounds of Elvis. We were kind of hugging each other to get into that bathroom. Then I made a remark that lately had become out of character for me, Nub, the rebel, the silent one. "I love you, Elvis," I said.

"Well, I love you too, Nub. I always will."

Back in his bedroom Elvis fished around for some money to give us. Of course we both declined, but Elvis wanted to give us something so we went along with it. "I want you boys to know you'll always be well taken care of," Elvis said.

"What are you talking about?" David asked, almost angry. "You don't have to give us anything."

"Take this," Elvis said. He gave us about a hundred and fifty apiece. I'm sure he meant it to be more.

That was the last time I saw Elvis alive.

23

"HOW GREAT THOU ART"

(August 1977)

Elvis called me a few days later. "Billy," he said. "This is bad. This divorce between Daddy and your mom is tearing us apart."

"I know it's bad, Elvis. What do you want me to do?"

"Arrange it so I can speak to Dee. She won't answer my calls. If you can set it up I'll give you ten thousand dollars."

"Bullshit, Elvis," I said. "I'll arrange it. But not for money."

"Nub. You don't understand. Arrange the call and come collect the money."

"No way, Elvis," I said. "I'm going to arrange it, but you don't have to pay me a thing for it."

Why was Elvis calling me? It was simple. Dee didn't want to deal with Vernon, and she wouldn't speak to Elvis. She had learned long ago, when we were small children, that he could talk her out of anything. Mom had no sense of business, felt she was betrayed by her husband, knew she had lost her children to Elvis, and needed some help. I just had to be there for her. I had become her spokesperson. Elvis respected that. And I felt it was my duty. Money was out of the question.

Dee had a favorite story she'd kept repeating to me. It was about the last time she'd been on tour, back when Elvis traveled by bus. "I'll never forget it," was the way Dee always began. It was a story about how they were leaving this motel in Las Vegas with Lamar Fike driving. He ran the top of the tour bus into the motel's marquee as they were pulling out. They were stuck for hours. When they were freed, and after Elvis had paid a substantial damage fee to the motel, Elvis grabbed the wheel of the bus and drove them all at breakneck speed far out into the desert until the bus ran out of gas. Then he turned to Lamar and said, "Now, you fat bastard. Fill it up!" Then Elvis went to his bedroom at the back of the bus, went to sleep, and left the rest of them stranded out there. For anyone who toured with Elvis this was normal behavior. Not everyday behavior, but the kind of thing that could happen, and would later be a good story that everyone laughed about. But Dee never got over it. She swore she'd never go out with this family again. She made a decision that night that she would never put herself at the mercy of Elvis's whims again. Of course she flew out to several of key show openings later, but she immediately flew back. And when Vernon, in his concern for his son, came out on the tour regularly it meant he came home to a separate bedroom.

More than losing her husband to Elvis, Dee felt she'd lost her sons to him. It was true. That's why I had to be there for her, even if my heart was with Elvis. So I set up the conversation. I don't know what came of it. A few days later I accompanied Dee to a hearing at the court. We met Vernon outside and he asked, "Son, what are you going to say?"

"I don't know, Daddy," I answered. "The truth, I guess, if they ask me." But I wasn't asked. And there was no resolution that day. It was just a preliminary hearing. Later Vernon and Dee and their attorneys worked out a settlement that avoided a full trial.

A couple of days after that, things seemed to have mellowed out. The crisis over, our torn loyalties were intact. Even the hubbub over Red and Sonny's book was easing. I was planning a going-away party for my brothers before they left on the next tour. Secretly, with all our problems seemingly worked out, I was enjoying the idea of rejoining the tour myself. Somehow the series of encounters had taken the chip off my shoulder. I was glad for that.

In the afternoon of August 16, 1977, I went with a few friends to a place called the Liquor Barn to pick up a keg of beer for the party for Rick and David. I'd been doing this for some time, giving them a farewell party—not before every tour, but usually after they'd been home for awhile and were about to start a series of tours. For some reason my friends walked in first. We all knew the owners, so when I came in a few minutes later I expected them all to be shooting the bull. Instead they were just staring at me. No one seemed able to say anything.

"What's going on?" I asked.

"We just heard that Elvis was dead."

"What?"

"The radio said they took him to Baptist Memorial and he was dead on arrival."

"Bullshit," I growled. "He may have gone in the hospital but there is no way that Elvis is dead. Is this some sick joke?" I demanded.

"Billy. It's on all the stations. You better call Graceland."

"I don't have to," I said, "because I know it's not true."

It was a hot afternoon, probably in the high nineties, and in that closed room there suddenly didn't seem to be any air at all. I must have been stumbling around a little or trying to say something, but I wasn't able to do either very well. I just kept feeling all these eyes staring at me.

"Billy, you better call," a voice said. I found a phone, or someone gave me one. I dialed Graceland and a voice answered, a secretary, I think, or it may have been Patsy.

"This is Billy," I said. "Is it true what I heard on the radio?"

"Billy!" the voice sobbed. "Billy, it's true!"

I dropped the phone and walked out. The heat, suddenly, was unbearable. The air was as thick as water. I felt I couldn't move my arms. And I felt my chest heaving convulsively.

"What do you want to do?" my friend Phil asked.

"Take me to Graceland," I mumbled.

So they got me in the van and drove down to Elvis Presley Boulevard. When we got within a quarter-mile of the mansion we ran into a colossal traffic jam. There were already hundreds of cars and people around Graceland and all traffic was stopped. I didn't know how to handle the situation. I couldn't have found my own way through. But some Memphis police saw me looking out the window of the van and recognized me. They got me out and into a squad car, put on the sirens, and in a few minutes we were through the gates to Graceland. I had them drive me up to the garage area, got out, and walked through the back door.

In the den I saw Rick and David, Charlie, and Billy Smith. They were all just sobbing with their heads down. I walked into the kitchen and Vernon was sitting at the table. He looked up and said, "Billy, Sonny is gone! My Sonny is gone!"

I looked into his eyes. He was so lost! Vernon rose halfway from his chair, and we embraced, and then I lost whatever composure I had left. We both started sobbing and probably would have fallen over, but there were other people there to hold us up. When I felt I could walk I went back to the den and looked at Rick and David. They got up and the three of us went out in the backyard. I could still hear Vernon wailing in the kitchen.

Outside, my brothers and I just stood together by the pool in an eerie silence. With the heat, the stillness, no breath of wind, and the sun still hanging high in the summer sky, it was as if time had stopped. We looked at each other but couldn't speak. And there was Lisa Marie, playing on her golf cart. "Uncle Rick. Watch this!" she commanded. I watched her, we all did, wondering what she knew and what she was blocking out. Only a few hours before, Rick told me, she had been screaming, "My daddy's dead." Now she was intent on driving that golf cart as hard as she could, laughing and demanding, as always, as if nothing had happened. Nine years old, deprived of her daddy, she was dealing with it any way she could. My heart went out to her. But what could we do but watch?

Somehow Debbie got through to Graceland and got me out. The sun finally set that day. It seemed to take forever. On the way back to our apartment I bought two bottles of Wild Turkey, and I finished one and was well into the second before I passed out.

When I awoke the next morning the first thought I had was that I didn't own a proper suit. And I needed one. I went to a friend's store in Memphis and bought a good dark suit and a black tie. No one said a word to me about Elvis, which I appreciated. I was glad I hadn't gone to a store where they knew who I was but didn't know me. Then there would have been questions.

I went back to Graceland and spent another day that lasted a month. At least now I could speak. I went in and helped the secretaries in the office for awhile. Man, were they overloaded! Calls came in constantly, and they didn't know how to deal with them. And Vernon couldn't help. So I took a lot of them. I'm sure I pissed a lot of people off. But the questions were so stupid! I had little patience for most of them. Then my brothers and I got together again. I had my own questions. Rick had been the last, outside of Ginger, to see Elvis alive. David had been among the first to find Elvis dead. I asked them what happened.

Rick had been on duty the night before Elvis died. They had plans to go to the Memphian to see the movie *MacArthur*, which Elvis had already seen three times. As was the case with any movie he liked, he was prepared to see it three more times. We must have seen *Patton* twenty times, and neither Elvis nor we ever tired of it. We knew our dad was in it, even if he wasn't mentioned by name. Normally I would have been part of the party, and driving Elvis's protective trouble-shooter car. But due to my position as Dee's advocate, I wasn't included. Something got screwed up at the Memphian that night and *MacArthur* wasn't shown. When they got back to Graceland Rick was sent out to fill a prescription Dr. Nick had written. Roughly it called for 100 Percodan, 100 Biphetamine (known as Black Beauty), 100 Valium, 100 Dexedrine (speed), 100 Amytal, 150 Quaalude, and 50 Dilaudid (a synthetic heroin, just as addictive and reportedly stronger). It was a lot of drugs, but Rick knew the prescription was meant to last through the forthcoming tour.

When Rick got back to Graceland Elvis was gone. He had decided to see his dentist, a Dr. Hoffman, and get some work done before he left on the next tour. He took Ginger, Charlie, and Billy Smith with him. They came back at around one in the morning and Elvis held a meeting. Elvis said he was concerned about the public's reaction to the book Red and Sonny had just brought out. He wanted to make sure that everything on the tour was set, in terms both of security and appearances. Quickly satisfied that the logistics were in order, Elvis adjourned the meeting, mentioning that he had to consider plans for his forthcoming marriage with Ginger—gowns, limousines, and all that. He was in an expansive mood. He said he was getting calls from Frank Sinatra, Muhammad Ali, and other celebrities decrying the "bodyguard book." But according to my brothers he was more concerned with the next tour and plans for his marriage to Ginger.

After dawn, Elvis asked Rick for his "nine-pack" of drugs. Rick reluctantly gave them to him. He also told Elvis that he had just been on the phone with his girlfriend, Robyn, a born-again Christian, who was then living with her parents in Florida. "Boss," Rick told him, "this is where I'm personally headed. I mean to serve only Christ. You know Robyn. And you know she's right. At least for me she is."

"Yeah, I guess so," Elvis replied, bowing his head. And then, to Rick's surprise he said, "Rick, we should all begin to live for Christ."

Then Elvis asked Rick about a new copy of the Bible that had been sent to him. When Rick found it for him Elvis told Rick that he planned to read, and didn't want to be disturbed for the rest of the night. Rick, knowing that Elvis wanted to be alone with Ginger, left him at about three in the morning.

Elvis was still agitated and unable to sleep. He called his cousin, Billy Smith, who still lived in a trailer in back of Graceland, and said he wanted to play racquetball. Billy and his wife, Jo, met Elvis at the court. Elvis was wearing a powder-blue jogging suit with the letters DEA (Drug Enforcement Agency). He tried to play a game, but he really couldn't play. He swatted at a few balls, hit himself on the shin, then went to the piano and started playing and singing gospel songs.

At around six in the morning he went back up to his room. Ginger, who'd been with him all this time, hit the sack. Some time later Elvis went into his bathroom and called downstairs. Either because he could find no one else available, or because he was afraid anyone else would deny his request, he somehow talked Aunt Delta into bringing him a second "nine-pack" of drugs from the kitchen refrigerator. Unaccustomed to this activity, but unable to deny Elvis's requests, Aunt Delta found the drugs and delivered them.

An hour later, Elvis, still unable to sleep, retreated to his bathroom to read a book on the Shroud of Turin. If Linda Thompson had still been there she would have been alert—she would not have slept until Elvis did. But Ginger was a kid really, not fully aware of the dangers. As soon as Elvis left her side she went to sleep.

David arrived at Graceland around noon August 16 to relieve Rick. Rick told him that Elvis had been up late, so David and his friend Mark went downstairs to shoot pool. Even if Elvis had been awake at the time David wouldn't have disturbed him. He would have waited for the set time, usually three-thirty, or until Elvis called him; before entering his room.

Ginger woke at around two in the afternoon. Apparently she made a few phone calls to friends; it was another half-hour before she remembered that Elvis had awakened her in the morning and said he was going to the bathroom. That had been several hours before, but still it was no cause for alarm. Elvis's bathroom was his own, a private retreat. He had had walls knocked out to enlarge it into a combination bathroom and study. One wall, fully mirrored, held the vanity counter and sunken sink, and the large circular shower. Elvis had the facing wall lined with a small library, a TV, and a couple of easy chairs. The floor was covered with a thick purple shag rug. Elvis would sit for hours in one of those chairs, reading his favorite books. This is what he had been doing that morning, in his powder-blue pajamas, when a heart attack struck.

Ginger finally concluded her "what's happening?" conversations with her friends. She went to the door of the bathroom, knocked, and hearing no response, entered. Elvis was on the floor in front of one of the leather lounge chairs, bent forward, with his head in the thick carpet.

"Elvis?" Ginger asked. She could see that something was terribly wrong. She ran to a phone. Al Strada answered it in the kitchen.

"Get up here!" Ginger yelled. "There's something wrong with Elvis!"

Al was up in a flash, with Joe Esposito, who'd just arrived to start making plans for the midnight departure of the group, right behind him. Joe immediately called for an ambulance, giving the address and instructions that the driver was to come straight through the gate. Joe then turned Elvis on his back and began giving him mouth-to-mouth resuscitation. Al Strada was on the phone to the hospital trying to have Dr. Nick paged.

Downstairs David was still shooting pool with Mark when Lisa and her friend Amber came running into the room. Lisa said, "David, my daddy's sick. I just saw him. David, come quick!"

Behind her, Amber said, "Elvis fell out of bed."

David bounded up the steps just as the paramedics arrived. He found Joe still giving Elvis mouth-to-mouth aid, and Charlie Hodge beating on Elvis's chest, screaming, "Live, Elvis! Live!"

Vernon, having been summoned from his office, was slumped up against a wall sobbing, "David, he's dead! My Sonny is dead!" David said, "No, Daddy. Elvis isn't dead. This isn't happening." But Vernon only gasped and sank lower against the wall. Fortunately, Sandy Miller was there and she quickly gave Vernon a quieting shot. Without her presence there well could have been two fatal heart attacks that day.

The paramedics tried heart massage and an injection of Adrenalin directly into the heart. But when David moved in closer he could see that none of it would do any good. Elvis's face was fixed and mottled with blue pools of blood. His tongue, grotesquely huge and protruding, was a deep purple. There was no breath. His knees almost touched his chin. Rigor mortis had set in.

They took him to Baptist Memorial where, absurdly, attempts at revival continued. Joe stopped a doctor and asked how long Elvis's brain had been without oxygen. "Too long," the doctor said. "Hours."

At 3:30 P.M. on August 16, 1977, Elvis Aaron Presley was officially pronounced dead. Vernon and Joe arranged a press conference to tell the world the sad news.

My brothers and I, in our dark suits in the ninety-five-degree heat, stood or sat on the steps leading up to our brother's room as the mourners filed into Graceland and out, all to view Elvis's lifeless body. Larry Geller had worked through the night before with the local morticians trying to make Elvis look like Elvis, but the blood that had collected in his face made him look grotesque even with all the makeup. Vernon had opened the gates because that had been Elvis's request. The line of mourners was unending. Many of them passed out in the heat; those that didn't had to endure hours of waiting for just a brief glimpse. No one complained. It wasn't just that Elvis was a star. For the tens of thousands who came that day, for the tens of millions across the country, for hundreds of millions throughout the world, a soul and spirit that they could call their own was lost. His mourners included those who had grown up in extreme poverty, like Elvis, and the 'billies, like myself, who grew up in the south with all the advantages but who still remembered their roots.

The casket was in front of the fireplace in the living room, which was reported by people who didn't know to be the "music room." I refused to walk up to the casket for some time, as did my brothers. It was as if once we did we had to accept what we couldn't accept. But it was inevitable and at some point we joined the line and filed past. David, the youngest, was in front, and when we got to Elvis, neatly attired in a white suit, blue shirt, and dark blue tie, he put his hand on Elvis's hand. I put my hand on Elvis's arm and my other hand on top of David's. Rick put one hand on Elvis and the other on top of mine. We paused like that. All I could think of was that I'd never said to Elvis, "I forgive you." Nor had he ever said it to me. I didn't say it then. I bent down and kissed his bloated, lifeless cheek and said, "Thanks for the good times, man." Then we moved on.

They closed the gates at six-thirty. Thousands of people had come to view Elvis. Thousands more waited outside. The crowds grew larger. Then a second tragedy occurred. At three in the morning some crazed idiot, loaded on beer, made a bizarre U-turn and crashed his car into the grieving crowd, killing two girls and critically injuring a third. It was absurd, useless. It saddened everyone all the more.

The formal ceremony was held the next day. By this time all of the important figures in Elvis's life had had time to get there. Priscilla arrived the first day to rescue Lisa Marie from the golf cart. Vernon or Joe had sent the *Lisa Marie* to pick her up in L.A. In addition to Priscilla, Linda Thompson was there, Ann-Margret, Ginger Alden— all the women Elvis had loved and who had loved Elvis. Charlie Hodge, sizing up the situation remarked, "What a stunt! Who else but Elvis would die just to bring all his girlfriends together in one room?"

I didn't laugh. I couldn't. But I appreciated the attempt at humor and the good fellowship it represented. We were there, after all, to honor the man, and the man would have joked. Charlie knew that, but he carried on the tradition almost alone.

A two-hour ceremony followed. The front door was shut and folding chairs were arranged back from Elvis's casket, through the front foyer, and into the dining room. About 150 attended the service, with another hundred thousand outside. Vernon, Priscilla, and Lisa Marie were in the first row. My brothers, Ginger, Debbie and I, and my mom were in about the seventh. Linda Thompson and Ann-Margret were directly behind us.

The organist started playing "Danny Boy," one of the first songs I'd ever heard Elvis sing when, as kids, we sat around the piano. Then Kathy Westmoreland sang "My Heavenly Father Watches over Me." The Stamps sang "How Great Thou Art," "His Hand in Mine," and "Sweet, Sweet Spirit." And then our pastor, C.W. Bradley of the Church of Christ, said, in part:

We are here to honor the memory of a man loved by millions. . . . Elvis can serve as an inspiring example of the great potential of one human being who has strong desire and unfailing determination. From total obscurity Elvis rose to world fame. Though idolized by millions, and forced to be protected from the crowds, Elvis never lost his desire to stay in close touch with humanity.

In a society that has talked so much about the generation gap, the closeness of Elvis and his father, and his constant dependence upon Vernon's counsel, was heartwarming to observe. Elvis never forgot his family. In a thousand ways he showed his great love for them.

But Elvis was a frail human being. And he would be the first to admit his weaknesses. Perhaps because of the rapid rise to fame and fortune he was thrown into temptations that some never experience. Elvis would not want anyone to think that he had no flaws or faults. But now that he's gone, I find it more helpful to remember his good qualities, and I hope you do, too.

The casket was closed and the pallbearers—Joe Esposito, Charlie Hodge, George Klein, Lamar Fike, Jerry Schilling, Gene and Billy Smith, and Dr. Nick—carried Elvis through the front door. Vernon, Sandy, Dee, and the three of us were right behind. (Dee and Vernon had reached a temporary cease-fire in their divorce wars. In fact, for two days they had been holding hands and crying on each other's shoulders. They still loved each other, but too many misunderstandings had gone unresolved, and separate courses were set for their lives.) At that moment we were all together. To me, it was still dreamlike, removed from time. As we left the house there was a loud cracking sound over our heads and a large limb from one of the oak trees came crashing down. It has been reported since that the limb was dead, and that circumstances, the heat, or something, caused it to fall at that moment. I know it wasn't the wind, because there was none. Later Uncle Earl examined the limb and declared it perfectly healthy. But at the time its fall didn't strike me as unusual in the least. The event reminded all of us close to Elvis of a promise he often made, "Wherever I am, if there is a way to communicate with you, I'll find it!"

The cortege formed. A silver Cadillac limousine drove in front, followed by several white Cadillac limousines. The first was the hearse that carried Elvis. Vernon and Priscilla rode in the second. My brothers and I were in the seventh. We commented to each other than seven was Elvis's favorite number. But we also wondered why we were so far back. In all there were sixteen white limos. Most people think that was an intentional reference to one of Elvis's songs, that has the line ". . . train I ride, sixteen coaches long." But I knew otherwise: I'd overheard Vernon say to someone, "That's all the white limos I could get."

It seemed to take hours to arrive at the Forest Hills Cemetery and reach the granite mausoleum shaped like a Greek temple that was to hold Elvis's remains. The pallbearers carried the casket into the crypt. Then Elvis's mother's coffin was interred with his. The mausoleum was sealed with concrete and marble by half a dozen workmen.

We rode back to Graceland, without Elvis, and I thought of what the pastor had said about remembering the good things. But I also thought of a couple of other matters. Colonel Parker had arrived the day before wearing a Hawaiian shirt, an admiral's cap, and his usual look of defiance. Apparently he had immediately made some licensing deal with poor Vernon, who was too weak with grief to resist the colonel's badgering. Colonel was heard to say, "Nothing has changed. This won't change anything." Maybe, for him, it was true. Colonel somehow never grasped anything that Elvis really was, as a person. It was incredible because he had known Elvis even longer than I had, and in my opinion he didn't care about the man, personally, at all. It was just business to him, always. Maybe it was a relief for Vernon to have him there. Because Vernon, when a crisis came up, would always say, "Boys, let's wait to see what the colonel has to say."

Then Colonel approached us. He said nothing about Elvis. Nothing about loss, grief, or sorrow. He said, "Boys, I don't want you getting involved in anything. Give me your phone numbers and addresses. I'm going to get in touch with you later about merchandising contracts. Believe me, the show is going to go on. And you're going to be a big part of it."

We said nothing to him. This wasn't the colonel who barked out orders on movie sets and gave three little boys, wondering who he was, cigars to smoke on the back set. We were men and we knew who he was. As David said later, "I should have decked him right there." I replied, "No, I should have."

And there was my recollection of Priscilla. Among the groups of lost and weeping souls uncertain how to behave, she remained so proper, yet so cold. If she spoke to me or anyone else at the funeral, it escapes my memory. And I'll never forgot what she said to my mom at Vernon's funeral less than two years later: "Why are you crying for him, Dee," Priscilla asked. "You didn't see me shed a tear when Elvis died."

24

"FUNNY HOW TIME SLIPS AWAY"

(1 9 7 7 ▬ 1 9 7 9)

Elvis had always said, "Death is the hardest thing for anyone to accept."

When we were kids he'd take us out at night and drive us down Highway 51 heading south.

"Where are we going, Elvis?" one of us would ask. It was the wrong direction for the fairgrounds or the cinema. Elvis wouldn't answer. He'd just keep driving until we got to Forest Hill Cemetery. Then, under clear, starry skies, he'd take us to his mother's grave. The gravemarker read:

Gladys Smith Presley
April 25, 1912—August 14, 1958
Beloved Wife of Vernon Presley
And Mother of Elvis Presley
She Was the Sunshine of Our Home

Elvis would say, "You've got to accept the challenge of death. Otherwise you'll live in fear of it." Elvis accepted that challenge with his mother's death, and he repeatedly said that we were never too young to start preparing for it. He often talked about his stillborn twin brother, Jesse Garon Presley, and the shotgun-style house where they were born in East Tupelo, Mississippi.

We knew from his tone that Elvis had hated that house, the poverty and alienation he'd been born to. But he loved the people who surrounded him. He never even thought to question his parents for anything that was lacking. When he found sudden fame and fortune Elvis immediately shared it with his family, making his family part of his life. Now Elvis, born of Vernon and Gladys, was dead. Were we prepared for it? Not me. In his final year he spoke often to Rick and David of his death. But to me he'd only mentioned it a few times, always vaguely. He'd talk about how we would be, along with Lisa, his legacy, taken care of, how we would tell his story. None of us paid any real attention to it. I don't know how many times Elvis told me he'd never get past the age of forty. When he got there he'd say, "Be prepared. I won't make it past forty-two." And he didn't.

In retrospect, the signs were evident. He wouldn't exercise, he only occasionally dieted, and then only with the help of powerful stimulants. And he could only come down from his performances with a widening variety of prescription drugs. By this time everyone was trying to warn him of the dangers. Elvis wouldn't listen. "I *know* what I'm doing!" he'd insist. But a couple of times in Rick's and David's presence he reversed the statement. "Man, what the hell am I doing?" he'd ask. He'd make a resolution to stay away from drugs, and it could last a few days, until something happened to convince him he needed them. The last several months on the tour, Elvis spent nearly all his time in bed. As soon as the *Lisa Marie* got them to a city, Elvis would go to bed. He'd remain there until shortly before his performance, when a series of powerful stimulants would arouse him. When that night's show was over he'd go back to his bed on the *Lisa Marie*. At the next town Rick or David or Charlie would sometimes wake him and say, "Elvis, it's a beautiful day. Get up, man. Let's do some exercises!" But Elvis could only get up for his next performance. He'd lost interest in everything else. His favorite songs that last year were "My Way" ("And now the end is near, and so I face the final curtain . . .") and Hank Williams's "I'm So Lonesome I Could Cry."

We took all that as a sign that Elvis was burned out from touring, and we saw his bad health as a sign that his body was burned out from the drugs he took to keep touring. All it would take to restore the old Elvis, I thought, was a healthy vacation from both. That never came.

What was the cause of Elvis's death? Within an hour of the announcement an autopsy was conducted. At its conclusion Dr. Jerry Francisco, the Shelby County coroner, had determined that the cause of death was a cardiac arrhythmia, a coronary disease. In short, Elvis died of a heart attack brought on by natural causes. But Elvis was only forty-two years old. "Natural causes" is a phrase usually reserved for someone in his seventies or beyond. When asked about drugs, Dr. Francisco stated that the only drugs detected were "those prescribed by Mr. Presley's personal physician [Dr. Nichopoulos] for hypertension and a blockage of the colon. . . ."

What had happened to the Percodan, Quaalude, Dilaudid, and other drugs that made up Elvis's "nine-pack"? I know that Rick gave Elvis his first pack of medication the night before Elvis died. I know that Aunt Delta gave him a second pack at about nine the following morning. It was unusual for Aunt Delta to give Elvis drugs, but everyone who regularly worked for Elvis would have refused him the second pack. How could all those drugs not show up in the autopsy?

Of course I was not the only one with questions. ABC did a news special questioning Dr. Francisco's report. It quoted Rick as mentioning the house for which Elvis loaned Dr. Nick money and saying that a Los Angeles dentist had given Elvis any drug he wanted. ABC pointed out that there had been no police investigation, no search for drugs, and that Elvis's internal organs had been removed and discarded. They demanded that Elvis's body be exhumed and a more thorough investigation begun.

The Memphis papers reported that Maurice Elliot, a Baptist Memorial vice-president, believed that "polypharmacy," an effect of several drugs working together, was the probable cause of death.

I don't believe Elvis died of a drug overdose. I believe he died of a heart attack. But I also believe that, right or wrong, the circumstances of Elvis's death should be faced. Just as Elvis should have faced up to his situation when he was alive. If he had, he might be alive today. If, when he had that heart attack, his body had not been so numbed and disoriented with those downers he might have been able to summon help or even find some way to help himself.

There were other strange things going on. First there was an attempt, several days after Elvis's and Gladys's remains were placed in the crypt, to steal his body. Vernon had both brought back to a new cemetery at Graceland. Then there were reports of two ambulances leaving in the middle of the night, bound for Tupelo, supposedly with the caskets of Elvis and Gladys. There were other rumors too numerous and bizarre to repeat.

Several months later my brothers and I were called in to testify at a grand jury investigation of Dr. Nick. I saw Vernon outside and I asked him what he thought I should say. "Just tell the truth, son," Vernon replied.

I did. But the only questions they asked me were, "Did you ever see Dr. Nichopoulos give Elvis a shot?" and "Did you ever see Dr. Nichopoulos give Elvis a pill?" To both questions I answered truthfully that I had not. But they didn't ask me if I picked up prescriptions for Elvis written by Dr. Nick. I did. They didn't ask me what drugs the prescriptions were for. They didn't ask me if prescriptions that were meant for Elvis were ever written and picked up in someone else's name. They were, by me, in my brother's name, in my name, and in many other names, principally at the Baptist Memorial Pharmacy and at the Methodist South Pharmacy. They didn't ask if Dr. Nick was on the payroll. He was. And if he was, why? They didn't ask but I knew the answer. His nickname was "Needle Nick." So Dr. Nick got his wrists slapped. The state medical board suspended his license to practice medicine and put him on three years probation. If they'd asked me the right questions it would have been a different matter.

They say that everyone has his price. I just hope that Dr. Nick, when he went home to his $300,000 house for which Elvis loaned him money, and as a pallbearer, carried Elvis's casket, realized that the kinds of drugs he'd prescribed had helped put Elvis where he was.

Then there was the will. Elvis had always told us we were in it. And he'd repeated to my mom, many times, "Dee, no matter what comes down your boys will be provided for." At one time I heard that Elvis's will provided one million dollars apiece for my brothers and me. I don't know. I never saw it. But Rick, who was with Elvis almost every day for the last six years of Elvis's life, once told he had seen it and that a substantial and equal amount was to be left to each of the three of us. However, in that original will there were grand provisions for everyone. All the TCBers were included—Joe, Charlie, Lamar, Red, Gene and Billy Smith, and others. Probably the will called for sums beyond Elvis's worth—that was always Elvis's way. Give it all back, it's only money.

Weeks before Elvis's death the will was changed. The change was inspired by Vernon's insistence that Elvis was spending his fortune before it could reach the proper dimensions of an estate and that too many people (whom Elvis considered family, but Vernon did not) were included. When Red and Sonny's book, *Elvis, What Happened?*, neared publication date Elvis gave in to Vernon's demands and changed the will. In its final form, read before Vernon, Priscilla (as Lisa's mother and guardian), and Charlie Hodge, the entire estate had one heir, Lisa Marie. Vernon was the sole executor and had the power to bestow cash on "close relatives in need," but there were no other provisions.

Why was everyone else suddenly cut out? Because of the book, mostly. It helped bolster Vernon's argument that no one outside the family could be trusted. The book gave Vernon the opportunity to hammer home the point that Elvis had spent so much he might not be able to provide properly for Lisa Marie. Vernon's argument might have made an exception for Rick, David, and me, but he was going through a divorce with Dee, so we fell, with everyone else, by the wayside.

Not that it mattered. At least, not for the money. None of us cared about that. Rick, now united with his Christian friend, and later wife, Robyn, was into spiritual evangelism. He didn't want or need the money. I may have needed it; I was heavily into alcohol and drugs. I only would have wasted it and maybe killed a few people, myself included, if money was available. David was somewhere in between, but still (in my opinion) too young to deal with a sudden large sum.

But there was the issue of pride for us. We would have liked to be in the will for any small amount. Just mentioned. And for Mom it verged on treachery. How many times had she been told that no matter what happened, her sons would be provided for? That if we were taken out of school to join Elvis on tour a college fund would always be available? She'd only given in believing that it was true. When she found out through the Memphis papers that in the end nothing was provided, she had a hard time, and she made it a hard time for Vernon. And that, really, was a shame, because they loved each other. They parted, forever, in the guise of enemies.

At a final divorce hearing that fall a compromise settlement was reached. Vernon got the Dolan Street house and Dee got enough money to buy a large house on a lake south of Memphis and a substantial cash settlement.

I only saw Vernon once again. For no particular reason I went to Graceland and found him, as I knew I would, in his office. Vernon looked very tired and I was careful not to mention any of the events of that summer. We just chatted for awhile about where our lives were going, and with Sandy's two younger children now with him I said, "Daddy, seems like you've got another long, hard road of parenthood ahead." And we both laughed. But I could see that he was not well.

Sometime early in 1978 Dee made a deal with Delacorte Press that included my brothers and me. We all met in Destin, Florida, in the early spring of 1979 to write, with Martin Torgoff, a biography of Elvis. The book that resulted, *Elvis, We Love You Tender*, was an embarrassment. As published it seemed to reveal only the bad or detrimental aspects of Elvis. The good was left out. It portrayed my brothers and me as slick-talking, dope-smoking, bourbon-guzzling hipsters who said things like, "The man was into drugs for sure, and so was I," and "Hey, man, it gets lonesome on that road because you live it." Maybe we did talk a little like that, because Elvis did, in public. But in private there was never any bombast or macho bleating from Elvis. There was only a loving, tender, and later, hurt and often angry soul. This didn't come out in the book. My brothers and I were portrayed as country bumpkins at best, mind-boggled idiots at the usual worst. And Elvis fared only a little better.

Martin Torgoff, in a later book, claimed he had written a more balanced presentation but that his editors had taken the famous blue pencil to any redeeming characteristics the Presley clan exhibited. Nobody wants to hear anything good about Elvis, he was advised. People just want to read the dirt. Let's make him look as bad as we can.

Beyond the one-sided personality portrayals, the book makes no sense. As with all lives, Elvis's included, one thing leads to another. But Martin had us accompanying Elvis in his own customized, luxury jets as soon as we joined the tour (that didn't happen for another five years), had David on the tour before Lisa Marie was born (David was in the eighth grade), and generally had nothing in the order it happened, with the exception of Elvis's death.

Fortunately, I contributed little to that book, first because I was close-mouthed and suspicious of the effort, but also because I couldn't go along with the depiction of Priscilla that my mother and brothers were determined to honor. "Priscilla is anything but a devious woman. Charades, facades, games with people's emotions, and clandestine love affairs are not her style," the text of the book reads. "Straight-shooter that she is, she came right out and told Elvis what was going on . . ." Dee is reported as saying. David, comparing Priscilla and Ginger, said, "Cilla outclasses her a hundred percent." And Rick says, "If there was ever a woman that walked the face of God's earth that fit the description of 'woman,' it's Cilla!"

Nobody's ever told the truth about Priscilla. She is always portrayed, or portrays herself, as forthcoming and honest. But her affair with Mike Stone had been going on for at least a year before she told Elvis. When I heard my mom and my brothers talk about her I just bit my lip. When I later read that on the day of Elvis's funeral Priscilla "was tender and yet impenetrably calm," I just laughed.

Why would they say those things? First because we all abided (me by my silence) by the rule of security and family protection. But more importantly because Rick and David believed what they were saying. They thought, and still do, that Priscilla was family. Dee knew better, but I believe bitterness over her sons' relationships with Elvis and the final will made Dee side with Priscilla, the woman who turned against Elvis.

The last time I saw Priscilla was at Vernon's funeral. That was in late June of 1979. No one was really shocked by Vernon's death. The biggest surprise was that he had lasted for almost two years after Elvis's death broke his heart. We buried our daddy at Graceland in the plot he'd reserved for himself next to Gladys and Elvis. His remains, and Elvis's, lie today in the little semicircle of white columns and stone next to the meditation garden.

Priscilla had acted cold at Elvis's funeral but this time she behaved differently. Because of Vernon's death, she was about to become the executor of the estate. But this time she didn't act as if she was going to boss everything.

After the services, Priscilla told us about a production company that wanted to make a TV special out of home movies that had been made, over the years, at Graceland. She said she needed us to sign a release on the rights and that there would be some money for us later when the special was aired. We signed the papers.

Then Priscilla took Rick, David, and me, along with her sister,

Michelle, out to dinner. After dinner Rick had to catch a plane back to Florida. The rest of us went on to an Italian restaurant where Priscilla kept buying us expensive bottles of red wine. She gave us one bottle unopened and told us to save it for a special occasion. We went on to another place, the Cock-Eyed Camel, and started talking about a lot of things we never had revealed to one another before. Laughing, Priscilla told me how angry her brother, Jeff, was that I had taken his girlfriend away in Las Vegas. That was the first I'd heard about it. I remembered the girl, quite a striking blond who was infatuated with the Elvis scene. But I didn't remember anything about her having come there with Priscilla's brother.

Priscilla was really letting her hair down. She told us about one time when she joined Elvis on the West Coast when she was only sixteen years old. She was scared of everything, particularly of Elvis's costars, but she didn't want to show it. One day she and Elvis were sitting in the living room of the first house he leased in Beverly Hills. He was reading her passages from the Bible, recreating voices of the characters. Priscilla kept snuggling up to him, anxious to consummate their love, but Elvis, obviously as anxious as Cilla but painfully aware of her age, kept reading passages from the Old Testament. As they snuggled and fondled each other Elvis's voice grew louder and louder. Suddenly, Elvis excused himself and went to the bathroom. For awhile Cilla was confused—didn't he feel the same passion? Then she was upset, and when the minutes dragged by and Elvis didn't return she became worried. She went to the bathroom door, knocked, and heard only a mumbled answer. So she went outside and around back and climbed a stone ledge that enabled her to see into the bathroom. There she saw Elvis, masturbating. She was back on the couch, crying, when Elvis finally returned from the bathroom.

Elvis, concerned but becalmed, asked, "Cilla, what's the matter?"

"You don't really love me," she cried. "You're finding your sex someplace else." Then, to Elvis's great discomfort, she told him what she saw.

We all laughed at that. It was a great story (unless you've never admitted to masturbation) and one that literally caught Elvis with his pants down. But a few minutes later Priscilla was crying. That stirred something in my heart. Made me remember I'd once cared for her like a sister. Later we got to laughing again and Cilla announced that she'd had enough of bars and that we should all go skinny-dipping.

She suggested that we might as well take advantage of the pool at Graceland.

Now I'm always for skinny-dipping at the drop of a hat, and I usually wear the hat, but I couldn't see going to Graceland, with Elvis's grave next to the pool and Vernon fresh in his grave next to Elvis. Michelle was, at best, lukewarm on the idea as well. We ended up driving out to the airport to make arrangements for their flight back to the West Coast. At the airport Priscilla suggested that Michelle and I go in to pick up the tickets. When we got back to the car we found Priscilla and David in the back seat wrapped up in what you could call a compromising position—very compromising.

We went to another bar, which was loud and hot. The skinny-dipping issue came up again. Finally we went to the pool at David's apartment. I stripped down first and jumped in the pool. Cilla stripped down to her bra and panties but she wouldn't get in at first. She just kept walking around the pool, laughing, and saying, "I don't know if I'm going to do this or not."

Michelle was walking quickly after her. "After all this you're going in," Michelle insisted. Then Priscilla decided to run away. Michelle and David were right behind her. I got out of the pool and joined the pursuit. It was after 2:00 A.M. but to anyone in the apartment complex who looked out their window we must have made quite a sight, with Priscilla in only panties and bra, David and Michelle fully clothed, and me as naked as a plucked chicken.

We caught Priscilla, carried her to the pool, and tossed her in. Then I jumped back in, with David and Michelle right behind me. When we went upstairs, the rest of us just put our dry clothes back on our wet bodies. In the Memphis summer heat that felt good to me. But Priscilla left the bathroom door open while she took her bra and panties off, toweled herself off, and dried her hair. Naturally, David and I couldn't help but watch. Then she came to the door, still naked, and asked, "David, have you got anything I can wear?"

We just laughed. We finally got Priscilla and Michelle back to Graceland at about six in the morning. The sun was coming up and I remember Priscilla saying, "I just hope we're getting back before Lisa wakes up." At Graceland's front door Cilla hugged David and me, saying she really loved us and that we had to stick together, not drift apart.

I recall that early morning scene quite well and how, even though I'd had no sleep, I thought how beautiful the sunrise was and what a great day it was going to be. And I remember it because, unlike my brothers, I've never seen Priscilla since, except on TV or on the cover of magazines and tabloids. The Elvis home movies did appear as a TV special about six months later, but I never got any money from it nor heard a word of explanation. And it was another nine long years before I again stood on Graceland's steps.

25

"HEARTBREAK HOTEL"

(1 9 7 9 ▬ 1 9 8 7)

At least the colonel's power was nearly at an end. He had his way for a couple of years while he could still control Vernon, taking (I've read) eighty-two percent of the money flowing into the estate. But with Vernon's death and the court appointment of Priscilla as the executor, that very soon came to a halt. Colonel was asked by the court to justify his large take and had no answer. He was cut off and cut out, left to answer difficult questions from the courts.

But what became of Billy Stanley? Well, my second wife, Debbie, divorced me. She had come with me to Destin, Florida when we all got together to work on Dee's book, *Elvis, We Love You Tender,* and even though I hadn't contributed much to the book, the experience of seeing me with my brothers, drinking and talking (maybe boasting) of all the things we'd done on the tour, was too much for her. She left early, and within two weeks had started divorce proceedings. The truth is that even before that meeting things had gone downhill. I was drinking too much, hanging out too much, taking too many drugs. I'd lost my job as a jet mechanic and did little or nothing in the way of attempting to find another. I couldn't blame Debbie. It occurred to me that this was the second wife I'd lost in Florida. But this time it was my fault.

After the divorce I lived on the money we got from *Elvis, We Love You Tender* for several months, and when that ran out I moved in with my mother at her house on the lake. I'd bought a speedboat and I exceeded every known limit on the lake, managing few run-ins with other lakefront homeowners. Then I got a landscaping job, got a little money ahead again, and shared an apartment with David in Memphis. Finally I got a good job as assistant manager at J.J. Morley's Clothing Store and things seemed to be going pretty good.

Rick had married Robyn, completed his ministerial studies, and was ordained as a Baptist minister. He moved to Dallas to establish his evangelical mission, Rick Stanley Ministries, and urged David and me to join him. I wasn't ready for anything like that, but David left for Dallas. I stayed in Memphis for a time and then went to Nashville to work for another recording company. Just as it had been with Casino records, my job was to use my name and connections to sign up new talent for the company. But I saw it as a way to keep the party going, and they got rid of me pretty quick. After my move to Nashville Dee sold her house and moved there too. She'd always preferred Nashville and, I think, she felt there was nothing left for her in Memphis.

Even before I worked for the recording company my main occupation in life had become being Elvis's little brother. The duties included going to parties, going to bars, talking with people, answering their questions, and taking drugs and drinking with them. Whatever the business, or scam, or deal was, there were plenty of people willing to furnish me with booze, coke, Quaaludes, or Demerols, just to have me around so that they could talk about the time they met or saw Elvis or about the Elvis movie we were all going to make. I listened to all the stuff people had to say about Elvis. How he touched them, how he did this, how he did that. Sometimes I'd correct their stories when I knew they were wrong. If I didn't know I'd just say, "Sounds like Elvis." Sometimes I'd laugh at the versions, like when I heard that Elvis was sitting in a room with JFK and Martin Luther King and that the three of them were going to return in 2001 because that was the theme Elvis used before he came on stage. Sometimes I must have gotten angry, particularly when they told me that they'd seen Elvis in the Bahamas the week before when they were on vacation, or that Elvis and his stillborn twin, Jesse, had been spotted on a UFO. That crap drove me crazy, but generally I must have suppressed my anger because I was usually a hit at parties, and only occasionally out of control with anger. My life-style got worse and worse. Rick knew I was in trouble; he called me regularly to tell me about his new awareness and his new direction. Then he'd ask me, practically beg me, to come to Dallas and join them. But I had to go my own way. It was the wrong way, but I'd bought the ticket and I was in for the full ride.

One night in July of 1981, after I'd moved back to Memphis, I ate thirty-six Quaaludes in a forty-eight-hour period. Why? I don't know. I was not like Rick, who got totally involved in drugs yet when it was over and the shame came, found a new direction—much to his credit. Rick had paid harder dues than any of us—he'd been a heroin addict. He had learned something from Elvis's seeking and from the masters Elvis respected so much. Rick had also learned something from the religious teachers who tell you to become fully involved in your faith, then emerge a new person. As Elvis bid us to do, Rick did. I couldn't. I meant to follow Elvis's example all my life, but I seemed to have picked up only the bad stuff, when I knew as well as anyone that the good things about Elvis were overwhelming. I was lost.

That July night Rick had a dream about me dying. He called my friend Randy, who came and found me passed out in my apartment. He helped me get on a plane to Dallas. Rick took me into his home for awhile; then I moved into an apartment with David.

David was making appearances with Rick, decrying the effects of drugs, alcohol, and the lost life. I knew I had to play that game myself, at least with Rick. So I was straight for a time, or rather I learned how to give that appearance and to avoid detection when I wasn't. But there were temptations in Dallas just like anywhere else.

I got a job with a landscaping company in Dallas. I moved out of David's apartment and took another with two new friends. We had a lot of good times. One day there was a fire. I don't know how it started. Everything I had was destroyed in it. My clothing, my TCB ring and necklace, my shirts, everything was destroyed. Of course I had no insurance. But how do you insure the mementos of an existence? They were just gone.

In August of 1982, something happened that changed my life. I got on a bus in Fort Worth, bound eventually for Nashville where I was going to visit Dee. I sat down next to a pretty girl named Connie. Connie and her younger sister, Donna, were bound for Humboldt,

Tennessee, to visit another sister, married and older than them. I had practically given up all hope of falling in love again, of having a permanent and lasting affair. But Connie was different. We talked for sixteen hours straight. She was seventeen. I was twenty-nine. But I was smitten. And before they got off the bus in Memphis I told her, "Connie, I'm going to marry you one day."

When I got to Nashville I called the number she had given me in Humboldt. Connie's sister, Judy, answered. I explained who I was and asked if I could speak to Connie. Judy said, "No, you may not. My sisters are out here to see me, not to have the likes of you bothering them the whole time. And please don't call back."

Whew! Obviously I wasn't going to get to see Connie again while she was in Tennessee. But I had her parents' phone number in San Diego as well and several weeks later I started calling her there.

Rather than return to Dallas I got a landscaping job in Nashville and moved back in with Dee. My biggest expense was the two to three hundred dollars in long-distance phone bills I racked up talking to Connie.

That December I took a bus to San Diego, took a motel close to Connie's parents' house (actually in Lemon Grove, a suburb of San Diego) and spent a week with her. I wanted to ask her to marry me but first I had to tell her about my background and Elvis. Telling a girl about Elvis before I knew how she felt about me was the last thing I wanted to do. But now I was sure, so I told Connie.

"You're kidding," she said. "You must be."

"Why?"

"Billy, don't you remember that guy on the bus who was all over Donna? He said his name was Champ Presley and that he was Elvis's cousin. Of course, later he admitted he was really Elvis's son, but that he couldn't tell anyone."

"Yeah, I remember him."

"And now you say you're Elvis's brother?"

"Stepbrother. But he always called us brothers."

"I can't believe it."

"Connie, it's true."

"I don't mean I don't believe you. I just can't believe you would let that guy carry on, let my sister half-believe him, and never say a word. What did you think of him? Weren't you angry?"

"No," I laughed. "I was so taken by you I hardly noticed him." And that was the truth. People claiming to be Elvis's cousin, or the like, were old hat to me. And how do you sort out the phonies when there are so many of them?

I asked. Connie accepted. But she needed time to break the news to her parents. I took a bus back to Dallas where we had a family Christmas. Dee and I then flew back to Nashville.

In late March Connie took a bus to Nashville. It was spring break of her senior year in high school; it seemed she had only been there a few days when she was due to go back. I had to make a quick decision. I cashed in her bus ticket and we got in my TransAm bound for San Diego. While Connie finished high school, I stayed with her in her parents' house, sleeping on the couch in the living room.

In July we returned to Nashville. Connie and I married and on July 6, 1984 our daughter, Brooke, was born. At the time I was working in the warehouse of a plumbing and electrical supply house and, part time, I drove a truck. I was following in the tradition of Vernon and Elvis Presley, although I never thought of that then.

I took a job with an Elvis impersonator. I'd go up on stage and give a personal remembrance and then he'd go into his act. When the guy started thinking he was Elvis, I couldn't handle it. At first I thought the show was a tribute to Elvis but finally I realized it was not something I wanted to do: the man didn't alter the show in the way that he and I had discussed.

I was looking for something better, preferably something in music. I went to see T.G. Sheppard, who was doing well in the music industry. I remembered when he'd call up to Graceland wanting to see Elvis. I knew Elvis didn't want to be disturbed. "Tell Elvis it's important. I've got to see him." So I'd say, "I'll see what I can do." Now I needed T.G. Sheppard to open some doors for me. But he literally closed his door in my face. I was running into a lot of that.

Of course you'd think that with a beautiful wife and a beautiful young daughter I'd just be more determined to overcome all obstacles. Often I felt that way. But just as often I got down on myself, my jobs, or my wife. And I had long before established an escape route. So I began once again to hang out, to drink too much, and to take drugs.

It didn't happen in one day, or one weekend, but gradually I lost it. For every step forward I took, I'd follow with two or three the other way. By January of 1986 I'd lost my last job and, according to Connie, showed no signs of even wanting another. By March we'd lost our apartment and had to move in with Dee. In June Connie left, taking Brooke, to move back to her parents' place in San Diego.

I followed, got another landscaping job, and found a place to stay with Connie and her folks. Her stepfather, Paul, was retired military. Like my dad, Bill, and everyone else I'd ever known from the military, he could enjoy a few drinks. So he and I could have a few beers together and at least discuss things.

"What's your problem, Billy?" he asked one night after we'd shared several beers.

"I have to bust my ass harder to prove I'm normal," I said. "It began in grade school football in Whitehaven. I had to hit harder just to prove I belonged on the team. And every time since, as soon as someone knows I'm Elvis's brother they take the attitude, 'Well, you're just here for a free ride.' Sometimes they gave me that assistance. But most of the time it worked against me. That was okay when Elvis was alive. Sometimes I'd tell him about it, most of the time I wouldn't. But he'd find out, and he'd make it right. Now I've got to do it on my own."

I was having an identity crisis. But Paul didn't understand it in those terms. He was concerned, probably sympathetic, but he had to express it in his terms. "Sounds like you've got a chip on your shoulder," he said. "You just have to try harder, Billy."

Then my friend Steve and I came up with an idea. The ten-year anniversary of Elvis's death was coming up in Memphis. Each year the crowds that returned to Memphis grew bigger but I'd never gone back, in part afraid to face it, but mostly because the idea of making money out of it rubbed me the wrong way. But Priscilla had opened Graceland to tours and had licensed various businesses to sell records, tapes, and memorabilia across the street. Millions were being made there, and in the week that marked the anniversary of Elvis's death all the major hotels were sponsoring booths that sold Elvis "remembrances." I decided it was time to get in on the act.

Steve paid a couple hundred dollars to reserve a booth for four days at the airport Hilton. I had 500 eight-by-ten copies made of a photo of Elvis, Vernon, Dee, and myself. Steve and I were going to drive cross-country in early August. There were some delays and then, for some reason, Steve couldn't go at all. He arranged for a friend to go with me. I didn't much care for the guy but my time and money were now too short for stops in motels along the way so we needed two drivers.

In El Paso we were stopped by the border patrol. For some reason they searched the car. In the guy's briefcase they found a half-ounce of marijuana and a half ounce of crystal Methedrine. At the police station my companion told them that both the drugs and the briefcase were mine. I had a friend arrange bail, and got out just in time to get to the hotel in Memphis for the dates we'd reserved.

I sat in the booth and sold the glossies, with my signature, for five dollars each. In a day and a half I sold out all 500 photos. I could have sold a thousand more if I hadn't run out. My pockets were bulging with cash. But I had a price to pay, too. For almost every picture sold there was a question to answer. "What was Elvis really like?" "When was the last time you saw him?" "Was he on drugs?" "Were you all on drugs?" "What was it like growing up with him?" One woman smiled as she handed me a five dollar bill. "What did you think of Elvis?" she asked.

"I loved him," I said.

Her face and voice tightened. "If you loved him so much then why did you let him die?" she snapped.

I'd hear questions like that many times over the years. Usually my response was to grow either angry or silent. But I rarely shot a smart answer back. In most cases I knew their sorrow was real. Mine was too. So I'd head for the nearest bottle.

But in Memphis in August the bars were no escape. Even among the old friends I'd looked up all the talk was about Elvis or the latest rumor that Elvis was alive, or that his stillborn twin, Jesse, was alive, or that Elvis, John F. Kennedy, and Martin Luther King were all sitting in that room somewhere talking. I was in an out of the way bar one afternoon and someone started talking about a tabloid article that said Elvis was spotted getting on a UFO.

"What do you think of that, Billy?" someone asked me. I just shook my head and laughed. But an older guy sitting next to me suddenly had an opinion.

"Wall—I know what I think of that," he drawled slowly. "It's a goddam lie! Elvis hasn't been up in no UFO all these years. And I'm the one who should know. 'Cause Elvis drives over to my trailer ev'ry Sunday and we sit there and read the gospel together."

I jumped to my feet. "You're crazy!" I yelled at him. "You must all be crazy. I've got to get out of here!"

What I meant was, "I've got to get out of Memphis." But I didn't. I just got out of that bar and into another. And later, with all that money in my pockets, and old friends everywhere, I got into more drugs. There was a carnival atmosphere in Memphis, almost a nightmare. I didn't have enough sense to walk away from it. I just stumbled blindly through it, going from one bar to another, one party to the next, until I passed out on someone's couch. The next day I'd start the pattern over again.

I didn't go back to San Diego. When the scene in Memphis died down and I called Connie, she told me that everyone there was upset about the drug arrest incident back in El Paso and that I should let emotions cool down a little before going back. So I went to my mom's place in Nashville.

Events had not gone well for Dee either. She had gotten involved in a land development enterprise and somehow was talked into putting her house up as collateral. When the company failed and went into bankruptcy she lost her house and now she was living in a small apartment. But Mom was never one to let things get her down. In tribute to her indomitable spirit, she was as determined then as she was when an athletic young Elvis pranced about the movie sets while she fussed about her young sons. She's as young today, twelve years after Elvis's death, as she was when she took us from Breezy Point Farms—and I think that is amazing. She took a public relations job with Cars of the Stars on Music Valley Road near the new Grand Ol' Opry. And since she never drank, loves to talk with people, and never could stand to look back in regret, she was (and is) doing just fine.

I was something else. When I dragged in from Memphis I must have looked a sight and Dee must have been horrified. My eyes were bloodshot, I was unshaven, hadn't changed my shirt in days, and probably reeked of booze. As the days went by I didn't get any better. I'd sit and drink beer and watch TV all day until Dee got home from work, then I might eat something, clean up, and hit the Nashville nightlife. Usually I'd get home at three or four in the morning, trying not to wake Dee while I crashed into the furniture. Some nights I didn't get back at all. I just didn't recover from the experience in Memphis, the carnival atmosphere, the accusations, the drugs, the booze, the confusion, and my renewed sorrow—now not for Elvis, but for myself.

"Billy, I can't stand this," Dee announced one day. "You've got to straighten yourself out. I know I tell you that every day, but you are the only one who can do it. And I can't have you living here like this. I can't sleep at night wondering when, and if, you're coming in.

If you're going to continue like this, you've got to find your own place."

So I moved in with a friend for a few days. Then his wife kicked me out. I moved into a hotel. All I wanted to do was go back to San Diego and make things right with Connie. But by this time I'd burned up all the money from the photo sales in Memphis. With Dee's help I got a job as a hotel bellman at the Ramada Inn on Music Valley Drive. At the time I thought that was the lowest point I could reach—taking a job as a bellboy at the age of thirty-four. I didn't realize that my life had already gone much lower. Or that worse was yet to come.

On October 1, 1987, I got on a plane for San Diego. My first paycheck, received the day before, was just a little more than enough to buy the ticket. I took the money and walked. I'd been calling Connie, telling her that when I got paid I was coming. I called again and gave her flight information. I had visions of Connie and Brooke at the airport to meet me. I hoped I wouldn't be disappointed.

But no one was there at the reception area when I got off the plane, and on the ramp to the baggage area it wasn't Connie, but two policemen who greeted me. Or, I should say, confronted me. They handed me divorce papers that Connie had filed, and a restraining order informing me that if I went within three hundred yards of Connie, her parents' house, Connie's place of work, or of my daughter, Brooke, I was subject to arrest.

I got a cab, got to a hotel, and tried to call Connie. At first I only got her parents. They wouldn't let me speak to her. But I persisted and Connie finally came to the phone. "Connie, what is this shit about a divorce?" I demanded. She hung up. After that there was no answer to my calls.

I bought a bottle and tried to knock myself out. It didn't work. I tried Connie all the next morning. Either the line was busy or there was no answer. Checkout time came at the hotel and I was down to less than ten dollars. I tried my friend Steve, but he was out of town and his girlfriend didn't want to speak to me. I tried others but it was a no-go situation. Finally, I called Dee at work. I tried to explain my situation.

"Billy, what airline did you fly out there on?"

I grappled for the ticket receipts, still in my pocket. "American," I said.

"Billy. Can you get to the airport? Good. Go to the American counter and I'll have a ticket waiting for you. But Billy. It breaks my heart to say this, but in the condition you're in you can't stay with me. I think you need professional help. Come and see me when you get back. As soon as you get back. But you can't stay with me."

"That's okay, Mom. I understand. Just get me back there. As long as I'm around friends I'll be okay."

I went immediately to the airport and got on the next available flight. I spent the remainder of my money on a few cocktails, but one of the stewardesses, based in Nashville, knew who I was and kept bringing me more beers even after my money ran out. All I could think of was the hurt and betrayal I'd been through. I couldn't believe that, after everything else, Connie would turn against me. I passed out sometime before we landed and they had to wake me and help me off the plane. I called a friend who came to the airport to pick me up. He took me to a bar where we had a few more drinks. I needed them. I was shaking from the experience in San Diego. He couldn't put me up, my friend explained. He was in too much trouble with his wife from the last time he'd been out with me. But he gave me enough money to get a motel room that night.

The next morning I had enough left for a few drinks. Now I really needed them, I was shaking so bad. But a few beers and a shot didn't do it. I was still in bad shape and the bartender wouldn't give me credit. I went to the phone to try another friend, slipped or fell, and had trouble getting up. When I did, my hands were shaking worse than ever. I just couldn't believe it. I'd seen lots of people like me and I'd just laughed. Drunks. Can't even walk or talk. I got to the phone and called Dee again.

"Mom. It's Billy."

"What's the problem, Billy?"

"Mom. I need help. I need professional help."

26

FROM ELVIS PRESLEY BOULEVARD

(1 9 8 7 ■ 1 9 8 8)

At the drug and alcohol abuse center in Florida they have what they call "burning the letter." After they'd done the tests I mentioned at the start of the book and showed me my profile on aggression, commitment, and self-esteem, and after we'd talked about these at length, they thought I was ready for it. "Burning the letter" involves writing a letter to someone you know who has died. In it you say all the things that you were never able to say. Naturally, mine was to Elvis. Your whole group goes out with you, like a funeral procession, and when you arrive at a "burial spot" you read the letter. Mine said: "Elvis, a lot has happened since your death and a lot of things have been said and done and some things have been left unsaid that should have been said earlier. I'm only sorry that we never found the way to discuss them while you were on earth. But now it's time for me to make amends. I forgive you for what's happened and I've forgotten about the affair. It was my fault as much as yours. And I love you, because you loved me more than you hurt me. You taught and advised me and I'm just now ready to understand some of the things you tried to tell and teach me all along. I hope you're happy in the place where you are now." I burned the letter and, at that moment, it felt like a ton of weight had lifted from my shoulders.

Of course, it didn't end there. One of the peculiar things about drying out is that you start to dream. Not that you haven't dreamed right along. But when you are abusing drugs and alcohol you never remember dreams. You don't know you've been dreaming. When you suddenly quit, they come at you with a rush. In one dream we are all at this crowded church and Elvis is in the front pew all by himself. I think, what's Elvis doing here? He never comes to church. He can't. But I look again. Ginger is there beside him, David is at his right, and Rick and I are to his left. And all of us are discussing music, gospel and rock and what we want to hear. In the background Elvis is singing gospel songs, but Elvis is still there with us, saying, "Listen to the preacher, listen to what he's saying." Then suddenly the service is over and we have to rush Elvis out of the building. Just like it was a concert.

In another dream Rick, David, and I are at Elvis's funeral. Everyone has been there to pay their respects. But Elvis is standing in the front hall thanking everyone for coming. Eventually they all leave to join the funeral procession. Only my brothers and I stay with Elvis. Rick says, "Elvis, this is heavy. They were all here for your funeral."

And Elvis says, "Aw, Rick. We've got it all under control. Let it happen." A last mourner appears and says what a loss it is. He doesn't seem to see Elvis, who smiles at his mistake. The mourner and his friends then leave. Elvis closes the door behind them.

Those two dreams, with variations, occurred several times at the clinic. But they already felt familiar the first time I remembered them. So I probably had been dreaming them for some years. Another dream that repeated itself at the clinic didn't have that familiar feel. In it Elvis and I were sitting on the couch in the den near the waterfall. I guess we were watching TV. We usually were. I ask him, "Elvis, are you reunited with your mother?"

"She's here, Billy," Elvis says, still looking straight ahead.

"Elvis, what's it like being dead?"

Then he turns and looks directly at me. "Don't you know?" he asks.

That one always woke me up in a hurry.

Of course I was in the Koala Treatment Center, in Bushnell, Florida because Mom, to my rescue as always, and my friend, Dennis, had arranged it. When they released me Rick wanted me to stay near his family in Fort Walton Beach. It wasn't exactly a request. Rick said, "Billy, this is what you're going to do when you get out." He paid the rent for a trailer for me to stay in and I went to work for him. Rick and Robyn's work is evangelical and inspirational. Through the Rick Stanley Ministries he travels around the country, mainly in the south, telling high school audiences of his journey from being the aide and brother to the king of rock 'n roll to becoming the instrument of the King of Kings.

Rick, heavily in demand as a speaker, arranged for me to tell my story before several high school assemblies. The idea was that youth would be interested because of my relationship with Elvis, so I would tell some stories about growing up with Elvis and then work into my problems with drugs and alcohol, reveal the lost, dark years, and then reveal how I finally came to see the light.

Telling the audiences about Elvis was easy. What I wanted to say was something like:

I'm a minor person in the tale of our times. But my brother, Elvis, was a great one. He changed the world as much as any musician could. He made a statement. He was the nonconformist. In a segregated world he united black and white American music. In a country that represented all the people but still said, "You can take this bull only so far, southern white trash and hillbillies should wait outside," he made a southern white trash hillbilly the heartthrob of all those northern WASP stockbrokers' daughters. And he made them all like it! In my opinion at least he helped bring this country together as much as JFK and MLK did. Elvis did all that because he could do all that. He was full of contradictions. He'd get explosive just before we left on tours. One minute he could be cussing us out or tearing the phone off the wall and the next minute he'd be down in the kitchen soothingly explaining to his grandma, Minnie Mae, that he was going off. Elvis never left Graceland without some words with the old woman he lovingly called Dodger because, as he said, "She's getting along in years, and you just never know."

One night, when he was in his decline, and when his mind and once proud body were both fogged by his abuse of prescription drugs, Elvis said to me, "Billy, isn't it a shame that some must die young so that others can learn from their mistakes?" I couldn't even answer him. Elvis had been referring to Jesus, President Kennedy, and a group of rock stars who'd met an untimely end. But I could sense he was also referring to himself, and I couldn't accept that. Now, if Elvis could hear me, I'd answer, "Yes, it is a shame. But it would be a greater shame if people died young and no one could learn from their mistakes." You see while Elvis was in school he never took drugs or alcohol or anything like it just to gain social acceptance. He didn't need it. But later he listened to some advisers and to some doctors who said, "Need some help? We've got a pill, or a shot, that will help you out." He was dead set against street drugs but he thought he was "a big boy," able to take care of whatever came his way. When those who loved him tried to warn him he replied, "I know what I'm doing." But he didn't. He tried to quit, several times. But he couldn't.

Even when Elvis was sick, overweight, and incoherent, I always thought, "Elvis will handle this. Just like he's handled everything else. He's not going anywhere he doesn't want to go." But I was as wrong as he was, and it was a fatal mistake. What I'm asking of you, based on my experiences, and Elvis's, is: Don't start down a road that may have no exits. Elvis did, and his only escape was death.

These had become my beliefs about drugs, and I think my high school audiences appreciated the message. They sure laughed at the part about the stockbrokers' daughters. I sometimes felt I was expected to say something about the glamour and excitement of the life with a rock star on tour and how that led to drug abuse and decline. But it hadn't happened that way. So I told it like it was. "I didn't get into drugs and alcohol abuse on the road," I said. "I got into them in my hometown with my high school friends. I wanted to belong. I wanted to show everyone that I was just as big and bold as my older brother, and that just seemed to be the easy way to do it. I faced the same situation many of you will face, or have already faced. And I made the wrong decision. I wasn't imitating Elvis. He always hated alcohol and drugs and he always warned us against them. If he was taking prescription medication for some of his physical problems when I was in school I sure didn't know it. He set up a model for us to follow. I failed to do it."

Where was I going? The truth was easy but shouldn't it be leading somewhere, to some conclusion? Not just for a high school assembly, but for myself. Rick could tie it all together. He had changed his life fairly soon after Elvis's death. It took David a few years more to get his life under control. But mine had been out of control for over ten years. In my opinion, a few months on the wagon hardly qualified me as an expert on the matter, even if the subject was my life. "Are there any questions?" I asked. Fortunately there were lots of them.

I realized I wanted to tell my story, but I wanted to do it in a different way. Since I'd never really contributed to *Elvis We Love You Tender* I knew I had something new to say. But I needed a professional writer. I couldn't do it on my own. And I needed to be near Connie and Brooke. I'd been calling Connie; I could sense she recognized the change in my life. Practically everyone objected to my going back to San Diego. All odds were against me.

But a way was worked out. I was to report to an abuse halfway house in San Diego, find gainful employment, and respect the restraining order regarding Connie and Brooke. That meant I couldn't go to them but they could come to me. I reported to the halfway house on December 27, 1987, got a construction job, and soon the order was forgotten, or ignored. My wife and I were dating again. This time I was playing it straight.

In March, a neighbor and friend of Connie's drove me up to Santa Barbara to meet an agent-writer, George Erikson (he's the guy writing these words down), and two months later we had a contract for a book with St. Martin's Press. By that time I was staying at George's house and doing long hours taping sessions on my life with Elvis. One night he broke off our session saying he had another appointment— at the Paradise Cafe. "Billy, it's a restaurant and a bar, but I'm going to meet my appointment in the bar. Do you want to come along?"

"I've been in bars before," I said. "I think I can handle it."

George seemed to know a lot of the crowd there that night. Before he wandered off to his meeting he introduced me to his friend Rick, an advertising and public relations man who was also the creator and "reverend" of the "Church of Monday Night Football." Rick's wife and I conversed long and hard about Elvis while George conducted his other business. While everyone else drank beer or cocktails I drank sodas. A crowd formed around us. I was just a little surprised at the amount of interest the sophisticated Santa Barbara people showed in Elvis.

Then Rick's wife said, "Billy, have you heard the latest on Elvis? Supposedly he's alive and hiding out in Kalamazoo, Michigan."

"That's not right," I laughed. "Elvis always hated Michigan."

"But this woman who claims it is bringing out a book. And she has tapes of Elvis's voice that some authorities say is Elvis's. Not that I believe it. But she was on the Larry King show last night."

Normally this would be the point at which I'd get angry. I'd slam down the shot glass of bourbon, or the bottle of beer, whichever I had in my hand, and say, "Do you think Elvis would fake his own death to cause his daddy's heart attack and his daughter's grief? Do you think he would hurt everyone he loved to make his own escape? You just don't know who the man was!"

Instead I said, "There's no end to the bullshit. But it's probably an honor, in that some people care enough to believe that crap. But they end up making money for jerks."

I was pleased at how I handled that one. But there was a tougher challenge ahead. A few days later George proposed that we go to Graceland. He said he needed knowledge of the physical background to write the book. "Do we have to go there?" I asked. I already knew the answer.

I truly feared it. Graceland had been my center, the core of my existence. Graceland without Elvis seemed to be more than I could handle. It had been nine years since Vernon's funeral, eleven since Elvis died. I wasn't sure I could face it. But a few weeks later I drove back to Nashville. A week after that George and his wife, Sandy, flew out. I called the VIP tour department at Graceland and they set us up with a guide named Patsy. We met in the offices across from Graceland at noon the next day. I almost can't express how scared I was. It was no longer mine yet it was everything. I dreaded the confrontation. A year before, Memphis had almost destroyed me, and that time I'd avoided Graceland altogether. Patsy, in the corporate offices, assured me that we'd avoid the crowds and the hype, and that she'd take us through between tour groups.

We drove in and parked against the wall to the left of the house, near the carport for all the cars I'd washed and waxed over the years. And they were still there! The pink Cadillac, the motorcycles, the three wheelers, the Stutz Blackhawk, the Ferrari and the Lincoln Continental were still there as if they were waiting for my attention, and for Elvis's command.

Patsy, George, and Sandy were out of the car, walking to the front drive, but I was nailed to the spot. Elvis had this expression, "Until you've walked in another man's shoes . . ." well, until you've walked in mine you don't know how badly I wanted a drink. I was prepared for a carnival, a sellout of Elvis and Graceland; I was prepared to question and fight the lies and hypocrisy I expected to find. Instead, even before going into the house I was crying, because everything was beautiful—just as we'd all left it.

It was so peaceful, with the smell of freshly cut grass, the shade of the trees, the glint of new paint from the walls. It was beautiful and serene and it was timeless. Graceland never looked, felt, or smelled so good. The crowds of tourist didn't offend me at all. After all, I was just one of them. My privileged position had ended eleven years ago.

We went through the tour, always within earshot of one tour director or another. Patsy would ask me, "Billy, have we got that right?" And they did, even to the color of carpets and in which year they were changed. I could only respond, "You've got it all right." I would have expected far less from something ultimately managed by outsiders. But it was great. It was respectful, and it was true.

In every room of the house, in the racquetball building, and in the slot car building that became the trophy room, I'd look at some object and memories of Elvis would rush to my mind. I looked at a sequined jumpsuit that I'd carried for Elvis; suddenly I saw Elvis in it, in his crowded dressing room after a Las Vegas performance. The tour group pushed against me and I could almost feel Muhammad Ali reaching over my shoulder and yelling at Elvis, "Man, we've got to be the two handsomest sons of bitches in the whole world!" Then my eyes swelled with tears. To fight them back I moved on.

After we walked by the pool, and spent a brief moment at Elvis's grave, I strolled out to the front pasture thinking about all the races, on foot, on bicycle, and on horses, that we'd had there. Then I spotted Uncle Lloyd standing guard out front. I moved toward him.

"Billy!" he cried.

"Uncle Lloyd! Man, you still work here?"

"Gotta do something," he said. Uncle Lloyd went on to spend twenty minutes telling any one who'd listen just how bad my brothers and I had been growing up at Graceland. Then he asked me if I'd seen Earl.

"Is Uncle Earl still here?" I asked.

"You bet he is. Right out back in the maintenance shed. You better go say hello to him."

Uncle Earl was there, just as I'd left him almost twelve years before. And so were many of the guys I worked with. Earl had worse stories about me, in part because I'd worked with him for so many years but also, in part, because he knew how to put a little relish on all of them.

"You've got air-conditioning in here now," I said, partially to divert the onslaught of "And then Billy did this . . . and then, would you believe it, Billy did that," stories.

"Gotta be some progress in this world, son," Earl said.

"What are you driving now, Earl?" I asked.

"Same old Buick. Two hundred and twenty thousand miles now and I'm going to drive it till the wheels fall off."

It amazed me. Uncle Earl, Uncle Harold . . . they looked and sounded the same. Where do these people find their strength anyway? Hell, they were old, in my opinion, twenty years ago. What were they now, timeless? How do you go on with an everyday life, unscathed? Everyone in the Presley family had been touched with tragedy throughout their lives. But to stay there, where they'd always been, with such determination and good humor. Obviously, they knew something I didn't—or hadn't. But I was finding it. And at the Graceland I loved.

An hour later I walked out of the air-conditioned shed. George was taking some notes on Earl's version of my childhood. I roamed out to the field near the back gate. It was one of those blue sky, hot, late June, Memphis days like the one on which Elvis had bought his customized Lincoln Continental. That day, when he returned to Graceland, someone was too slow in opening the front gate. Elvis, impatient as always, swung his new prize and pride to the back gate. "Don't go back that way," they yelled. "They have that gate closed!" But Elvis was so mad he went that way and just drove through the closed gate. We were all back there, I can't remember why, and as pieces of the gate flew through the air David yelled, "Elvis, you crazy, don't hit my TransAm." Elvis had bought the car for David only a few days before, and he would never have considered it if David hadn't issued the challenge. But as soon as he heard David's words he spun the Lincoln around, sliding through the grass, and headed exactly in that direction. He slammed on the brakes at the last moment but still bumped into the TransAm, denting a few panels. David slumped to his knees and held his hands over his face. Elvis jumped out of his new Lincoln, athletic, on top of the world, and said, "Nobody tells me what to do."

As I looked over that field, it was the same. It smelled, looked, and felt the same. For a moment I expected Elvis to come charging through the gate. I wanted him to. But he didn't.

At the time I was one year out of the rehabilitation program; now I'm two years into the road back. I know that I'm just beginning. But I know who I am, who Elvis was, who we were together, and who we now must be separately. It hasn't diminished my love for him. I'm rebuilding my relationship with him, too. Because now I know as well as anyone the forces that can bend and crush the best intentions and the strongest will. Now that I know how hard it is I marvel at his accomplishments and his spirit. Like his fans, who shared a similar love for him, I forgive and forget his shortcomings. To use one of Elvis's favorite expressions on his flaws, a subject he didn't really like to talk about, "They didn't amount to all that much, anyway." To this day his spirit is still at Graceland. As soon as I go to sleep he's with me, either back when he really was alive or alive with me in the present world. We'll be driving around Memphis, just like the old days, and I'll point some things out to him and he'll say, "Nub, I can't believe the way things have changed. And that's good!"

I'm proud to say Elvis was my brother.

POSTSCRIPT—The day after I visited Graceland I called Connie. The next day she and Brooke started driving east and five days later they arrived in Nashville. We've been together since.

INDEX